for Saha & um,

Love Tam

*By Tahir Shah*

Godman
Jinn Hunter: Book One – The Prism
Jinn Hunter: Book Two – The Jinnslayer
Jinn Hunter: Book Three – The Perplexity
Travels With Nasrudin
The Afghan Notebook
Hannibal Fogg and the Supreme Secret of Man
Paris Syndrome
Casablanca Blues
Scorpion Soup
Eye Spy
Timbuctoo
Three Essays
Travels With Myself
In Arabian Nights
The Caliph's House
House of the Tiger King
In Search of King Solomon's Mines
Trail of Feathers
Sorcerer's Apprentice
Beyond the Devil's Teeth
Journey Through Namibia
The Middle East Bedside Book

# TRAVELS WITH NASRUDIN

## In Search of the Wise Fool

# TAHIR SHAH

# TRAVELS WITH NASRUDIN

## In Search of the Wise Fool

## TAHIR SHAH

SECRETUM MUNDI PUBLISHING

MMXIX

Secretum Mundi Publishing Ltd
PO Box 5299
Bath BA1 0WS
United Kingdom

www.secretum-mundi.com
info@secretum-mundi.com

First published by Secretum Mundi Publishing Ltd, 2019

TRAVELS WITH NASRUDIN: IN SEARCH OF THE WISE FOOL

Visit the author's website at: www.tahirshah.com

ISBN 978-1-912383-32-0

*This book is for Dr Riad Kocache.*
*The most sensible of men, whose soft-spoken*
*wisdom never ceases to amaze.*

A conceited customer approached Nasrudin in the teahouse.

'Why do you always answer a question with another question?' he asked.

Narrowing his eyes, Nasrudin sipped his tea, and replied:

'Do I?'

THE WISE FOOL of Oriental folklore, Nasrudin is known across a vast swathe of the globe – from Morocco in the west, to Indonesia in the east.

Appearing under different names and in all manner of guises, he's universally admired for his back-to-front brand of genius – so much so that at least a dozen countries insist he was one of theirs. In reality, he is of course found everywhere, even in regions where he has no name.

Tales of Nasrudin's wise-foolery have been told in caravanserais and teahouses since ancient times, just as they are recounted in cafés, office buildings, and homes the world over today.

In the Land of Nasrudin, the wise are foolish and the foolish are wise. Leading the listener through a keyhole into a realm that's back-to-front and inside out, the stories turn what we think we know and understand on its head.

At the same time, Nasrudin tales form a cornerstone in an ancient and advanced psychology. As you laugh at the off-beat humour, the subconscious turns the puzzle-joke around, working away at it like a terrier worrying a rag doll.

Nasrudin has been in my life since the day I was born. He's travelled with me, chatted to me, laughed with me, and consoled me, as I have wandered the world, doing my best to make sense of it.

As the ground beneath my feet has slipped past,

I've found myself considering familiar stories from the corpus of Nasrudin in fresh ways. My journeys have been a key that opens a door to the Land of Nasrudin, just as the Land of Nasrudin has been the key to make sense of my journeys.

By directing my attention to the methods of the wise fool, I have found that new dimensions reveal themselves to me, both in lands I thought I knew, and in fresh dominions.

*Travels With Nasrudin* is a book no one else could or would have written – not because I am better or worse an author. But because I've set it down as I experienced the world, as a consummate wise-fool-traveller myself.

Had Nasrudin sat down to write a travel book, I like to think this is what he would have come up with. As back-to-front as it is inside out, my hope is that it challenges the reader as much as it has the writer, turning common convention on its head.

Tahir Shah

# PART ONE

# THE GHOST ZONE

## One

n need of funds, Nasrudin made a sign and hung it on the back of a chair.

It read:

ANY TWO QUESTIONS ANSWERED
FOR ONE GOLD PIECE!

Sitting on the chair back-to-front, he waited for customers.

It was only a matter of time before someone approached. Well-dressed in a lovely silk robe, he looked at the chair, the sign, then at Nasrudin, and parted with a golden coin.

'Do you really answer two questions for a single gold coin?' he asked.

Nasrudin slipped the coin into his pocket.

'Yes, I do,' he answered. 'And your next question is...?'

LANGTON HOUSE, 1972

On the eve of my sixth birthday, my father tucked me into bed.

'Are you excited for tomorrow?' he asked.

'No,' I whispered.

'Why not?'

'Because I'm frightened.'

'Frightened of what?'

3

'Of the monsters under my bed.'

Stooping down, he peered into the darkness.

'Nothing there.'

'That's because they're invisible monsters.'

'If you don't think about them, they'll go away.'

'But they'll just hide under someone else's bed, and that doesn't seem fair,' I said. 'You see, that's how they came to my bedroom in the first place.'

Perching on the edge of my bed, my father smoothed the blanket with his hand, and said:

'I'll tell you something... something that will protect you throughout your life.'

'From monsters?'

'Yes. And all kinds of other things... things that frighten you, or that you don't understand.'

'What is it, Baba?'

'A suit of armour.'

'Like the one down in the hallway?'

'A little bit like that, but different as well.'

'Will I wear it?'

'Yes you will.'

'Can I see it?'

Leaning back, my father grinned, the kind of magical grin that preceded something special.

'This suit of armour isn't like others that you've seen before. It's different because it's not made of metal.'

'Then it won't stop the arrows and the swords.'

'Ah, but it will… in its own way.'

'How?'

'By protecting you from the inside out.'

I didn't understand. All my friends had fathers who said things simply, while mine spoke in riddles.

'What's it made of, then?'

'Of stories.'

'What kind of stories?'

'Stories about the bravest and most amazing fool who ever lived.'

'What's his name?'

Dark eyes reflecting the lamplight, my father replied:

'His name is Nasrudin.'

## Two

asrudin had got a reputation for being rude to wealthy self-important women. As his reputation preceded him, he received fewer and fewer invitations.

One day a very rich and exceedingly conceited woman moved to town. Hearing about Nasrudin, she invited him to dine at her mansion.

'If I was married to you,' she said gruffly, 'I would feed you meat laced with poison!'

Nasrudin mused for a moment, and riposted:

'My dear madam, if you fed me meat laced with poison, I would eat it!'

THE YEARS PASSED, and eventually I broke free from the shackles of childhood.

While my former classmates set about getting sensible jobs, fat salaries, and supposed trophies of success, I embarked on an altogether different path.

I decided to devote my life to the restlessness that filled me from the tip of my heels to the great swathe of nut-brown hair that then crowned my head.

A restlessness borne out of my need to escape into a realm of fantasy.

So, I wandered.

Through Africa, Central Asia, and the Far East, through the Americas, Europe, and the distant Antipodes... zigzag journeys more often than not made without a clear destination.

All the while searching for stories and for myself – embarking on explorations and quests as I went.

I studied magic with the godmen of India. Searched through the Peruvian cloud forest for the lost city of the Incas. Scoured war-torn Afghanistan for the treasure of Ahmed Shah. Mounted expeditions to locate King Solomon's mines. I even lived with a former head-shrinking tribe on a mission involving primitive flight.

The books and documentaries recording my adventures were outward proof of where I had been and what I'd done. Forming a body of work, they kept those who assumed I would never amount to anything at bay. But the books I wrote and the films I made were of little consequence to me. At best they were a cover story, a smokescreen masking the real reason for embarking on adventure.

A reason shrouded in total secrecy.

By announcing it, I feared that I would be signing the death warrant of my research and my fantasies. Only now, long since those nights beset with monsters, I am ready to lift the veil on the hidden thread running through my travels and my life...

An abiding quest through the eye of the needle for the wise fool.

### *Three*

The most miserly man in the kingdom invited Nasrudin to dine.

'Come to my home next week,' he said, 'and we shall have a bite to eat!'

Amazed at being offered anything by such a wretched member of society, Nasrudin arrived on the appointed day, made polite conversation, and waited for the food to arrive.

When at last it did, a ragged servant stumbled in with a tray on which were two plates – a single mouthful of pilau on each.

Reprimanding himself for having expected greater hospitality, Nasrudin swallowed the mouthful and wondered how to escape.

At that moment, a beggar passed the house, calling out:

'A little food for a blind veteran of war!'

Enraged by the disturbance, the host leapt up and yelled:

'If you don't stop making such a racket, I'll come out there and strangle you!'

Nasrudin leapt up and called out:

'Brave warrior, I beg you to take the threat at face value, for the man whose mouth spoke it has proved himself true to his word!'


NEW YORK, 1994

In the early 'nineties I was a frequent visitor to the US, and for a while lived on New York's Upper West Side.

There were two things I adored about Manhattan:

The first was that oddity was celebrated rather than shunned.

The other was the curiously Oriental way of thinking that prevailed.

Although broke, I did my best to find an apartment for next to nothing – a tall order in one of the most popular cities on Earth.

The search led me to sublimely squalid corners of the city, rife with crack dealers, pimps, and gangs. Ever the optimist, I was sure that sooner or later I'd get the perfect deal.

And, I did.

A writer friend put me in touch with an associate of hers who worked in television and lived in Brooklyn. She had a rent-controlled flat on West 72nd Street – between Broadway and West End – that she didn't want to give up. She was willing to give me the place for a nominal rent.

There was one condition, however.

I had to agree to vacate the apartment on Wednesdays and Thursdays between six and nine p.m. The reason was explained to me in a mumble – the lady was a part-time psychotherapist, and needed to hold sessions in the apartment two evenings a week.

Thrilled at having a place to live, I readily agreed, and my New York days began. Through weeks and months, I explored the city, desperate to claw my way down to the bedrock of life.

Manhattan is much more sanitized these days than it was back then. The creative class has largely been forced out, replaced by the well-heeled elite. There are exceptions of course – many of them in the guise of the homeless. They tramp down the great avenues with sleeping bags wrapped over their shoulders, like coronation robes of the dispossessed.

Back in the early 'nineties, if you saw someone talking – or ranting – to themselves, it meant they were probably part of the psychedelic and psychotic underbelly. These days they're more likely to be chatting to a far-flung friend through ear pods, than to be paid-up members of what a New Yorker explained were 'Whacko Warriors'.

In many ways 1994 was the last gasp of Manhattan's true psycho zone – a realm so perfectly evolved – like a scientific experiment gone right, rather than wrong.

As the seasons progressed, I made my way through the catalogue of curiosity advertised in free newspapers and on tear-off sheets stapled to telephone poles.

I got to know the so-called 'Guerrilla Girls', who dressed in gorilla masks to protest about male-dominated art galleries. I was taken in by Santería devotees way up in Harlem – invited to their parlours to attend sacrifices and the 'seating of the saints'. And, I toured the sewers beneath the streets, guided through the labyrinth by a flute-playing Russian émigré on the trail of the perfect echo.

By nature I'm pre-programmed to search. Most of the time I don't know why I am so restless – especially as my quests tend to dredge up far more questions than answers.

My time in Manhattan was intoxicating because there was so much oddity crammed into such a limited geographical field. In a single day I could attend blood-drenched chicken sacrifices, tour emporia abundant with medical marvels, and chitchat to the homeless man who sold bottled dreams down in Greenwich Village.

Each week, a special time was pencilled into my diary... the bewitching hours between six and nine on Wednesday and Thursday nights.

Unlike any other time, those two slots were mandatory. I had to leave the apartment whether I liked it or not. Indeed, I might have gone to the movies, or lain low in a bookshop to kill a few hours. The way I saw it though, the 'Ghost Zone', as I came to call it, was reserved for investigations that more normally might have slipped through the net.

When it came to the Ghost Zone, I didn't choose it. It chose me.

The only rule was that a Ghost Zone lead could not be direct. Instead, it had to reach me by refraction, through a zigzag trail.

That's how I came to meet Philomena and George.

Having lived in New York for about five months, news spread I was in town.

It wasn't of course a matter of my name being recognized, but rather that the son of Idries Shah was there.

At times I felt like a character from *Men in Black*, passed secret messages by alien sleepers in the guise of mankind.

A Rastafarian handed me a scrap of paper while I was relieving myself in the toilets at the New York Public Library. Opening it, I read three familiar words: 'Seeker After Truth'... a reference to the Sufi Path, and the title of one of my father's best-selling books.

Another time, I was standing in the crisp autumn sunshine at Strawberry Fields in Central Park, when a guy sweeping fallen leaves paused, strolled over, and said sotto voce:

'Look not at my outward form, but take what is in my hand.'

The aphorism was my father's favourite and, not long after, found its way onto his headstone.

Another example began with an encounter in the Strand Bookstore down on Broadway with Twelfth.

Having asked one of the sales clerks whether they stocked a book on shrunken heads, I was directed to a shelf with the standard works on the Shuar tribe. While poring through the volumes, I heard a low guttural cough in the shadows behind.

Turning, I made out a figure doing their best to hide behind a cart packed with books. Frowning,

I went back to my search for M. W. Stirling's 1938 monograph on the head-shrinkers.

The cough came again.

It was followed by the sound of nimble feet moving fast over boards.

Again, I turned.

'It's a secret,' said the woman standing over me. 'A secret I'm not supposed to tell.'

Swathed in tie-dye and of retirement age, she had long, fluorescent-pink pigtails and matching lipstick.

'Excuse me?' I said.

'I will tell you the secret,' she said.

'I'm not altogether with you,' I replied. 'Think you're mixing me up with someone else.'

'I've read all his books.'

'Whose books?'

'Idries Shah's.'

'Oh,' I said.

In similar situations I'd learned to reply with a shrug and the words, '*Who's he?*' But I got the feeling the woman with pigtails had done her research.

'May be best to keep the secret to yourself,' I said.

The woman appeared crestfallen. Her pink lips parted:

'Please let me say it!' she begged.

Standing, I stepped backwards, so as to put a good yard and a half of bookshelf between us.

'All right…. What is it?'

13

It was as though a light had been turned on in the woman's mind. Grasping a fist to the end of either pigtail, she announced:

'The eagle will come at dawn.'

'Ah,' I responded knowingly.

'Shall I repeat it?'

'No, no. Not necessary, got it the first time.'

'What am I to do now?'

I swallowed hard.

'Go back home and get on with your life.'

'But how will I know whether the secret's been of help?'

'I'll make sure it gets passed on,' I said.

'Do you promise?'

I nodded.

'Promise.'

The woman with the secret was about to go, when she gasped.

'I almost forgot!'

'Forgot what?'

Rummaging in her daypack, she pulled out an envelope. Browned with dirt, it was sealed, and had my name scrawled on the front.

'For you.'

Again, I frowned.

'Who's it from?'

'From Philomena and George.'

'*Who*?'

The names were repeated, louder than before.

'Who are they?'

'Friends,' the pink lips mouthed darkly.

'But... but how did you know I'd be here? I only dropped in as I was passing.'

'Can't tell you that.'

The woman with pigtails left, and I opened the envelope.

Inside was a single sheet of paper folded diagonally. Written over it in large capital letters were an address and a date. Below the address were the words 'NASRUDIN HEALS' and the now familiar names – Philomena and George.

I never found out whether it was coincidence that the invitation was for a Ghost Zone night.

My gut told me that in such matters there was no such thing as happenstance. Needing a quest for the regular three hours of limbo the following Thursday, I made my way to the Upper East Side brownstone, and rang the bell for apartment 4C.

Five minutes later, I was cross-legged on oak boards wondering what was going on. A dozen others were in attendance, each of them excited to the point of delirium. Unlike me, they appeared to have an idea of the routine.

An officious woman with an exceedingly firm handshake had let me into the apartment. When

I asked if she was Philomena, she let out a great raucous wail of laughter, following her like a vapour trail as she turned and strode away.

A timid man was cross-legged beside me. Making conversation, I enquired if he was George. He didn't answer, but instead broke down in tears.

Candles were lit, as was incense, and a recording of what sounded like muffled Buddhist chanting was put on. The fluorescent-pink pigtails and matching lipstick from the Strand Bookstore appeared, embraced me in a spine-numbing hug, and read what she said was an Inuit fertility prayer.

Sitting there politely, I wondered desperately how to extricate myself.

Thirty minutes of Buddhist-style meditation came and went.

Then our hosts swept in.

Philomena was wearing a rainbow-coloured kaftan, and many strings of beads – around her neck, her waist, and twisted over her arms.

George was dressed in a pinstripe suit, a black bow tie, and superior calfskin brogues.

Having greeted their guests, they made their way over to me.

'A real honour,' said George, the muscles of his face clenched tight.

'I can feel your aura,' Philomena added. 'It's so intense.'

Mumbling an uncertain reply, I feigned a smile.

'Shall we begin?' George intoned.

'The healing?' I answered.

'You got it.'

'Great,' I said.

The woman with the firm grip clapped three times.

'Who wants to go first?' she cried.

The participants seemed bashful, like children asked to read at the front of class.

'I will,' said the frail man who'd wept when I spoke to him.

The next thing we knew, he was lying on the floor, with the group around him. Eyes closed, hands crossed over his chest like an Egyptian mummy, his feet were splayed a few inches apart.

'Ready,' he said from the corner of his mouth.

Philomena fell to her knees, the kaleidoscope of colours wafting down. Then, once she was in position, George stooped to hand her something.

A book.

A book I recognized at once.

My father's book, *The Pleasantries of the Incredible Mulla Nasrudin.*

Opening it at random, and with the audience pressing forwards, Philomena read:

'Every Friday morning, Nasrudin arrived in a market town with an excellent donkey, which he sold.

17

'The price which he asked was always very small; far below the value of the animal.

'One day, a rich donkey-merchant approached him.

'"I cannot understand how you do it, Nasrudin. I sell donkeys at the lowest possible price. My servants force farmers to give me fodder for free. My slaves look after my donkeys without wages. And yet I cannot match your prices."

'"Quite simple," said Nasrudin. "You steal fodder and labour. I merely steal donkeys."'

When the story had been read, Philomena held her hands over the patient's face like a magician working a spell. The audience sat in absolute silence, the recorded chants of the Buddhist monks bathing them.

As soon as the first patient had been treated, a stream of others volunteered.

At the end of the healing session, I asked some of them whether they felt better than they had done when they'd arrived. They all swore they did – as though touched by some secret alchemy.

One by one, those who had ventured to the brownstone drifted away. Although I hadn't meant to stay till the end, I found myself sitting alone with Philomena and George.

The candles were put out and the lights switched on.

'I've never seen Nasrudin being used like this,' I said.

'You mean in healing?' said Philomena.

'Well, doing what you're doing.'

George tugged the end of his bow tie.

'We've read your father's books for twenty years,' he explained. 'And in all that time we've been profoundly affected by their wisdom.'

'Profoundly,' Philomena echoed.

'We've begged our friends to read his books,' George went on. 'Some of them do, but over time we saw they were craving something else.'

'Such as what?'

'Attention,' said Philomena blankly.

'That's all they want,' added George. 'We've tried to explain where they're going wrong – hankering for the container rather than the content... longing insatiably for an audience.'

'An audience for what?'

'For their interminable needs.'

'Sounds as though they're better left alone,' I said.

'Perhaps,' Philomena answered. 'But the way we see it, we're giving them attention with a message.'

'What message would that be?'

'That it's wise to be foolish,' George stated, 'rather than foolish to be wise.'

## Four

asrudin had left school without any qualifications whatsoever. Unbothered by his lack of scholastic paperwork, he had no concern in this regard until he was ready to get married.

In the teahouse he overheard that the father of the girl he wanted to marry was an old-fashioned calligrapher, who took qualifications very seriously indeed. He supposedly inspected all school certificates before he even allowed a suitor to meet his beloved daughter.

Next day, Nasrudin tracked down a master calligrapher and enquired how much he charged for lessons.

'The first month costs five gold pieces,' he said. 'Then the second month is two gold pieces, and the third month is a single gold piece.'

'Very well,' Nasrudin said. 'I'd like to begin with the third month of study, please.'

LANGTON HOUSE, 1974

My childhood was divided in two halves.

The first was the one I came to loathe. It consisted of schoolwork I couldn't do, sports I couldn't play, and games at which I failed. Continually lampooned by my peers, and roasted by the masters, I was scruffy, confused, and all covered in ink.

The second half was a fantastic realm where I spent almost all my time. Before and after school, on the weekends, and increasingly during class – a realm free from monsters, and conjured from the stories I so loved to hear…

I called it the 'Land of Nasrudin'.

Adults are taught to learn things in a practical way – starting at the beginning and finishing at the end. But children do things differently – in a way that's the default setting with which we are born.

That's how I learned about Nasrudin…

Not in a linear kind of way, but upside down and from the inside out. Whenever I asked about the wise fool, the reply came in the form of a story, or a fragment of information that seemed to make no sense at all. The suit of Nasrudin armour my father gave me in the shape of stories, took other forms as well.

Among them was an awkward stuffed puppet of Nasrudin on his donkey, made by a band of Argentine troubadours; a glass eye whispered by my aunt to have been given to Nasrudin in payment for a dream; and a lump of quartz supposedly cut out of a rear hoof of Nasrudin's donkey while on a journey in Tibet.

As the years passed, and as I found myself less and less able to be the person I was expected to be, I slipped deeper and deeper into the Land of Nasrudin.

In class, the form master would beat me, order me to face the corner, or write out lines after school. In the playground, I was shunned by the other boys at the insistence of the master so dead set on making my childhood hell.

With time I came to see that the kids at school who were given an easy ride, and the adults who aren't knocked about by life, have something in common with each other: the inability to succeed in the face of desperation.

At the same time, there was something that the brutal form master, my classmates, and all the others, never grasped.

Something amazing.

Something magical.

Something that made me who I am.

It was this:

The more they punished and heckled, lambasted and ridiculed, the more I sought refuge in the Land of Nasrudin.

And, the longer I spent there, the better equipped I became for the world – because the stories prepared me by teaching me how to think in an original way.

A way that mirrored how my father perceived the world…

*Five*

asrudin had become a celebrated psychologist.

Patients came from far and wide to avail of his expertise, for it was said there was no condition he couldn't cure.

One morning an elderly judge arrived at his surgery. On the face of it he seemed quite normal, and had achieved high office through a long and distinguished career.

'How may I help you?' the wise fool asked once the two men were together.

'I'm afflicted by a horrifying phobia, doctor,' explained the judge.

'What is the nature of your fear?'

'Long words!'

'*Long words?*'

'Yes, yes… the mere thought of them fills me with terrible dread. In my line of work there's no end of long words to set me on edge.'

'Fascinating,' declared Nasrudin, frowning with interest. 'I can imagine the difficulty you face.'

'It's terrible, doctor,' the judge responded. 'I don't know what to do.'

'I'll prescribe a strong medicine to remedy your condition,' Nasrudin asserted.

'*Medication*?' the patient asked, pleased by the idea.

'Yes… although it may not be the medication you were expecting.'

Scribbling something on his prescription pad, he handed it to the judge.

'To be cured you must understand your condition,' Nasrudin said. 'Say this word ten times in the morning, and ten times before bed, and your symptoms will be gone within a week.'

Glancing at the prescription, the patient screamed.

'Read it!' Nasrudin yelled.

'Hippopotomonstrosesquippedaliophobia.'

'Excellent, you're improving already!'

'Is it a talismanic charm to protect me?' the judge enquired.

'No, no,' replied the wise fool. 'It simply means "the fear of long words".'

UPPER AMAZON, 1999

I first read about the Shuar tribe in one of those annuals kids were given at Christmas in the 'seventies – the kind containing an endless stream of little-known facts.

The book explained how the Shuar were savages who shrunk the heads of their enemies to the size

24

of grapefruits. Devoid of real possessions or proper culture, it said, they romped through the jungles of the Amazon hacking off heads.

The only time they broke off from head-hacking raids was, the annual informed, when the tribal chief gave the order for a fiesta. Covering themselves head to toe in feathers, they flapped about like wounded birds until the sun went down.

I'd been drawn to the Peruvian Amazon under the guise of an expedition on the trail of primitive flight. After a boat ride of several weeks beyond Iquitos, I found myself at an encampment. The journey upriver had been a hard one – or so I imagined. In hindsight, I blush at my rawness, and for complaining at what I imagined were miserable conditions.

To experience the Upper Amazon is to be touched by the most extraordinary magic, and to observe oneself as though from a great height. Wayfarers such as me from the Occidental world arrive burdened with supplies, unnecessary equipment, and by a mindset that grinds against achieving anything at all.

Through the long weeks spent on '*Pradera*', the rotting, rusting vessel, I came to understand how supremely unsuited I was to undertake an expedition of that kind.

Not until I ventured into the actual undergrowth did I fully understand my true wretchedness.

By the time the rat-infested craft pulled up at the Shuar village, we were on a small tributary of the mighty Amazon. If the main river was a tree trunk, the waterway we'd navigated over the previous handful of days was no bigger than a twig.

As soon as we arrived at the precipitous mudbank, a gaggle of children scurried down. Laughing and whooping, they were gripped with a sense of splendid occasion. I gave the order for gifts of food, cloth, and beads, to be made ready. When the head of the village arrived, we plied him with the tokens of friendship.

His sinewy form was the product of the same habitat that had reduced me to a pathetic, feverish state. Unlike me, he'd been strengthened by an environment in which almost every living thing was doing its damnedest to end your life so that it could devour what was left.

The gifts were met with mile-wide grins, and reciprocation.

Even before we had left the riverbank, a pair of roasted monkeys was brought forward. A leg and an arm were ripped off by the village chief, and presented ceremoniously to me.

Over the years I have found myself dining on monkey far more often than I would wish – in Latin America, Africa, and the Far East. Affection for our primate cousins makes me a reluctant champion of their meat.

My rule of thumb is always the same: eat anything in the name of courtesy. Compared with the roasted tarantulas that would come later, a little charred monkey meat was no great test.

My expedition to the Peruvian Amazon was focused on whether ancient peoples might have flown, or at least glided, long before breakthroughs in modern powered flight. Following a trail woven through literature and folklore, I'd learned that the Incas had 'flown over the jungle like birds'.

Months of research led me deep into the Amazon. It was there my eventual conclusion was formed: that a complex hallucinogen known as 'Ayahuasca' had given the Spanish Conquistadors a sense that they were actually flying.

In recent years, Ayahuasca has become a fashionable drug of choice with party-goers in Europe and beyond. It's used by therapeutic practitioners, too. Although outspoken in my distaste for recreational drugs, I was profoundly moved by the role of the hallucinogen within the confines of the Shuar world.

As I'd first read as a child in my Christmas annual, the tribe had historically shrunk the heads of their enemies to tame a victim's avenging soul. For them, the trophies themselves were of little importance. More often than not, once they were completed, they were simply tossed away. All that changed with the advent of Ripley's Believe It or Not!

A great many of the small Shuar communities dispersed through the deepest regions of the jungle had already been converted by the time I arrived. Landing in flying boats, missionaries from Alabama penetrated the most remote areas, bringing with them shallow vestiges of the modern world, along with the Seventh-day Adventist faith.

The frail community at which we stopped on that searing summer afternoon had shunned all advances from the missionaries. As a result, they were far less endowed than the others. Almost everything they owned had been sourced in the jungle. The long-houses were fashioned from chonta palms and bamboo; the scarlet paint adorning their cheeks, made from crushed achiote seeds. They hunted with squat bows and elongated arrows, and ate anything they could catch.

In the days and nights we stayed at the village, the crew and I took part in an abundant fiesta. As always, these centred around drinking gallons of 'masato', a white milky beverage served in bowls made from gourds. Hugely popular with everyone, the drink is prepared with boiled manioc. Mashed up, it's chewed by the village's oldest crones, who spit mouthfuls of it back into the bowl. Water is added, and the liquid quickly ferments, saliva playing the part of yeast.

On the third evening of our visit, I was sitting in the chief's long-house, the remains of a roasted peccary on the bamboo floor. With darkness, a haunting nocturnal cacophony rang out from the jungle undergrowth, reminding me that real life is not limited to how we imagine it to be.

The chief's head was crowned in a corona made from the wings of a scarlet macaw. The previous night we'd taken Ayahuasca together, and I had flown over the jungle just as I imagined the Spanish Conquistadors had once done.

The chief drew slowly on a mapacho cigar as thick as a man's wrist, made from pure black tobacco grown in the jungle. I hoped he would not suggest taking the potent hallucinogen once again. Unlike the rave culture on Mediterranean shores, the Shuar reserved the so-called 'Vine of the Dead' for solemn occasions – a blessing as I saw it.

For the tribe, the hallucinogen was a way of leaving the illusionary world in which we live, and soaring into the realm of reality to seek answers by which to solve the trials and tribulations of life.

My interest in the connection between Ayahuasca and primitive flight was very much genuine. But another interest had lured me to the Amazon.

I'd read in an ethnographic monograph from the 1930s that the Shuar had a sophisticated folklore. The abiding fascination with their head-shrinking sadly sidelined any research being done into what was certain to be a folkloric treasure trove.

A sentence in the monograph had stuck in my head. It went, 'Shuar mythology is founded on the belief of a wise fool'.

As with so much that is of real value, I knew from the start that the only way to get information was to make the journey to the land of the former head-shrinkers.

The way I saw it, material mined from even the most reliable books or websites, lacked layers – the kind needed to understand something from the inside out.

The chief smoked the cigar until his face was glazed. A little girl of about six pranced over the bamboo floor, dragging a dead sloth behind her.

Recognizing it was not the perfect moment, I set about enquiring after the wise fool, doing my best to shape the question in my limited Spanish.

The chief did not respond.

So I translated the question back into English and played it over in my head, my mind's eye grimacing at the faulty construction.

I was about to have another go, when the chief drew long and hard on the mapacho cigar and replied:

'To be wise is to know the language of the trees.'

I scribbled the choice soundbite in my journal right away.

'Can a wise man be a fool?' I asked.

Again, the chief inhaled, his expression clouded by haze.

'Of course,' came the reply. 'Because wisdom and foolishness are the same. Wisdom is foolishness, and foolishness is wisdom.'

Scribbling fast, I spluttered another question:

'Does the wise fool teach the Shuar?'

'Yes, he teaches,' the chief agreed.

'And do you tell stories about him... about the wise fool?'

'Yes, we tell stories.'

Moving at lightning speed, my hand scribbled an indecipherable jumble of scrawl.

'Would you tell me a story about the wise fool?' I probed, anxiously.

Again, the chief inhaled and, in his own time, he replied:

'The wise fool travelled from far away and came to the jungle. By the time he arrived he was sick and his body marked all over with sores. He brought with him a lot of objects that we had not seen before... objects with no use. He thought he was intelligent because he had been to a city. That is why he was wise. But at the same time he was ignorant because he had no reason to come here. That is why he is a fool.'

The chief looked at me and grinned, mapacho smoke curling up into his eyes.

'Am I the wise fool?' I asked, a little piqued.

'You are the latest one of them,' the chief answered. 'But I am certain you will not be the last.'

## Six

After years of social climbing, Nasrudin was promoted from a lowly official to chief judge. Thrilled at his success, he took his place in court and heard the first case.

Two men were led in.

The first claimed that the other had bitten his ear.

The second asserted the first man had bitten his own ear.

Anxious he might be seen as not giving appropriate consideration to the first case of his career, Nasrudin ordered a recess of an hour. While the court waited for its judge, the wise fool slipped into his chambers and experimented.

For an entire hour he tried to bite his own

ear. But, every time he lashed out, his teeth snapping sideways, he overbalanced, fell on the floor, and bumped his head.

At the end of the recess, one side of his head was badly bruised. Smugly, Nasrudin took his place back in court, and ordered for his assistant to step forward.

'Make a full and thorough examination of the defendant's head,' he whispered. 'If it's found to be black and blue with bruises, we will know the defendant is innocent of the charge!'

ALGECIRAS, 1987

Curvaceous, big-boned, and a shameless flirt, Doña Fernández did her level best to shock everyone she encountered.

More often than not dressed in a super-tight t-shirt and an ultra-skimpy miniskirt, with a spectacular beehive towering above her head, the *doña* may once have been a beauty of sorts. But time had been cruel to the face that, I liked to imagine, had broken a thousand hearts. Half an inch of foundation cream, mascara, rouge, the blonde-dyed bouffant, and pearly dentures made it challenging to accurately deduce her age.

Pouting, she insisted she wasn't a day over forty. My own guess was that number and at least the same again.

Like all the other travellers taking refuge at her modest pension, I'd wound up under its roof having fallen victim to thieves.

The longest-serving resident, an American student, had been accosted at knife-point while hitching outside town.

Another, a Dutch artist, was mugged in the public toilets down at the port.

Three more – a trio of French street musicians – claimed to have been pickpocketed on a local bus. While queuing to report the incident at the police station, they'd had their instruments pinched.

As for me, I'd dozed off on the overnight sleeper from Madrid. Waking as the train screeched its way into Algeciras, I found myself relieved of my luggage, valuables, and even my shoes.

With no money or passport, and wearing a pair of borrowed sneakers, I drifted from hotel to hotel. But none would take me in as I didn't have ID, let alone funds with which to pay.

So, like all the other misfits lying low in the backstreets of Algeciras, I found the only sanctuary with an open door was the inimitable Hostal Magnífico.

Having recently arrived, my stock value was still high, as was the shock value in reacting to Doña Fernández's cleavage – which was thrust in my direction as soon as I crossed the threshold.

I remember huffing and puffing on that first morning, declaring optimistically how I'd be out 'within a day or two at most'.

Looking back, I see why the other residents did their best to keep straight faces. Some had been stuck in the Algeciras limbo zone for weeks or even months.

My room there resembled a cell in a Pakistani solitary confinement block. Unfortunately, I know that for certain. At the time, I didn't give the lack of comfort much thought, however. Mounted high on the back wall, the only window was the size and shape of a dinner plate. No amount of jumping up and down ever revealed its view.

For three days I lined up at the police station and waited to be seen. A line of freshly robbed travellers snaked out the door and around the block, hinting at the scale of the local crime wave.

When I finally got to the front, the duty officer seemed unimpressed by my tale. Rolling his eyes, he suggested I call my parents by reverse-charge call.

I did so, and they promised to send funds by express transfer.

Unfortunately, Andalucía's banking system was as incompetent as its thieves were capable. Despite endless visits to the bank, I was holed up in Algeciras for weeks.

At times during my long residence at Hostal Magnífico, I wondered whether the voluptuous

Doña Fernández was somehow caught up with the ring of thievery preying so adeptly on unsuspecting young travellers. Our communal misery ensured her business boomed.

The unintentional stay in Algeciras, with its vantage point over the Straits to Africa, may well easily been a footnote in my travels. But an encounter took place there unlike any other, leading me to ponder whether the theft of my belongings was somehow preordained.

Having been installed at Hostal Magnífico for about ten days, I was no longer shocked by Doña Fernández's cleavage. Nor was I interested in playing cards with the French street musicians, who were desperately attempting to win funds through poker. Like most of the residents, they'd long since given up on ever landing a transfer from faraway friends or family.

I filled the days by reading crime novels borrowed from the hostel's bookshelf, and by planning the books I hoped one day to write.

Days passed slowly.

As the first week edged towards the second, time slowed yet more.

Late one morning, a woman called María arrived.

For two reasons she was different from everyone else taking refuge at Hostal Magnífico.

First, she hadn't been robbed.

Second, despite what everyone thought and said, she was a truly good person.

Sitting in the reception when she arrived, I observed from a distance whether she recoiled at Doña Fernández's bust.

To my surprise, she did not.

Nor did she balk when the Dutch artist strode out the door wearing only a pair of painted-on boxer shorts.

María's journey had begun in her native Ecuador, and taken in more than fifty countries between her home village and the Sea of Okhotsk.

Slightly built, she was hollow-faced and prim in an unusual way. Her eyes were emerald green, and her smile was utterly intoxicating. Ten minutes after her arrival, the French musicians enquired if she wanted to play poker. As graciously as I have ever seen an invitation passed up, she declined. A moment later, when each of them tried to chat her up, María held up her ring finger, with the words, 'Already taken, boys.'

A couple of days came and went before I spoke to María myself. Although my funds still hadn't arrived, I did a deal with Señor Chen, the owner of a Chinese takeaway across the street from Hostal Magnífico. A hole-in-the-wall by any standards, it was roach-ridden, and stank of raw sewage. I swore that when my transfer came in I'd buy him a new set of frying pans.

Señor Chen may have been a rogue of the first order, and possibly the worst chef that ever lived, but he was my saviour for dishing out two daily bowls of leftover soup.

Three days after her arrival, María came in at lunchtime and joined me on the one and only table at Señor Chen's.

She asked what was good.

'I always have the "house soup",' I said.

'Is it delicious?'

'Not exactly.'

'Then why do you order it?' María asked.

'Because it's what Señor Chen gives me as his part of our deal.'

'And what do you give him in return?'

'I've promised him a set of new frying pans.'

María frowned – not a frown of displeasure so much as one derived from bewilderment.

'I'm in Algeciras because I was robbed,' I explained. 'Was on my way to Morocco... to visit the house where my grandfather lived.'

'Where was that?'

'Tangier.'

'Which street?'

'Rue de la Plage.'

María smiled graciously, as she'd done when the French musicians asked her out. Ordering a bowl of the house soup, she scratched at a patch of grime on the spoon placed before her by Señor Chen.

'Tangier's the crossroads of the winds,' she told me. 'It was there my journey began... and there it ended last week.'

'How long have you been travelling?' I asked.

María looked across at me hard, as though her mind was making a connection.

'For twenty years,' she said. 'Since the summer of 1967... when I was young and headstrong and guided by a dream.'

I asked a question, something about favourite destinations, but María didn't answer it. Instead, peering deep into my eyes, she said:

'The dream got me to leave a village in Ecuador, and set off in search of wonder.'

'Did you find it... the wonder?'

'Yes, I did.'

'Where?'

Again, María smiled, a little more intently than before.

'I found it on Tangier's rue de la Plage.'

My eyebrows rose.

'My grandfather lived at number seventy-one... at Villa Calpe.'

The leftover soup arrived at that moment, steaming more than usual.

'Yes, I know,' María countered in a slow, firm tone, when Señor Chen had sloped away into the kitchen.

'*Really?*'

'Yes. Because it was he who sent me on the journey.'

'You knew him?'

Raking the rim of her spoon over the soup's fatty surface, María nodded.

'Back then Tangier was a melting pot of people and of secrets,' she said, 'blown there by the prevailing winds. But he was in a league of his own.'

'He moved there after my grandmother died, in 1960,' I said. 'Utterly broken, he chose Tangier because he wanted to be in a place they'd never been together. He lived there until November 1969, when he was struck by a reversing Coca-Cola truck outside Villa Calpe.'

'That's right,' said María, as if affirming the veracity of my information.

'How did you come to meet him?'

'Through the actor James Coburn. They were inseparable friends as you surely know. At the height of his fame, Coburn was in Tangier making a movie called *Duffy*. I was involved as a lowly production assistant.'

'I heard that Coburn was a disciple of my grandfather.'

'Yes, he was. There were two great masters in his life. One was Bruce Lee, who instructed him in

40

the Way of Kung Fu. The other was Sirdar Ikbal Ali Shah, who instructed him in the Sufi Path.'

María stirred her soup, hoping to cool it.

'We used to meet in the afternoons and sit in the garden of Villa Calpe,' she said. 'He would tell me about his life, and I'd listen with rapture, like a child hearing magical tales.'

'What about your journey?'

The question caused María to freeze, the rim of the spoon hovering at her lips. Very slowly, her hand lowered, and she said:

'That's a very odd thing.'

'The journey?'

'Yes, and the way it came about... all of it.'

'In what way?'

María looked across at me hard again, her eyes twin oceans of emerald green.

'One afternoon your grandfather was complaining about a leak in the bathroom,' she said. 'The plumbing at Villa Calpe was in a terrible state. A week before, the boiler had exploded – blowing off half your grandfather's moustache. A plumber was called. As soon as he arrived, he began tearing up the floorboards.'

'Did he find the leak?'

María nodded even before the question was spoken.

'Yes, he did. But that's not all he found.'

My mind's eye caught a flash of a treasure trove secreted under the floor.

I shrugged.

'Treasure?' I whispered, hopefully.

'Yes... and no.'

'Beneath the leaking pipe a card was discovered.'

'A playing card?'

'Kind of... you see it was a tarot card... a very wet tarot card.'

'Which one?'

María sighed.

'The Fool,' she said.

No doubt visualizing the frying pans I'd promised him, Señor Chen cleared away our bowls.

María and I sat at the table for a good long while, our faces glinting with perspiration from the heat.

'The card was brought down into the garden by Zohra, the maid,' María explained. 'She presented it to your grandfather, who was sitting across from me in the shade.'

'What did he make of it?'

'I remember watching as he held it up to his face. I half-expected him to make a joke, after all it was The Fool. But he didn't. Instead, he appeared profoundly moved.'

'Do you know why?'

'Not exactly,' María answered. 'But what he told

me took centre stage in my mind, and has been rooted there for twenty years.'

'What was it?'

He explained that during a journey in the Himalayas in 1924, an astrologer divined a fool would come to him in the most unlikely of ways. A fool with a feathered hat and all dressed in green. It was then that the professor turned the card to face me. The Fool was wearing an olive-green cloak, and a cap onto which a peacock feather had been pinned.'

As though plucking the name from my mind, María asked whether I knew of Nasrudin.

'He's one of the family,' I replied.

'Your grandfather placed the tarot card on the low table between our chairs,' María said. 'He explained how the discovery of the card was an event to be unfurled over coming weeks, months and years... an event that would involve me.'

'How?'

Awkwardly, María twisted the gold band on her finger, her eyes trained down at the scuffed table-top.

'He ordered me to leave, and to return only when the filming was over. Although saddened, I did as he asked.'

'How long was it before you were done with *Duffy*?'

'About a month. A month of curiosity. From time to time, I would bump into your grandfather down in the souq. He'd greet me, but had no interest in conversation. I was very sad... sad, and yet curious.'

'So what happened at the end of filming?'

'As soon as we were done I rushed over to Villa Calpe,' María said. 'I was so excited and nervous. Opening the door, Zohra took me through to the garden where your grandfather was sitting in the shade. Tea was served. I sat there, waiting for some kind of explanation.'

'Did he explain?'

'After a long silence, he dug a hand into his jacket pocket and fished out the tarot card. To my surprise, he handed it to me. "For you," he said. I thanked him, wondering out loud if he thought me foolish.'

'What did he reply?'

María's eyes welled with tears.

'He said I was to leave on a journey.'

'Where?'

'Anywhere.'

'*Anywhere?*'

María nodded.

'A journey without a clear destination – a journey in search of Nasrudin.'

'And did you go...?'

'Oh yes, I did.'

'Where?'

'Anywhere and, at times, what seemed like *everywhere*... To every corner of the earth where

Nasrudin was found. Of course I had to tune myself to recognize his various incarnations. As you know he appears under different names between here and the farthest reaches of the East.'

'What was the purpose of the journey?' I enquired, wondering whether my grandfather had wanted to rid himself of green-eyed María from Ecuador.

'To find myself. By finding the wise fool.'

A stream of questions came to mind. Before I could pose any of them, María held up a hand, signalling she had something to tell me.

'Your grandfather said the journey would give me the experience needed for the next phase of my life. He said it was the clay with which I'd sculpt a masterpiece. Before I left, he told me to make a solemn promise.'

'What?'

Again, María's eyes glinted with tears as she looked across at me.

'That I would return to Villa Calpe at the end of the journey, and pass The Fool on to someone.'

'Who?'

'"He who answered to his name."'

Fumbling to make sense of it, I sat there in confused silence, before blurting out:

'I was supposed to visit my grandfather's house last week.'

María had already made the connection. But

it didn't explain how she'd known to find me in Algeciras.

Unbuckling the leather satchel hanging from her chair, she took out a journal. It was battered and worn, and was packed with scribbled notes, sketches, and mementos of a thousand destinations.

With extraordinary care, she shuffled to the middle of the book, and removed a tattered rectangle of card.

The Fool.

'This is for you,' she said.

'You should keep it.'

'No, no, no… it's time for me to pass it on, as your grandfather instructed.'

'So that I can continue the journey in search of Nasrudin?'

'Yes!'

'Am I to roam the earth for twenty years as you've done?'

María grinned, her emerald eyes bright again.

'Take all the time you need,' she said.

## Seven

ne of Nasrudin's students asked him what he considered Truth to be.

After thinking for a long time, he answered:

'Truth is something I have never in my life been found guilty of speaking.'

LUXOR, 2003

Ancient Egyptian folklore describes an Elysian realm known as 'Aaru', the so-called 'Field of Reeds', to which the souls of mortals journey after death.

Although ever-curious when it comes to folklore, I didn't know much about the treasury of myths dating back to Ancient Egypt. That is, not until the friend of a friend pointed me in the direction of a small village lost in the desert between Luxor and the Red Sea.

The details provided were sketchy:

A foreigner who didn't speak Arabic was living with the locals, and was behaving in a very strange way.

I remember thinking it wasn't worth investigating, and being told by my informant that I'd 'thank the heavens' if I went.

Having been holed up writing a novel in the

Winter Palace Hotel in Luxor for as long as I could remember, I was ready for a break.

So, although dubious, I agreed to go take a look.

Spend any time in Luxor and you can't help but acquire hangers-on. Within an hour of arriving at the railway station, I had a money-changer, a barber, a fixer, and a guide. Egypt's unwritten rule is that hangers-on give the traveller preferential treatment in return for availing of their services rather than those of the competition.

I'd been a regular visitor to Luxor, and a guest at the gloriously faded jewel of the Winter Palace, since my teens. Taken to Upper Egypt first by my parents, I found the city perched at the edge of the Nile to be a pleasure dome of exotic adventure.

Random attacks, revolutions, and the general instability of the Middle East had caused fickle khaki-clad tourists to go elsewhere for their Oriental fix.

Although it shames me to admit it, part of the draw of Luxor was the lack of tourists. My travels tend to zigzag between destinations low on security and high on the unusual. As far as I'm concerned, there's nowhere quite as perfect to lie low and write than in the faded grandeur of a cut-price palace hotel.

That's how I found myself in a spacious suite, the floor hardwood parquet, with a vintage fan whirring round on the ceiling above.

Over the weeks I stayed at the Winter Palace, I engaged more and more hangers-on – dozens of them.

On the scale of retainers none could compare with Mustapha.

A goliath of a man, a life-long passion for mutton kebabs had got the better of him. As he reminded me frequently, he was the finest taxi driver in all Upper Egypt.

Whenever I'd step out from the Winter Palace's revolving door and stroll down one of the curled twin flights of stairs, Mustapha would screech to a halt on the street below. The tyres of his battered old Peugeot 504 would be smoking, the exhaust belching out clouds of poisonous gas.

Quite how Mustapha knew I would be exiting the hotel when I did was one of Luxor's great mysteries. I put it down to a kind of magical telepathy between us.

On the morning of the journey into the desert, I casually mentioned the plan to the bellboy on the way down to breakfast. By the time I was ready to leave, I found a line of the hotel's staff poised to the right of the door.

The manager wished me good fortune and reminded me to trust no one.

The concierge provided me with a map, on which danger zones had been marked in red felt-tip pen.

The maître d'hôtel bowed, and clapped his hands twice.

A pair of staff with small feet shuffled out, lugging an oversized hamper forwards at double-speed.

'A little light lunch, monsieur.'

Before I could reach the revolving door, the concierge scrutinized the directions provided by my informant. Checking them against the map he'd given me, he scowled, his expression disapproving.

'Please forget this unwise journey,' he urged. 'Go out to the pool and lie in the shade.'

Thanking him, and his colleagues, I made my way through the revolving door, emerging in the dazzling morning light.

A minute later I was down on the street, where Mustapha's decrepit Peugeot was waiting for me.

Clambering in, I handed over the directions. Mustapha studied them intently.

'Will this car make it?' I asked.

As though I were enquiring whether a war-horse was capable of enduring a battle, the veteran driver tugged a rag from his wrist, mopped his brow, and gave a double thumbs up.

'Very good,' he affirmed. '*No broblem!*'

Three hours passed, in which the Peugeot shrieked and groaned along metalled roads pocked with holes, then down telescoping tracks. Either side of the oily smog-trail belching out behind us, the desert spanned out from horizon to horizon.

Mustapha put on a tape of rousing love songs by the vintage Egyptian heartthrob, Hafez.

From time to time he would glide to a halt, mop his brow, and glance wearily at the instructions.

Whenever I offered the map, he'd wave it away, as though swiping a fly buzzing around his head.

Like all Egyptian taxi drivers, Mustapha had no faith at all in cartography. The only thing he trusted was information provided by word of mouth.

That meant screeching to a stop as soon as anyone was spotted herding sheep near the track. More often than not it was a child of six or seven.

Having exchanged elaborate greetings, shared water, conversed, laughed, asked, listened, commiserated, and thanked God half a dozen times, we would press on a little further... until the next underage shepherd came into view through the Peugeot's cracked windscreen.

The sun arced its way up into an empty sky.

We passed a large, dented, sand-swept sign. It featured a hand-drawn skull and crossbones, against what appeared to be an illustration of an explosion.

'The danger zone!' I roared, jabbing a finger to the map.

'*No broblem!*' Mustapha shot back.

'Are you sure?!'

The taxi driver nodded, then shook his head.

'Very good!' he muttered. 'Very very good.'

Another hour came and went before the Peugeot overheated. While waiting for the engine to cool, I unbuckled the hamper and scattered the Winter Palace's feast over a picnic blanket on the rock-strewn ground.

Eyes lighting up at spying food, Mustapha chomped his way through three plates of sandwiches, half a leg of lamb, and a cherry trifle – its dish designed to be cooled by an in-built ice basin. Long since melted, the ice had transmuted through desert alchemy into boiling water. Discovering it, Mustapha let out a cry of joy, and brewed a flask of tea.

Eventually, the engine cooled and we pushed onwards, faltering and jerking on for another hour and a half.

As I drew breath to give the order for retreat, Mustapha's index finger motioned at the horizon.

Drowned in mirage up ahead lay a cluster of homes.

'D'you think that's it?' I asked.

Mustapha cackled and whooped:

'Very good! Very good!'

Veering off the track, the Peugeot 504 navigated a zigzagging course between boulders and ditches, until it reached the clutch of frail stone houses.

Villagers streamed out as we appeared.

A minute or two after that, Mustapha and I were staggering through the searing heat from the vehicle to the shade, calling greetings as we went.

I wasn't sure whether to reveal right away the reason for our expedition, or to let things naturally progress. My travels had taught me when possible to favour the second option.

Having reached the villagers, we shook hands, thanked God, and ran through the catalogue of pleasantries preceding the rituals of desert hospitality. We were coaxed into one of the stone houses, to drink tea, and to rest.

In the Western world unexpected visitors may well be regarded with suspicion; the opposite is true in the vast expanse of desert in which we found ourselves. Another difference that often struck me was the balance between chatter and silence.

In the Occident, a newcomer might expect to be bombarded with questions and drawn into protracted conversations. In Arab lands, silence is more revered than even the most enlightened exchange of words.

So, we sat there, drinking tea, with no enquiry as to why we had come or where we were going. Poised beside me, Mustapha broke the silence by thanking God.

Resorting to the magical telepathy between us, I pushed him to enquire about the foreigner. Before any such question could be voiced, the villagers spoke:

'He arrived a month ago,' said the first.

'With little luggage, no shoes and dressed in rags,' added a second.

'He doesn't speak our language,' explained a third.

'Where is he now?'

'Under the ground,' the first villager said.

'He's *dead*?!'

'No... not dead...'

'Then what is he doing underground?'

'Sleeping.'

'*Sleeping*?'

'He sleeps a lot of the time.'

'Why?'

The villagers conferred, argued, agreed and, in unison, replied:

'We don't know.'

'Can I meet him?' I asked.

'If God wills it.'


The villagers led me out into the blazing light.

As we crossed the patch of empty ground, circumventing a low hill, I tried to imagine what they must have thought of the mysterious foreigner arriving on foot.

On the far side of the hill, one of the villagers strode over to a crude stone doorframe set at an angle against the gradient. Pulling away a sheet of corrugated iron, he led the way down a set of steps carved into the rock.

At once the insufferable heat was replaced by extreme refrigeration, ice-cold shadows, and a faint scent of rotting meat. Following the others down, I readied myself for the unexpected.

But that certainly didn't prepare me for what came next.

The stairs led down to an antechamber. As I descended into the darkness, I tried to work out if the structure was a remnant of the Ancient Egyptian era. In some ways it was like the tombs I had visited in the Valleys of the Kings and Queens. But there were no hieroglyphs. Instead of the plaster favoured by the ancients, it appeared as though the walls were rendered in cement.

My eyes calibrating to the lack of light, I paced through the antechamber, and down a long corridor – a conduit into the main chamber.

The room was illuminated by a dozen shafts of blinding light. Somehow channelled from ground level, they took my breath away. I remember puzzling at being so impressed. After all, a few minutes before there had been abundant light. But only now that it was limited, did I notice it at all.

Mustapha's silhouette strode through to the centre of the chamber which, I suppose, must have measured about a hundred foot square. As I drew closer, and as the others moved out of the way, I caught first sight of what I was later to describe as the 'altar'.

Crafted from a series of stone blocks, it reached chest-height.

Outstretched upon it, was the body of a blond man.

Bare feet together, both arms were crossed over the torso in mummy stance. His eyes were closed. Had I not been told he was alive, I might have assumed the reverse.

We stood there, watching.

Succumbing to the talc-like dust, I sneezed, automatically excusing myself.

The foreigner opened one eye, and then the other.

Lifting his head, he scanned the chamber.

'Someone speak English?'

'Sorry,' I said. 'It's terribly dusty down here.'

Sitting up, the man appeared intensely sleepy, as though he'd been hibernating all winter.

'What are you doing here?' he muttered, an accent to his English.

'Just passing by,' I replied, adding, 'what about you?'

The foreigner jumped off the altar, completed the ritual of shaking hands, and said:

'I'll tell you over a cup of tea.'

So we left the chamber with its glorious shafts

of light, and retraced the route back into the realm awash with illumination.

'I am Dieter... Dieter from Switzerland,' the blond foreigner said, leading me to a low stone shack at the edge of the hamlet. 'They've given me this to use.'

'What about the cavern down there?' I asked, looking over my shoulder. 'What's that all about?'

'First tea, then I will explain.'

So Dieter cooked up a pot of tea. Then he clicked his neck, his shoulders, his finger joints, and his toes, inhaled and exhaled, and regarded me through ocean-blue eyes.

'Wish I could tell you I'm a crackpot,' he said. 'I'm sure that's what you think of me. After all, being out here as I am, lying on a slab ten metres under the desert... I can imagine it would look odd.'

Dieter folded the mop of hair from the left side of his head to the right. As he did so, I wondered how old he was. I guessed about thirty-five.

'I've seen stranger things,' I countered.

Studiously, Dieter the Swiss narrowed his eyes and let out half a laugh.

'I should like to hear about them.'

'I'm more interested in hearing how you ended up in the desert,' I replied.

'Through a journey that began with a hunch.'

Dieter explained how, as an anthropologist with

an interest in Pharaonic Egypt, he was obsessed with their notion of 'Aaru', the so-called Field of Reeds to which the souls of mortals venture in the afterlife.

As Mustapha the taxi driver dozed out in the shade, Dieter the Swiss described the route thus far.

A journey from the town of Aarau, in the canton of Aargau, to the remote desert hamlet in which we'd met.

'"Aaru" sounded rather like "Aarau",' he said at the end of the explanation, 'which is how I came to be interested in Ancient Egypt as a child.'

'Why don't you just study the hieroglyphs like everyone else?'

Dieter rubbed a thumb to either eye, and sighed out of the corner of his mouth.

'Because I want to understand it in a different way.'

'Is that why you arrived here barefoot and without any backup?'

'It's part of it.'

I asked how he came to hear of the chamber.

'It was left by a Swiss field unit who were doing work here back in the 'sixties,' he said. 'My PhD supervisor had been involved. He told me all about it, and even gave me the key. I didn't want to freak out the villagers, so I turned up in the most discreet way possible. To my delight it was still here. The only problem's been trying to explain what I'm doing.'

'They think you're a nutcase,' I said.

'Yeah, I know.'

'They're wondering how long you're going to stay.'

Dieter the Swiss coaxed the mop of blond hair from the right side of his head back to the left.

'Wish I knew the answer to that myself.'

I accepted a second cup of tea, my mind struggling to frame questions.

'Don't quite get how lying down there in the dark is going to magically transport you to the Field of Reeds,' I said.

Again, Dieter sighed through the corner of his mouth.

'I've spent the last ten years with anthropologists, psychologists, students of philosophy, and a never-ending cast of serious men and women. Each one of them tackles the research in exactly the same way. Once in a while one of them branches out and poses what appears to be a radical new approach. Yet, even at best, they never stray from the path mapped out by those who came before them.'

'So you're blazing an entirely new trail?'

'Yes, in some ways I am.'

We sat in silence for a few minutes, listening to the stray breeze tearing over the desert. In different circumstances I might have given voice to my many questions. Somehow, though, it didn't seem like the right time.

But there was something I needed to know.

When the breeze had died down, and our ears were both tuned in to Mustapha snoring outside once again, I asked Dieter how he'd come to think like he did.

The answer that came was not the one I had been expecting.

'When I was a kid,' he said, 'at bedtime my parents used to read me stories about a very funny man. He wore a big, white turban on his head, had a long, flowing beard, and rode a donkey backwards. Sometimes he was the king, and at other times he was a beggar. But no matter whether he was rich or poor, he always saw the world in a fresh "back-to-front" way.' Dieter paused, as though wishing to make a point. 'His name was "Nasrudin",' he said.

A shiver coursed down my spine.

'Amazing,' I whispered.

The Swiss anthropologist from Aarau rummaged in a daypack and pulled out a hardback book. The covers were desperately scuffed, as if they'd withstood a sandstorm.

'This is it,' he said, passing it to me.

Opening it to the title page, I read:

'The Exploits of the Incomparable Mulla Nasrudin, by Idries Shah.'

## Eight

Nasrudin had lost his job, and resorted to taking work as an interpreter of dreams. Finding himself in a new country, he was ordered to get a licence. Annoyed at the petty officialdom, he went to the government office that dealt with licences and waited in turn.

'I'd like a licence to interpret dreams,' he explained when his turn had come.

The official looked him up and down and scowled.

'Complete these papers, then lie down there, fall asleep, wake up, and interpret your dream.'

'Very well!' Nasrudin snarled.

Lying on the ground, he quickly fell asleep, and found himself dreaming that a mysterious benefactor was paying gold coins on to his hand. It was the most wonderful dream he'd ever had. As he watched, nine gleaming coins were piled up on his palm. Just as the tenth coin was about to be paid out, he woke up and found all the gold gone.

Cursing himself, he mumbled he'd have settled for nine.

'What did you deduce from your dream?' the official asked.

'That I'm a greedy good-for-nothing,' replied Nasrudin.

London, 1986

A favourite tale I heard in childhood was about an old woman who fell into a fast-flowing river.

As the villagers raced downstream in the desperate hope of finding her, the woman's husband hurried in the opposite direction.

'She'll be swept away with the raging current!' someone yelled.

'You don't know my wife!' the man shot back, running upstream.

The story, which describes how the old woman did things differently from everyone else, has always made me think of Nasrudin.

But, that's not all.

You see, year after year, decade after decade, as I turn it over in my mind, my subconscious has linked it with my aunt, Amina.

Like the old woman in the tale, she did things contrary to others.

She dressed differently, spoke differently, observed things differently and – most importantly of all – she thought differently from everyone else… as though her circuits were wired up back-to-front.

Amina was six years older than my father, but

watching them together I used to get the feeling he was far more of what kids would call a 'grown-up'. Although capable of reducing his audience to howling laughter, or joining in with the fun, it would be accurate to say he was superbly considered in almost everything he did.

My aunt, on the other hand, had managed to reach maturity with her child's eye on the world still firmly intact.

While her generation grew up, and got on with their lives against the backdrop of war, aunt Amina embarked on an existence untouched by the difficulties of adulthood. Centre stage on the grand rumpus of delight that was her life, was an imagination quite unlike any other.

Amina could be called upon to tell stories from morning till night. Whereas most adults might find regaling an audience with tales a task, for her nothing was quite so pleasurable.

The reason is, of course, that adults need to prise themselves away from their reality, before 'descending' to the level of children. Having never sloughed the mindset of her younger self, Amina could perceive stories in the way they were appreciated by kids.

Clinging hold of far more of my childhood persona than was expected of me I, too, managed to emerge with my default imagination intact.

As I pushed out into the world, I would turn to Amina and observe how she acted in, and reacted to, given situations.

A yardstick by which I learned to behave, I saw how she succeeded in navigating a path of her own. For her there was only one thing to bear in mind – the resolute conviction that nothing was so important as being true to oneself right to the core.

I remember once accompanying her to a plush cocktail party in aid of a charity. Having miscalculated the dress code, she'd arrived in a crumpled tweed suit. All the other women there were dolled up to the nines in cocktail dresses. My aunt glanced at me as we strode in through the door and, in a loud voice, exclaimed:

'She who is different is the mistress of her fate!'

One of the great joys of life is getting to know oneself.

And, knowing oneself is a secret to happiness. It might sound obvious, but in my experience it's definitely not.

Over the years, I have cross-referenced myself with other members of my family. I like to think that I have my father's productiveness, although our minds were not the same. His was the epitome of an analytical engine – dazzling in speed and efficiency.

Although not as fast or as perfectly calibrated, my mind is configured to champion the fantastical.

Now that I know myself well inside and out, I can state with certainty that my aunt Amina and I were reflections of each other. We shared a mutual adoration for spontaneity, oddity, and for zigzagging journeys.

Like her, I yearn for unplanned and random expeditions peppered with eccentricity, and with peculiarity guaranteed.

There is a dark side, too.

As with myself, my aunt Amina was famously disorganized, messy, with handwriting that was indescribably challenging to read.

Like me, she was obsessed with the role of the wise fool... perhaps, as I've said, because she was wired differently from everyone else.

I often ask myself why my aunt was as she was, and whether she was shaped by nature or by nurture. My conclusion is that it was a mixture of the two.

Aunt Amina was born on Halloween night 1918, eleven days before the Armistice. Her father, my grandfather, was the author and roving diplomat, the Sirdar Ikbal Ali Shah. Her mother was Elizabeth Louise MacKenzie, a member of the Scottish aristocracy who, aged eighteen, eloped to the Hindu Kush.

Like those of my father, Amina's childhood and adolescence were spent in constant flux. The storm-clouds of the 'thirties led to all-out war, and shaped my aunt's life.

Trained to shoot a bolt-action Lee Enfield .303 as a child by my grandfather's Pashtun bodyguard, she was a crack shot. A karate champion, too, she was daring in an almost unhinged way. The only other person I have ever encountered with the same utter nonchalance for fear was an SAS commander who'd been dropped behind enemy lines in the first Gulf War. So, it came as little surprise when I discovered in a declassified file that aunt Amina had been considered for a covert parachute operation in 1944.

Rather than attempting to curb his daughter's eccentricities, my grandfather seemed to encourage them. It was he who took her on mysterious missions on behalf of governments and monarchs of the pre- and post-war Middle East. And, it was he who strove behind the scenes to shape the course of aunt Amina's life.

A close friend of the deposed King Zog I of Albania, my grandfather worked tirelessly to marry his daughter to Crown Prince Leka. While no doubt flattered, my aunt was at the same time aghast – for Prince Leka was twenty years her junior.

Having published her first book, *Tiger of the*

*Frontier*, aged nineteen, Amina continued to write over a span of seven decades. Her abiding passion was for folktales. While her written stories reflect the back-to-front wise-foolery, her paramount gift was as an oral teller of tales.

So it was perfect when Amina was elected as chairman of the College of Storytellers in London in the early 'eighties. Although my father's brainchild, he left it to her and a close-knit troupe of storytellers to shape.

Whenever I was free, I would accompany aunt Amina to the College's sessions. Sitting cross-legged on Afghan carpets, I'd absorb tales from all corners of the earth. While listening, I trained myself to observe the way each speaker handled the task of telling. There were some talented contributors, but none had the back-to-front-ness and the inside-out-ness of my aunt.

At the end of one evening session, as we strolled through the deserted streets of north-west London on the way back to my aunt's flat, I asked her what made a good storyteller.

Amina stopped.

I wondered for a moment if I'd caused offence.

'Storytelling's something you are born with,' she said. 'In the same way that learning a language in adulthood will result in an accent, the same is true for storytelling. You can learn to mimic, but you'll never speak in the same way as someone born with the language inside them.'

I asked something else, but Amina was still thinking about my first question.

'You've got to understand something,' she said as we pressed on. 'The secret that's central to everything. The mortar that binds the human existence together, into a shape that makes sense.'

'What is it?'

Again, my aunt paused, mahogany-brown eyes reflecting the lamplight.

'Almost everyone you'll ever meet is fearful,' she said. 'They're frightened – not necessarily of danger... but rather of what others think of them. Stumbling through life fitfully, they're terrified they'll be lampooned. The condition begins in the crib and continues to the grave. Of course, some people learn to mask it – to pretend they're not scared. But it's always there, suppurating like an ulcer.'

Amina closed her eyes for a moment and inhaled through her nose, as though magnificently inspired.

'If you can detach yourself from caring what others think,' she said, 'not in a superficial way, but right down to the marrow of your bones, all kinds of doors open. The more people single you out as an oddity, or a fool, the more strength you'll take on – like a storm-cloud sucking up water from the ocean. Embrace the folly and foolishness, harness it, and

like some ancient alchemy it will transmute... into a
wisdom of the purest kind.'

## *Nine*

A friend stopped Nasrudin in the
town square and described the most
delicious lamb stew in the world –
cooked in a far-off kingdom by a princess more
lovely than any other alive.

'I beg you to share the recipe with me!'
Nasrudin pleaded. 'As I surely won't live
another day without tasting such a succulent-
sounding dish.'

After much imploring, the friend scribbled
down the recipe and handed it to Nasrudin.

'Don't forget to buy the very best lamb you
can find,' he said, 'because only lamb fit for a
princess will do.'

His mouth drooling with anticipation,
Nasrudin stuffed the recipe under his belt and
hurried to the bazaar. Instead of going to his
usual butcher, he began patronizing a stall at the
far end of the market, which was ten times as
expensive, but sold meat fit for a king.

'I'll have five pounds of the best lamb,' he
said. 'And be sure to not trick me!'

The best cut of lamb was weighed out, and Nasrudin parted with all the money he had. Setting off for home, he imagined the first bite of the royal stew touching his lips. Then, breaking into a run, he tripped.

The packet fell onto the ground.

A giant eagle swooped down, snatched it in its talons, and soared into the sky.

'O feathered fool of a bird!' he bellowed, waving his fist at the sky. 'You have the meat, but you won't be able to make the princess's dish! Come back and take the recipe!'


LANGTON HOUSE, 1976

For my father, Nasrudin was not so much a personality – fictional or otherwise – but a mindset.

As far as he was concerned, the wise fool was like an equation – not a scientific one, but a cultural one… a mechanism by which to challenge conventional thinking and transmute the way people thought.

For him, it was a secret code.

A code that could be harnessed to resolve almost any situation.

As children we were obsessed with chocolate.

It's all we thought about, talked about, and wished for. Whenever guests came to the house to visit my parents we would rate them on their generosity in bearing chocolate gifts.

In times when there was no chocolate, we would go to our father's study and stand in the pool of sunlight beside the door. He would be lost in his own concentration, clattering away at his typewriter. Eventually, he would look up, see us there, and pause.

One of us would be pushed forwards by the others and say:

'Baba, we need chocolate, and we need it badly.'

'How badly?'

My sisters and I would exchange pained glances.

'Desperately!'

One blistering afternoon in the long, hot summer of 1976, when I was nine, we went to beg for chocolate as we used to do. Instead of dishing out a handful of coppers, our father beckoned us in to where he was hunched over the typewriter.

'Today I'm going to show you something,' he said. 'Something very important indeed.'

Craning forwards, we listened.

'One day I won't be here to give you money to buy your precious chocolate with,' he said, 'so I'm going to show you how to get enough coins yourselves.'

I remember feeling worried, as though we were about to be tricked. Before I could voice my concerns, my father opened a small drawer on his desk and took out a stack of miniature envelopes – the size and shape of a shirt pocket.

He gave them to my twin sister, Safia.

To Saira, who was the oldest, he passed a sharpened pencil.

'These are the tools you will need,' he said.

'I don't have a tool though, Baba,' I moaned.

'Well then, I'll give you one. Hurry into the garage and fish out the old pram and dust it down, because it will be important to what you are going to do.'

'And what are we going to do, Baba?'

'You are going to go into the garden, from plant to plant and bush to bush, gathering seeds. Put some from a single plant in each envelope and bring it back to me with samples of its leaves.'

We trudged away, sure that we were being duped. An hour later we were back at the study door with a stack of rattling envelopes.

Examining the contents one at a time, our father called out the name of a plant, which Saira wrote down on the front of the packet in her best handwriting.

Once the envelopes were ready, we were given further instructions:

'Put them neatly in the pram, make a big sign which reads "Finest Seeds For Sale At Discount Prices By Children In Need Of Chocolate" and wheel it through the village.'

'But Baba,' Safia intoned fretfully, 'we don't know how much to charge.'

My father scratched his head.

'Well, how much is chocolate?'

We conferred.

'About 5p a bar.'

'And there are three of you, right? So you need about 30p to buy two bars each – right?'

We nodded enthusiastically. Two bars each was better than right.

'How many envelopes do you have?'

I did a count.

'Twenty-one.'

'So charge 2p per envelope, and give some out to good customers… because people always like getting stuff for free.'

We set off, pushing the pram through the village. Although it was hot, we managed to sell twenty packets of seeds within an hour and a half.

Delighted, we returned to the study door with the coins.

'Always remember this day,' my father said, 'because you learned how to think in an original way.'

## Ten

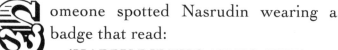

omeone spotted Nasrudin wearing a badge that read:

'HAPPY BIRTHDAY TO ME!'

'How old are you this year?' a friend asked.

'I'm fifty-three.'

'But you said you were fifty-three when I asked you last time!'

'Exactly,' Nasrudin gloated. 'As everyone knows, I'm a man of my word!'


APPALACHIA, 1994

As I steered the compact rental car off the main road, and caught a first sight of the rickety church silhouetted in the distance, the full moon broke free from its heavy mantle of cloud.

The group I'd come to meet might have regarded it as a sign from God, but I saw it as an omen. The frail Chevy heaved along the rutted track, like a sacrifice about to offer itself to a supreme being. As it did so, I tasted bile in my mouth, my mind questioning whether such a reckless investigation was really necessary.

Even before I was out of the car, which I'd parked at the side of the church opposite a row of monster trucks, my ears caught the strains of euphoric celebration.

A moment later, fortified by curiosity, I was standing in the doorway, my elongated shadow projected down the aisle.

On my travels I've witnessed all manner of unworldly things…

A godman in Tamil Nadu swallowing pebbles.

A preacher in Manila performing 'psychic surgery'.

An Amazonian shaman apparently walking on water.

A Moroccan exorcist cavorting about in a trance.

But compared to what was taking place in Appalachia on that moonlit night back in 1994, none of it impressed me.

Wood-framed and ramshackle, the timber church was lit by dozens of neon tubes, bathing the congregation in ghostly light.

At the front of the hall six young men were standing on a stage, each of them with an instrument. A stream of early Elvis numbers were relayed to giant speakers hanging from the beams. Instead of ripped jeans and t-shirts, they were dressed in button-down shirts like all the other men.

The women wore plain white dresses ranging from the top of the neck down to their heels.

But it wasn't the lighting or the band, the orderly

dress-sense, or even the monster trucks outside that struck me.

It was the snakes.

A friend who'd grown up in Appalachia first told me of the services he had experienced as a child. As 'Melungeons', his family were regarded as outsiders, descended from mixed African, European, and Native American stock. Melungeons were taunted – for looking different, and for the way they viewed the world and experienced it. Most of all, they were ridiculed for occasionally being born with six fingers on either hand.

Although intrigued by the Melungeons, what stuck in my head was what my friend told me about the way some congregations in Appalachia proved their faith.

Slipping into a pew at the back, I watched.

The band was whipping out a ballad of lost love, their faces and button-down shirts drenched in sweat. At the pulpit, the preacher's hands were raised to the heavens, his body forming a capital 'Y'. The congregation – about three hundred men, women, and children, were in their seats – consumed by the electricity that charged the room.

Had I been told the neon tube lights, the instruments, and the oversized speakers weren't powered from the mains, but from current tapped from the air, I would have believed it.

As I watched the band, the preacher, and his flock,

shaking and quaking, whooping and shuddering, three men and a woman stood up in the pews. Each of them was holding a miniature wooden crate above their head, ventilation holes pierced through the sides. Overcome by emotion, they shook the crates hysterically, tears rolling down their cheeks.

Whipped in their hysteria to the point of no return, the audience went wild with delight. Some were screaming. Others jumped up and ran around babbling in tongues. More still collapsed to the floor, their bodies writhing and squirming as though electrocuted.

Craning my neck to get a good view, I observed.

Amid the frenzied backdrop of wailing and flailing, the shallow crates were unfastened.

One by one, the contents were fished out.

The band fell silent.

The preacher praised the Lord.

Held high above heads, the dozen serpents were waved about, goaded and mocked. Some were copperheads, and the rest were timber rattlesnakes. Coiling and wheeling in alarm, they licked the air, no doubt wondering what was going on.

The band struck up again, and the snakes were passed around. The music blaring, the preacher and his flock were roused in the most spectacular way.

Some of the congregation didn't take part, but a great many did. Savouring their time with the serpent in their grasp, they dared it to strike them. Others sipped at hipflasks, filled with what I learned later was strychnine poison.

The snake-handling tradition is said to have arisen in Appalachia a century or more ago, when a preacher started taking a New Testament verse literally (Mark 16:17-18). It says:

*And these signs shall follow them that believe: In my name shall they cast out devils; they shall speak with new tongues. They shall take up serpents; and if they drink any deadly thing, it shall not hurt them.*

On the night I visited the Pentecostal church three people were bitten. Fortunately none perished – although I heard that one of them was struck down at another service soon after.

Not until now have I described the scene I witnessed that night a quarter of a century ago. At some points during the intervening years I've questioned whether I actually saw what I thought I saw in moonstruck Appalachia. The reason I haven't published my memory of the event until now, is that I've been at a loss for words to describe the interwoven layers of emotion.

Every so often we encounter things in our lives that form perfect bite-sized chunks, the kind that provide a choice anecdote. But despite shaping them in our minds, they're out of reach, as if defying the power of description.

The snake-handlers of Appalachia are an example. While it was no trouble to sketch out the general scene, I've never felt capable of portraying the deeper sense of it all. The constituent parts were obvious enough, yet when thrown together, the experience touched me in an extraordinary way.

Over the years I have frequently revisited my memory of that night, reflecting on the players and their motives.

The way I perceive it has depended on my own condition, experiences, and the stage of my journey.

Sometimes I shake my head in despair that anyone could be so foolish as to wave snakes around. Other times I've tried not to judge, but rather absorb what I remember through a kind of inner osmosis.

On yet more occasions I've questioned whether it was me who was the fool.

Or indeed, if, as the fools, the snake-handling congregation were the wise.

*Eleven*

Nasrudin was walking home from the teahouse late one night when he dropped his key. Not wishing to wake up his wife, he got down on his hands and knees and started searching.

It was so dark, and the ground was so stony, he quickly gave up. While running a hand to his sore back, he noticed a streetlamp on the other side of the road, beneath which was a lovely smooth patch of ground. Scampering over, Nasrudin got down on his hands and knees once again, and started looking for the key.

A few minutes passed and a man who lived in the same area saw Nasrudin on his hands and knees.

'What are you looking for?' he asked.

'The key to my house. I don't dare wake my wife up as she'll yell at me. So I'm out here searching for it.'

Being kindly, Nasrudin's neighbour crouched down and helped to search as well. A little later, another friendly neighbour stopped and gave a hand.

Then another, and another.

Within an hour, twenty people were all searching for the key in the pool of lamplight. Irritated that they hadn't located the key, the first man stood up.

'Nasrudin!' he growled. 'Where exactly did you drop the key?'

'Over there on the dark stony path.'

'Why aren't we looking there, then?!' demanded the crowd.

'Because,' said Nasrudin, 'there's so much more light over here!'


ORINOCO 1988; SWAKOPMUND, 2003

On a long, twisting journey through Latin America, I once met a Texan sitting on the palm-fringed porch of a café on the banks of the Orinoco.

He was hunched over what looked like an impressively thick dictionary. In one hand he had a red felt-tip pen, and in the other a magnifying glass. Intrigued, I watched as he thumbed through the book, checking off words with a tick.

He glanced up at me.

'Learning some new vocabulary?' I probed.

He frowned.

'It's not a dictionary.'

'Oh.'

'It's a gazetteer.'

'You mean a list of places?'

The man nodded.

'That's right.'

'Are you marking places you'd like to go to?'

'No,' said the traveller. 'Places I've been. Some people collect postage stamps... I collect places.'

'You mean places you've been to?'

'Yup. Or been through. And, my oh my, there's been a lot of places these last couple of days. Gotta catch up.'

The man thumbed through the book fast, the pages animated with red ticks.

'Looks like you've been everywhere already,' I said.

'Nope. Not yet. But give me some more time and I will.'

'If you go back to a place, do you tick it twice?'

Slamming the gazetteer shut, the Texan swivelled around.

'I *never* go back!' he riposted angrily.

'Why not?'

'Because once it's done, it's done.'

Unlike the red-tick traveller on a quest to visit the whole known world, the joy for me is venturing back to the same place time and again.

Sometimes I find myself returning to a city or a town over and over, limiting the journey to a single quarter. Should I ever tire of it, I would move on to another part. But it rarely happens. For, by training one's senses in the right way, magnificent wonders can be revealed almost anywhere.

A journey at speed is a sure-fire way to ensure it's made blind.

True, some places need less time to unlock their

secrets. Of course, perception of a place is down to chance, and to the conditions of an encounter. Some destinations require extra time... time in which the conscious mind and the subconscious can peel away the layers.

The way I see it, perception is not so much about the place being perceived, so much as the person observing it. One's ability – or indeed *inability* – to make sense of a place is a reflection of oneself more than it is of the destination.

The Texan man and his gazetteer piqued me.

In the days after our encounter, my daydreaming mind would pick out the image of that brawny right hand ticking off names in red felt-tip.

At the same time, that part of my brain so often called to work overtime on calming, nudged me to relax. 'You'll never see him again,' it said. 'So let's think about something else... like the sun slipping into the ocean as viewed from a jungle shore.'

Several years elapsed in which I undertook all kinds of quests. More often than not I was far from home. So much so, that I often found myself wondering where home was. One especially dark night, while camping in the Atacama, I got chatting to a traveller who said he'd been born in Saskatchewan. Silhouetted against the fire, his lean frame was a reflection of every inch of ground that had passed beneath it.

'Where's your home now?' I asked.

'Home is where I am,' he answered.

A few months later, I reached the Namibian town of Swakopmund. Although not quite certain why, I'd found myself there often in the preceding years. Namibia's vast open expanses, coupled with excellent German-built roads, made for a pleasing combination.

On my first night in town, I dined at my favourite restaurant on Sam Nujoma Avenue. The last time I'd visited, in 1992, it was still called 'Kaiser Wilhelm Street'.

Taking a seat at the back of the restaurant, I ordered a glass of *weiss* beer and a steak, and leaned back in my chair. Two tables away, an elderly man was crooned over a thick book, his shoulders rounded forward. In his right hand was a red felt-tip pen, and in his left a magnifying glass.

I did a double take.

'Incredible!' I thought to myself.

Leaping to my feet, I went over, gushing apologies for the intrusion.

The man looked up.

'I'm sure you don't remember me, but we were at the same café on the Orinoco quite some time ago.'

'Got some great names on that trip,' he replied.

'So how's it going?' I asked. 'You know, in the red-tick business?'

The Texan put down the pen.

'Had an emergency three years ago in Haiti. Worst trip of my life.'

'Why was it so bad?'

The Texan slapped a hand to the gazetteer.

'Got stolen,' he said, the words echoing pain.

'But you got it back, right?'

'Nope. Didn't.'

'Oh?'

'Bastards. The whole damn lot of them.'

'So what d'you do?'

'There was only one choice. Had to get another copy and mark all the names off from memory.'

'Are you near to finishing?'

The traveller choked at the question.

'Hell no! I've got all of India to do next.'

'Big country… a lot of places,' I muttered.

The Texan seemed displeased at hearing such information.

'When I started the Gazetteer Challenge twenty years ago,' he said, 'I thought it'd be a fantastic way to experience the world.'

'And have you reconsidered whether it is?'

The traveller ran a thumb down the book's fore-edge.

'I certainly have,' he replied.

'Then why do you keep going? You could give up.'

'That's impossible.'

'But why?'

'Because if I did,' he said, 'it'd send a message to all the other fools out there that they could give up, too!'

## Twelve

Nasrudin entered a competition for profound observations.

One by one the contestants gave voice to a deep matter. It was evident the standard was very high indeed.

When it was Nasrudin's turn to make a profound observation, he clapped his hands, and begged everyone to listen well, declaring that his observation was wiser than anything spoken by any man in history.

The judges, the other contestants, and the audience clustered around.

'The moon is more useful than the sun,' the wise fool said.

'That doesn't make sense!' someone called out.

'Of course it does,' Nasrudin responded. 'Because you need the moon's light to see at night, don't you?!'

# TRAVELS WITH NASRUDIN

BUENOS AIRES, 1948, 1988, 2008

The first time I heard the word 'Argentina' was as a child, when a troupe of puppeteers came to Langton House.

They had read bootleg Spanish translations of my father's books, and were feverishly excited at having arrived at our home in a quiet corner of Kent. Even though they were from Argentina, they were dressed in sheepskin coats from Afghanistan – something that made no sense to me at all.

But then I was only four and a half.

They showered my sisters and me with gifts they'd made themselves from scraps and junk. Sequinned bags and tie-dyed waistcoats, lamps fashioned from old tin cans, spinning rainbow discs, mobiles, and stained-glass wigwams lit by tea lights.

The thing I liked best of all was the stuffed toy one of the Argentinian visitors brought me. His name was Rudolfo and he said he'd made it himself...

A soft toy of Nasrudin on his donkey.

Skewed awkwardly to the side, it was stuffed with second-hand stockings, and it smelled unlike anything I had experienced before. My mother grimaced when she saw it for the first time. She said it was how Argentina smelled, and that I ought to wash my hands after playing with it.

When the puppeteers left, my father slumped in a low leather chair, and seemed lost in despair. Even though I was young, I could see something was wrong.

So I asked what the matter was.

My father sat up, his head bowing down to my level.

'Show me your Nasrudin,' he said.

I held the stuffed toy up by the donkey's foot.

Pressing his nostrils into the fabric, my father breathed in, lids lowering over his eyes as though he were experiencing the most delicious perfume.

'Smell it,' he said.

'I already did. Mummy says I have to wash my hands after touching it. She thinks it smells like dirty old sacks.'

'She doesn't know what she's talking about.'

'Why not, Baba?'

'Because she's never been to Argentina.'

'The place the puppet men come from?'

My father nodded.

'That's right. Argentina.'

Pulling the toy away from him, I hugged it tight and nudged my nostrils into it.

'That's right. Smell your Nasrudin,' he said, 'and never forget that smell... because one day you'll go there.'

'To Argentina?'

'Yes.'

'What will I do there?'

My father grinned.

'You'll go in search of Nasrudin,' he said.

With time all dreams come true, and I finally got to Argentina.

The first time I went, forty years had passed since my father had lived there, reaching the Argentine capital by boat. About my age at the time of his arrival, he had accompanied my grandfather on a humanitarian mission on behalf of the India Office, to source halal meat for Muslim soldiers. As ever, they were shadowed by spies, who regularly filed disparaging dispatches to Whitehall.

After several months in Argentina, they made plans to leave, their mission completed and their funds spent. The day before the ship set sail back to Europe, my father was sitting alone in a café on Avenida Santa Fe when a young man stumbled in, touting lottery tickets.

Spotting a foreigner, he made a beeline for him.

'Señor, your last chance to buy a ticket!' he announced breathlessly. 'The national lottery is to be picked this afternoon!'

'I won't win. You know it as well as I.'

The ticket-seller clicked his tongue.

'No, no, señor, on the contrary... I am absolutely certain you are going to win!'

'How can you be so sure?'

The vendor selected one of the paper squares, holding it in his fingers as though it were treasure.

'Because this is the winning ticket, that's why.'

My father sipped his coffee.

'If it is, then why don't you buy it yourself?'

The young man sighed.

'If I did as you suggest, and buy the winning ticket for myself,' he answered, 'I would be robbing you of your destiny.'

So, my father handed over a coin and bought the lucky ticket.

That afternoon, he won the lion's share of *La Grande de la Nacional*, the Argentine National Lottery.

Next day, my grandfather set sail for Southampton, leaving my father to spend a bale-and-a-half of peso notes. Had he taken the money out of Argentina, it would have been devoured by tax.

From time to time in our childhoods, he would reminisce, describing the suite in the Plaza Hotel where he lived, the cut of the suits he'd had made, or the parties he attended at the invitation of Evita and Perón.

Only after his death did I learn another side of the story.

Six months after my father's fatal heart attack in November 1996, a letter arrived at my London flat.

The front of the envelope was plastered with large postage stamps, my name and address written in a precise cursive script.

It was from Rodolfo, the puppeteer who, thirty years before, had given me my beloved home-made Nasrudin.

Through pages of handwritten text, he described how he'd been selling lottery tickets on Avenida Santa Fe one morning, and how he had sold a winning ticket to a young foreigner sitting alone.

'You must think me mad to write this,' he wrote, 'but I saw something in his eyes – something I had not encountered before. It was as though they were burning with anticipation: a most desperate and urgent need to complete a body of work.

'Selecting a lottery ticket, I informed him it was the winning one. As I said the words, I felt deep in my heart it was true. Next day, after the massive win, I found him looking for me on Avenida Santa Fe. On seeing me trudging up and down with the tray of lottery tickets hung around my neck, he said he needed to speak to me urgently.

'So we went to a café nearby. Not one of the grand haunts on Santa Fe, but one that was a little more comfortable, and we drank coffee together. I had no idea that he had struck gold. The tickets were just numbers to me – numbers to sell so that I could pay my family's debts. When he told me of his success, I was happy. As I said, I felt his need – and a destiny far greater than mine.

'The next thing I knew, he'd paid my family's debts, given us savings, and even bought us a car. In the following weeks and months, we became firm friends. Your father was invited to all the fashionable receptions, where he made a name for himself – he was unlike anyone high society had encountered before.

'Early one morning he came to my apartment on the edge of Buenos Aires, an attaché case under his arm. He said it was full of banknotes – money he wanted to give away to change lives. Over a period of a year, I helped him to locate people in need. A baker who required money to open a shop. An artist who couldn't paint because he had three dead-end jobs. A young mother who had no funds with which to send her children to school. One by one, he helped them, always making sure the gifts were made anonymously.

'We continued in this way for a full year. At the end of it, there were several bricks of peso notes left. A year to the day of the lottery win, your father packed his bags, and put the remaining money in a cardboard box. Having given me a hug, he passed me the box and an envelope "These are instructions on whom to help with this money," he said. We hugged again, and then he was gone.'

The Buenos Aires of 1988 was not the same Buenos Aires of 1948.

The glitz and the glamour of the post-war days when Argentina was the richest country on Earth were long gone. The military junta and the Falklands War were recent memories. Distraught mothers paraded through Plaza de Mayo in front of the Casa Rosada, clasping enlarged photos of their disappeared sons. The streets were filled with rubbish. The currency had just crashed – yet again.

Soon after my arrival, overland from San Paulo, I found myself strolling down Avenida Santa Fe in the flat light of late afternoon. Without thinking, I was drawn into a café, the doors open wide to the street.

Taking a table at the front, I ordered an espresso, and smiled.

'I'm here, Baba,' I whispered. 'I'm in Buenos Aires at last.'

At that moment, as though cued to do so, a young man swept in, a tray of lottery tickets suspended around his neck.

He strode over.

'Will you choose one for me?'

He picked out a number. I took it and paid.

'Is it a lucky one?' I asked, as he turned to leave.

'Yes, of course it is,' he replied.

Unlike my father, my fate was not to win a share

of the Argentine National Lottery. Despite this, it was my destiny for a long-anticipated dream to come true…

…but not for another twenty years.

I longed to meet Rudolfo, the puppeteer who'd made my Nasrudin – the tatty old toy stuffed with stockings and my first scent of distant Argentina.

Even though I returned to Buenos Aires again and again, and roped everyone I met into the hunt for him, there was still no luck. He'd long since moved from the address on the front of the envelope, and no one could even say whether he was alive or dead.

In the winter of 2008, I rented an apartment in the suburb of Palermo Soho, and hid myself away to write a novel, *Casablanca Blues*. The short days were packed with long writing sessions, as they always are when I'm working on a book.

A week passed; then another.

I rarely left the apartment, and only then to buy provisions. For, as every writer knows, nothing is so important as getting past the mid-point.

On the night of the fifteenth day, I had a dream.

A fabulous and fantastical dream.

I dreamt I was seated with Nasrudin on his donkey, flying through space and time…

Back to a bright spring morning in 1948.

Peering down through the cloudless sky, I saw Santa Fe curving round to where it met Avenida 9 de Julio. We soared past an open-air café where my father was scribbling notes, and on to the magnificent Teatro Colón.

A performance was about to begin.

The great and the good of Buenos Aires were streaming urgently from limousines in sable coats, white tie and tails. Inexplicably, my father was there as well – strolling towards the steps, Rudolfo at his side.

On waking, I found the dream waiting in my mind. However hard I tried to forget it, it hung there, like a curtain, as if begging me to observe it.

Condemning myself for slacking, and uncertain quite what I was in search of, I grabbed my overcoat and hurried down to the street.

Fifteen minutes later, I stepped from a taxi outside the Teatro Colón.

Unlike in my dream, the *grande dame* of Buenos Aires was silent, shrouded in scaffolding, as the restoration struggled on.

I stood there for ten minutes, my coat keeping out the wind.

'Where are you, Rudolfo?' I asked, the words lost on the breeze.

Then I remembered something… a stray comment my father had once made. It was so trivial that my mind had hoarded it away in a thick file marked 'insignificances'.

'Argentina is one of the most civilized nations on Earth,' he'd told me many years after the puppeteers had come and gone. 'They treat creative people like kings. In Buenos Aires there's even a sanctuary for actors and those connected to the arts. One day you may see it for yourself.'

Pacing fast, I wove my way through the backstreets to Avenida Santa Fe, pausing at number 1243.

La Casa del Teatro – 'The House of Theatre' – had been established in the 'thirties, as an Art Deco refuge for retired performers down on their luck. It featured guest rooms for residents, and even its own theatre. High above the grand stone edifice, the masks of comedy and tragedy peered down at those hurrying by – landmarks in their own right.

Eaten alive by guilt for escaping my desk, and yet refusing to give in to doubt, I pulled the door open and initiated the kind of doomed enquiry that has characterized my life.

Even when certain there's no chance at all, a trident jabbing inside me always goads me to ask… just to be sure.

It can be credited with most of my successes, and for reuniting me with Rudolfo Fernández Peña… the puppeteer.

As soon as I mentioned his name, I was rewarded with an ear-to-ear grin.

'He's like my father, and I am like his son,' spouted the doorman.

'Does he live here?'

'Yes, of course.'

Sighing, I exclaimed joy.

Calling a lift finished in hardwood and brass, the doorman dispatched me to an upper floor. A well-dressed orderly met me there and enquired if Señor Fernández Peña was expecting me.

I responded in the negative.

'Does he know you?'

'He did at one time.'

Not wishing to put the puppeteer on the spot, I wrote a message, folded it, and asked for it to be passed on.

Three days slipped by in which I burrowed deep into my unlikely plot in far-off Casablanca.

A watched kettle does not boil, so I slipped my phone into the desk drawer and forgot about it.

On the morning of the fourth day, the phone rang, and a distinguished yet elderly voice spoke my name.

An hour later, the same voice was greeting me face to face.

Since selling the winning lottery ticket and ensuring the proceeds went to the needy, Rudolfo had lived a life of high adventure.

He'd cycled overland to Afghanistan; had sailed across the Pacific in a boat he built himself; and had got lost in the Sahara in a home-made hot air balloon. The journeys were mapped out on a face shrouded by a wind-chapped sheet of leather.

As soon as his mouth had spoken my name, Rudolfo pulled me to him in one of the longest and most satisfying hugs of my life.

When at last it ended, my neck was damp with his tears, and I was left feeling as though I'd been baptized and born again.

Rudolfo took me to a splendidly shabby café on Avenida Santa Fe five minutes' walk from La Casa del Teatro. The walls were stained yellow from decades of cigarette smoke, the light fittings smashed, and the floor re-laid in the cheapest lino.

Two or three elderly regulars were sitting at the bar staring into space, no doubt reminiscing about the glory days.

As soon as the heels of his shoes were through the door, Rudolfo's mood changed. While overcome with emotion when we hugged, he was now overcome with passion for the room.

'Every time I come in here I weep,' he said. 'Can't help it. The more I try to stand tall, the greater the cascade of tears.'

'Why does it make you sad?' I asked.

The puppeteer held up a hand, the fingers as leathery and wind-chapped as his face.

'No, no...' he said fast. 'There's no sorrow. Only joy. You see, this is where I began my first incarnation.'

'Which incarnation was that?'

'As the lad who stumbled from one end of this great avenue to the other, selling lottery tickets from a tray hanging around my neck. The incarnation in which I came through those doors over there one bright morning, and sold a young man in a rather crumpled linen suit a rectangle of paper.'

'*My father?*'

Rudolfo blinked.

'I can see him sitting at this very table, making notes.'

Unable to reply, I sat there profoundly moved, staring into Rudolfo's eyes.

After a long expanse of silence, I explained that I still had my beloved stocking-stuffed Nasrudin, although he was a little worse for wear.

The puppeteer seemed pleased.

'In stuffed toy years he's an old man, and his donkey's even more ancient,' he said. 'But then, I suppose, everything has its time.'

As my ears took in the words, I cast an eye around the café, wondering how long it had left.

I spent all afternoon chatting to Rudolfo, listening to his life's narrative, played out in extraordinary detail. The episodes continued over many more days, until it was time for me to leave Buenos Aires.

The first draft of my novel done and dusted, and my luggage packed, I went to meet the puppeteer for the last time.

'I'll be back soon,' I said, knowing full well that I would not.

'Then I'll wait for you,' he said.

Three years later, arriving once again in Buenos Aires, I made a beeline for Avenida Santa Fe.

To my great sorrow, the café was gone.

So was Rudolfo Fernández Peña…

Ticket-seller, raconteur, adventurer, puppeteer, and maker of the most unusual soft toys the world has ever known.

## Thirteen

As everyone knows, Nasrudin's wife was as greedy as she was lazy. Nothing pleased her quite so much as gorging herself on platters of kebabs.

One afternoon, the mayor agreed to visit Nasrudin's home for dinner. Eager to inveigle his way into the administration, the wise fool wanted to make a good impression. So, he hurried to the butcher, bought five pounds of the best steak, and rushed home.

'Wife! Wife!' he called. 'I have to go and find clothing suitable to receive the mayor. Please cook this special meat in the way your mother used to do and, before we know it, our fortunes will have been reversed.'

That evening, when the mayor arrived, he found Nasrudin dressed in fabulous robes. Once worn by the king, they'd been discarded, before finding their way onto a third-hand market stall.

Calling in a favour, Nasrudin instructed his neighbour's son to practise his flute out in the street, so as to create something of an ambience.

Straining to entertain his respected guest with elevated conversation, the wise fool hurried back and forth to the kitchen to check on the meal. Every time he reached the stove, his wife shooed him away.

After waiting an eternity, a huge platter was borne in by both Nasrudin's sons. Pulling off the silver dome, a large meatless bone was revealed on a bed of lettuce.

Scarlet from embarrassment, Nasrudin charged into the kitchen, where he found his wife picking her teeth.

'I gave you five pounds of the finest meat!' he screeched. 'Where is it?!'

'The cat ate it,' replied his wife.

Grabbing the animal, Nasrudin threw it on the kitchen scale. The cat weighed five pounds.

'If this is the cat, where is the meat?' he demanded. 'And if this is the meat, then where is the cat?!'

SWAT VALLEY, 1983

In the lush glens of Swat, on the North West Frontier, they have a saying:

'He who has feasted on autumn pomegranates may die from both sorrow and joy – for having tasted heavenly perfection, he will never know the experience equalled again.'

I had travelled to Pakistan for a family wedding. Or, at least, that's what I told people when they asked. Aged sixteen, and as enthusiastic as I was raw, I was desperate to be blooded by adventure.

Slipping away from the wedding party in Peshawar, I made my way to Swat, where I first experienced the awe-inspiring beauty that has wowed wayfarers for centuries.

The summer's interminable heat was dissipating, and it wouldn't be long before the winter's white mantle would descend.

As is the way of things there, I was passed down a line of trusted warriors, intermediaries, relatives, and friends.

The chain began with Major Hassan Shah. Retired hero of Britain's Indian Corps, he had clambered over bodies in the scramble up the hill to take Monte Cassino, back in '44.

He passed me to his blood-brother, Rustam Khan, whose mother had suckled him, and whose life had been dedicated to upholding the family name.

In turn Rustam Khan passed me to his nephew, and he to his wife's brother – a studious young man with horn-rims and a limp.

At twilight he delivered me to an encampment of Mujahedeen, freshly arrived from subduing the Russian Bear over the border in Afghanistan.

Having sworn to guarantee my protection, but unsure quite what to do with me, they sent me on an expedition to Swat.

There it was that my journey in the Land of Nasrudin began.

A cross between a military base and a caravanserai, the camp was the first of its kind I had encountered. Like something from the pages of a nineteenth-century novel, it was awash with caricatures:

Brawny guerrilla fighters armed to the teeth, weighed down under giant turbans and bandoliers. Crates of ammunition, stencilled lettering on the sides. A hotchpotch of tents lit up like Japanese lanterns by squealing paraffin lamps. Great chunks of meat roasting on spits, thunderclouds of fatty smoke boiling into the evening sky.

Green tea was served, so sweet it made my lips turn numb.

Once the supplies had been secured, the commander came over to where I was sitting. All I knew was that he'd lived for many years in Britain, but had returned to fight the war raging in his homeland.

About sixty, he was dressed in camouflage, with a white woollen Chitrali cap at an angle on his head. Tall even for a Pashtun, his face was silhouetted against the fire, his features like those sculpted from stone.

At his approach, I clambered to my feet. Flopping down onto an Afghan rug, he slapped it.

'Sit here beside me!' he commanded. 'Don't worry, I won't bite!'

Gripped by youthful fear, I did so. And, having downed more tea, I strained to make conversation – asking about the situation across the border.

The commander, whose name was Aslam Shah, stared into the fire. He didn't reply – not at first anyway. Lighting a cigarette, he held it tight between his knuckles, inhaling through his fist.

I assumed he hadn't heard my question.

In his own time, he said:

'The land of our ancestors is a reflection of us… a part of us, like a limb. But unlike an arm or a leg, it can't be amputated – not even by the cruelties of war.'

I asked the commander about his training camp – which had got plenty of press in both East and West. Reflectively Aslam Shah drew on his clenched fist.

'Young men imagine they're wise,' he replied. 'And thinking you are wise is more dangerous than any minefield, or Russian helicopter attack.'

The second-in-command approached, gave greeting, and took his place. He had evidently heard the leader's comment.

'There's nothing quite so reliable as a fool,' he said.

'Because he doesn't surprise you?' I asked.

'Because he behaves exactly as you would want him to.'

Silence prevailed for a long while, shadows roaming through the camp.

'There's an exception, of course,' Aslam Shah declared. 'The secret weapon of Afghanistan… the weapon by which we Afghans shall defeat the *Rouss*.'

'What's that?' I whispered subversively, craning forwards.

'You mean, *who's* that?'

'The secret weapon… it's a person?'

The officers exchanged a wry smile.

'Shall we tell him?' the commander probed.

'Think we can trust him,' countered the second-in-command.

Aslam Shah grinned, tombstone teeth framed by a foaming mass of smoke-grey beard.

'The secret weapon is the wisest fool who ever walked the earth,' he said. 'A man so dazzling in his foolishness he surpasses the intellect of any genius alive.'

'Who is he?'

'Nasrudin!'

'I was brought up with him,' I said, confused that my beloved Nasrudin was being advertised as the saviour in a war against a superpower.

The commander turned his head to cast an eye over the camp. Either side of him his men were attending to their chores. Some were stripping down AK-47s, checking the mechanisms and cleaning the parts. Others were repacking equipment, or preparing the evening feast.

'I'll tell you something,' said Aslam Shah at length. 'Something that you may care to remember in the future – thirty years from now when I myself am long departed. It is this: to win a war you need weapons. But as any successful commander will tell you, knowhow is far more powerful than even the most accurate rifle, or the most modern helicopter gunship.'

'What kind of knowhow?'

'The kind which turns the tables on the enemy by using weaknesses as strengths. The kind that allows a band of men like those behind me to move fast over mountains as high as any on Earth. The kind that enables them to hide in the shadows and to hit the target every time. And, the kind which leads them to ultimate triumph, despite having the odds stacked against them.'

'How do you teach it?'

Again, the commander grinned.

'By not teaching it.'

'I don't understand. If you don't teach it, how will the men know it?'

'They don't need to be taught it because it's already inside them. It's seeded in every cell… lying dormant. It's merely our job to coax it out, develop it, and harness its strength.'

A young soldier no older than myself slipped over and served more green tea. When his shadow had melted away, I breathed in as if about to ask another question, but Aslam Shah cut in:

'The Russians think in a straightforward way,' he said. 'However hard they try it's always the same… like a chess player who only knows one game. They're like robots – robots following orders. They just can't break out of the shackles.'

'What shackles?'

'The shackles of pre-programmed thought. A kind

of thinking so linear it holds them prisoner… a kind of thinking that can be trounced by simply thinking in an Oriental way.'

'Thinking like Nasrudin?' I said.

The second-in-command winked.

'Exactly.'

'What do you think Nasrudin would make of the war?' I asked.

Aslam Shah turned to me, one side of his face in shadow, the other tinged rose-red from the fire.

'Nasrudin was the greatest warrior of his age,' he said. 'So fearless was he that stories of his bravery were told at bedtime in every home across the land. The mere thought of him would cause the Russians to quake in their boots. But then, one day, the unthinkable happened – Nasrudin was captured in an ambush. Taken in chains to the torture room at Pul-e-Charkhi jail. The implements of torture were made ready. Gleeful at having captured the much-feared Nasrudin, a Soviet general presided over the torture session.

'"We are going to peel back your skin and cut you limb from limb," he yelled.

'"Excellent," Nasrudin replied, "before you get started, can I ask you a question?"

'"Very well," the Russian growled. "But make it quick!"

'"Please can you tell me how Comrade Lenin is?"

"'He's dead!" cried the commander.

"'Then can you tell me how Comrade Stalin is?"

"'Dead, as well!" boomed the general, his expression displeased.

"'Oh dear," Nasrudin responded. "So, can you tell me how Comrade Brezhnev is these days?"

"'Dead!" roared the Russian. "It's common knowledge. Surely you know all three are no longer alive!"

"'Yes, yes, I do," Nasrudin declared, beaming.

"'Then why do you ask such questions?!"

"'Because hearing the answers is music to my ears!'"

# PART TWO

# IN THE LAND OF NASRUDIN

inding himself penniless, Nasrudin sat down on the ground, and put a sign on his lap which read:

'PATIENT MAN FOR SALE'

Hundreds of people passed before someone bothered to stop.

'How much is the patient man?'

'The price of a bowl of soup,' replied Nasrudin.

'That seems reasonable.'

'A bowl of soup... a steak and a platter of fruit,' Nasrudin said, correcting himself.

'Now that seems rather expensive.'

'Listen!' Nasrudin scowled. 'Can you please decide the right price because the patient man in question is about to snap?!'

London, 2006

Nasrudin and his blend of back-to-front wisdom is found throughout Central Asia, but it took a Russian to bring him to the silver screen.

The celebrated director Yakov Protazanov, regarded as one of the founding fathers of Russian cinema, released *Nasreddin in Bukhara* in 1943, at the height of the war. A huge critical success, it was

Protazanov's last film. Within two years of its release, he was dead.

My interest in Nasrudin was what first led me on a treasure trail for the film. For fifteen years I searched for it, writing hundreds of messages to collectors, archivists and cinema enthusiasts all over the world. These days, of course, anyone can find it online with a few clicks of a mouse.

As is so often the case, the trail twisted and turned for so long I began wondering why I was subjecting myself to what had become a mania. Over coffee one spring morning a close family friend begged me to forget about *Nasreddin in Bukhara*, and to get on with what was important. Holding a mirror up to my life as he always did, he said it would lead to an abyss.

I promised that I would do so.

Then, on the afternoon of the same day, I received an email out of the blue – not from Moscow, or even Bukhara – but from Notting Hill… a mile or two away from where I was living at the time.

'Heard on the grapevine you're interested in Protazanov,' it read. 'If indeed you are, come and see me. Make sure to come alone, and to wear green.'

The next afternoon, I found myself in a private screening room off the Portobello Road. Just as I'd agreed to wear green and go alone, I promised not to write about the gentleman who'd extended the invitation.

All I can say is that the house had a private cinema and a vault, the shelves packed with cans of vintage films.

My host was terrifically fond of discretion, of the colour green, and the early works of Russian cinema.

I arrived wearing a bright green sweater, and a pair of green suit trousers bought at a charity shop that very morning. The gentleman made no mention of my clothing. He was dressed in a green tweed jacket, a green tie, green corduroys, green shoes and socks. Almost everything that I saw in the house – from the walls, to the flowers, to the books on display, was green.

Evidently disinterested in small talk, he led me straight down into the basement, where he instructed his green-clad assistant to dim the lights and screen the film.

There were no subtitles, and I don't understand Russian. No matter – for from the first moment to the last, I was transported to the distant mindset of Uzbekistan.

Dated by modern standards, *Nasreddin in Bukhara* captures the back-to-front 'Zigzag Think' on which I had been raised. That it was made in Russia – and by such an important director at the height of his career – fascinated me.

At the end of the screening, I commented on

how exciting it was to glimpse a Soviet telling of Nasrudin.

My host replied with something that has stayed with me for being so insightful.

'Nasrudin is everywhere,' he said. 'He's in every country and every city, in every town and village in the world. Sometimes he has a name, and sometimes he does not. Sometimes he's fêted, and sometimes he's neglected, or even condemned. But he's always there. It's because Nasrudin isn't a person but a way of thinking. He's the content rather than the container, the essence of humanity in its most perfect form.'

## Fifteen

Nasrudin decided he had lived in his kingdom long enough, so he saddled his donkey and clambered onto it. But the animal was so small, and he was so large, it took a lot of wriggling before he was comfortable. And, while jostling about, he turned around so that he was facing the animal's tail. Undeterred, he rode backwards to the next town. Seeing him approach, people started asking what kind of a fool would face backwards on a donkey.

'I'm not facing backwards,' Nasrudin spoke out, 'but rather my donkey is going the wrong way!'

BUKHARA, 2007

Almost a year after my visit to the green man of Notting Hill, I arrived in Uzbekistan.

In the preceding months I'd read all I could find on the connections between Nasrudin and the former Soviet republic. Eventually, I'd discovered the life of Leonid Solovyov, the Russian author whose novel, *The Tale of Hodja Nasreddin*, formed the basis for the film I'd watched in the private screening room the year before.

Solovyov had been born in 1906. His adolescence was played out against a backdrop of turmoil, as the Revolution's anarchy gave way to purges, and the road to war.

As a young man, Solovyov had been immersed in the folklore of Soviet Central Asia – which had got into his blood in a way I fully understood. Recognizing the precariousness of the time in which he lived, it seems as though he grasped hold of Nasrudin, as a way of effecting change from the outside in.

Three years after the triumphant release of the film based on his book, Solovyov was arrested and charged with conspiring to wage terror against the Soviet State. Along with so many other writers of his generation, he was convicted and imprisoned. During his confinement in a gulag at Dubravlag, he completed the second part of his *Tale of Hodja Nasreddin*. In 1954, eight years after his arrest, Leonid Solovyov was released without explanation.

And so it was that I arrived in Bukhara on a chill spring morning, overwhelmed with the same sense of wonder that has wowed wayfarers for centuries. As I see it, no one can claim to be a traveller until they've set eyes on Uzbekistan.

My father always asserted that Nasrudin was Afghan. Indeed, a great many Afghans I've met claim the wise fool, too. However, from the moment I arrived in Bukhara, and stood at the foot of its colossal fifth-century fortress, I felt as though I had at last arrived in the Land of Nasrudin.

Perhaps I shall come to my adventures in Uzbekistan later, but for now there's an encounter that's coaxing me to record it here.

Ever since it took place, it's hung heavy in my mind. Observed from every angle, I've dissected it a thousand times, drawing parallels and conclusions with my own life.

The event took place in a small town on the road from Bukhara to Samarkand.

My translator and guide was an enthusiastic man

with no neck and overly muscular hands called Abdullo. With the perfect physique for a nightclub bouncer, he'd been a champion wrestler in his day. It was no surprise when he told me he had been selected for the 2004 Olympics. Alas, though, injured a week before the competition, he'd been forced to withdraw.

Abdullo had a great deal to say about the history of his country, or at least elements of its history connected to his obsession with wrestling. I didn't bring up the subject of Nasrudin until the second day of our journey.

'He was a wrestler,' Abdullo revealed sternly, as the vehicle trundled north-east on the road that eventually led to Samarkand.

'Was he?'

'Oh yes, everyone knows it.'

'Was he any good?'

Abdullo grinned.

'A champion, even though he was terrified.'

'How did he overcome his fear?'

'He used to put strong industrial glue on his fingers and jab them up the opponent's nostrils.'

'Did the move help him win?'

'Yes and no.'

'Huh?'

Abdullo winked.

'His challengers used to pass out from the smell, but Nasrudin couldn't ever receive the trophies

119

because his fingers were still glued up the opponent's nose!'

Although I liked Abdullo, I feared that by the time we reached Samarkand I might be super-saturated in wrestling talk.

Late on the morning of the second day, he phoned a cousin who lived in a small town just north of where we were driving. I listened as Abdullo erupted in joy at hearing news of the family. One by one he asked after every relative, only moving to the next when sufficient information had been received on the last.

Suddenly, the wrestler-guide's voice seemed to crack with sorrow. His face flushed beetroot-red, he ended the call abruptly.

'Everything OK?' I asked.

A single tear welled in Abdullo's right eye and tumbled down his cheek.

'Yes. OK,' he said tautly.

'Really OK?'

A tear welled in the other eye and began the journey south to Abdullo's chin.

'Family,' he said, the word a cauldron of emotion.

Unsure of how to answer, I winced and nodded in a knowing kind of way.

'There's a problem,' Abdullo said. 'Well, it's more of a situation between two brothers, rather than a problem. It's causing a lot of sadness to my father.'

I asked what the situation was.

'Calligraphy,' he replied.

'What do you mean?'

The wrestler-turned-guide wiped his eyes.

'I am the only wrestler in my family,' he said. 'The others are all calligraphers. They're well known throughout Uzbekistan for their skill in writing in the old Arabic script. The greatest calligrapher of all was my ancestor who died more than a hundred years ago. He wrote thousands of complicated calligraphic designs.'

'Are they sayings from the Qur'an?'

'No, they're part of an ancient body of wisdom passed down since prehistoric times.'

'Are the calligraphies beautiful?'

'Yes, so beautiful!' Abdullo riposted at once. 'And that is where the problem lies.'

'I don't understand.'

The wrestler-guide scratched a thumbnail to his nose.

'My family isn't far from here,' he said. 'If you don't mind too much, I would like to take you to meet them.'

Less than an hour later, we reached the town where fifteen generations of the family had plied their calligraphic trade.

We were welcomed with pomp and ceremony, by a stream of Abdullo's relatives spilling out from modest houses all around. No matter of their age, all the men had the same neckless muscular physique as my guide.

As is so often the case with Central Asian hospitality, we were corralled into a formal sitting room, floral-covered sofas running along three walls. Ornate rugs obscured the floor, and framed Arabic calligraphies loomed down.

Tea was served, while a feast was prepared.

Holding court, the wrestler's father explained how his family had been master calligraphers for five centuries.

'In the distant past we were entrusted an ancient book by a Sufi saint,' he said, his thick-set face a ripened facsimile of his son's. 'Over centuries my ancestors have written out the pages of the manuscript. Although doing justice to the wisdom contained through calligraphy, we have always been cautioned to remember that the book itself is only a container… that the text is the real value, the thing which can bring knowledge and transform lives.'

'This is the cause of the problem,' Abdullo said, excusing himself for speaking out of turn.

I shrugged enquiringly, as if hoping to know more.

The master calligrapher cleared his throat as one would do before making an announcement.

'From earliest childhood my brother received the same instruction as me,' he said. 'We were taught how to form the letters with nibs we cut ourselves from reeds. And, we were shown how to decipher the patterns back into text… text containing profound philosophical advice.'

'Sounds like a wonderful chain of transmission.'

Our host shook his head.

'No,' he replied.

'*No*?'

'No.'

'Why not?'

'Because once in a dozen generations you get a lame ram.'

'A "black sheep"… a disgrace?'

'Yes.'

'Your brother?'

'Yes.'

'What's he done to disgrace the family?' I asked.

'Why don't you go and see for yourself?'


Having been advertised as a light snack, lunch lasted more than three hours, with every member of the extended family in attendance.

Everyone, that is, except for Abdullo's wayward uncle.

We were showered with gifts, triumphant expressions of affection, and begged not to leave.

'Stay with us and marry my youngest daughter!' the master calligrapher exclaimed.

'But I'm married already.'

'But Islam allows you four wives!'

'Alas, though, my wife doesn't allow it,' I said.

Abdullo fended off the surge of neckless relatives blocking the way to the car. Once strapped into our seats, we set off through the backstreets.

'What about your uncle?' I said.

'You really want to meet him?'

'Yes! I'm intrigued.'

The wrestler-guide heaved the steering wheel sharply to the left, continued for a few hundred feet, and pulled up at a mansion of infinite proportions. Outside were parked a pair of Rolls-Royces, a Ferrari, and a stretched Hummer.

Even on the scale of Central Asian bling, the scene was super-charged.

Mirrored in symmetrical reflection-pools, the front of the building was dominated by six pairs of Corinthian columns, each one overlaid in gold. Sheering up behind them was a home that would make any drug lord salivate.

'He lives *here*?' I asked.

Abdullo grimaced.

'It's one of his houses,' he replied. 'And those are *some* of his cars.'

'Where does he get the money?'

'From the minions.'

'*Minions?*'

'You'll see.'

Crossing a golden bridge, we made our way to the front door.

It opened inwards as we approached, and I followed the wrestler inside. Awkward at having arrived unannounced, I'd begun to wish we hadn't come. Unlike me, Abdullo was unimpressed.

In the entrance there was a free-standing waterfall, multiple peacocks strutting about, and white tiger skins tossed over a Carrara marble floor. The ceiling was painted gold, as was a vaulted passageway leading through into a ceremonial hall.

Rose petals rained on us from a carved balcony, thrown down by an invisible hand above the door, as we entered the vast vacant space. Strains of recorded chanting were broadcast from speakers hidden in the floor. Six gargantuan chandeliers hung from the ceiling on gilded chains, each one a bohemian crystal triumph of bad taste.

As for the walls, they were covered with supersized calligraphies executed in Arabic script.

'Recognize them?' Abdullo whispered.

'They're like the ones I saw in your parents' place.'

Before the wrestler could reply, the far wall of the hall lowered into the floor. I watched it descend without any sound at all. As it disappeared, I caught first sight of a second chamber, identical to the one in which we were standing.

It was packed with people – hundreds of them.

Dressed in matching lilac robes, they were barefoot, overexcited, and were clearly not from Uzbekistan.

'Who are they?!' I said, the words voiced in hushed exclamation.

'The minions,' said Abdullo.

'Thought your uncle was a calligrapher.'

'He is. Or, rather, he was.'

'So what is he now?'

The wrestler-turned-guide cracked his neck.

'He's a man who mistook container for content,' he said.

Right then, Abdullo's uncle appeared, taking me by surprise as I hadn't seen him come in. Unlike his followers, he was wearing pink robes, the cuffs delicately embroidered in gold.

Minions fussing around, like bees attending to the queen, he greeted his nephew and then me.

Apologizing for turning up unannounced, I praised the proportions of his palatial home.

'This is of no significance,' he remarked wearily.

'Well, it looks very impressive to me.'

'It's merely a vessel to hold the sacred artwork.'

Resentful their leader was neglecting them, a swell of minions swept forwards, petitioning him with questions, problems, and what sounded like petty grievances against one another. From what I could make out, they were a mixture of nationalities – North and South Americans, Europeans, and more than a few from the Far East.

Abdullo's uncle invited us to observe the ceremony about to begin. Accepting, we followed him into the second hall, a lilac sea of minions lapping around us.

As soon as the leader was installed on his dais, tranquillity prevailed.

Over the next two hours, I observed first-hand how the precious document, passed down by the ancestral line of calligraphers, had been reduced to a hollow entertainment for attention-starved devotees.

When the ceremony was over, one of the minions led us outside, back over the golden bridge to our car.

As she sprinkled rose petals ahead of us, I noticed an Islamic calligraphy tattooed on the back of her neck.

'What does it say?'

The woman, who was from Chile, shrugged.

'What do you mean?'

'Well, isn't it writing?'

'No, no, no,' she responded firmly. 'Only the foolish believe it can be read.'

'And what do the wise believe?' I asked.

'That it's a sacred symbol of the saint, a magical energy that keeps the world in alignment,' she said.

Almost three years after I left Uzbekistan, Abdullo called, asking for me to help with a subscription to an American wrestling magazine.

Having promised to look into it, I enquired how his uncle's calligraphic cult was going.

'He passed away unexpectedly six months ago,' Abdullo said.

'Sorry to hear it, but in a way I imagine your father must be relieved.'

'Oh no! Not at all!'

'Why not?'

'Because his son – my cousin – is running it now. He's turned it into an even bigger money-making machine.'

'Don't you think your cousin secretly wishes he had a normal job?' I asked.

'Perhaps,' said Abdullo. 'Then again, maybe not. You see, my cousin was a failure at calligraphy, and even worse at wrestling.'

'*So?*'

'So this is the one way he can feel important,' Abdullo said.

## Sixteen

ne morning while trying to entertain his children at breakfast, Nasrudin managed to swallow his pocket watch. Despite being seen by a number of leading specialists, the wise fool couldn't get the object to pass from his stomach and out through his digestive tract.

In despair he went to a surgeon, widely regarded as the one with a proven track record at remedying such conditions.

The doctor asked Nasrudin to take a seat while he got ready for the consultation. One by one, he laid out an assortment of clamps, hammers, scalpels and tongs.

At the sight, Nasrudin was overcome with terror.

Clasping his stomach, he moaned and groaned, rocking back and forth as he did so. As the doctor took his seat, the patient retched violently, and the pocket watch shot from his stomach and onto the floor.

Delighted, Nasrudin asked for the bill.

'But I didn't even treat you,' the surgeon said.

'Yes you did,' the wise fool replied. 'And what a marvellous treatment it was! I had expected you to use those horrid instruments – but instead you resorted to an implement far more ingenious.'

'What?' the doctor asked in confusion.

'Fear,' said Nasrudin.

LANGTON HOUSE, 1973

As a small child I had a battered old cardboard box in the corner of my bedroom.

On each side was a picture of two giant upright bananas, a hammock slung low between them, along with the words 'Welcome to Bananaland!'

The box arrived when I was about six, and was still there in the corner of my bedroom when Langton House was sold seventeen years later. In that time, it got more and more bashed about, but was much prized for what it contained.

*Expedition equipment.*

I'm not sure if it was the banana box that first sowed the idea of exploration or whether it was the precious objects inside that stirred me. I like to think it was a mixture of the two.

For as long as I can remember, the banana box was a receptacle for the kind of gear I imagined would be needed on an ambitious expedition. As I'd never been on an expedition, I relied on word-of-mouth information passed on by the full gamut of characters who visited us.

Whenever an elderly lady or gentleman strode through into the hallway, I'd slink out of the shadows and ask if they had been on an expedition. Sometimes they replied politely that they had not, or that they had but it was too long ago to remember the details. But not infrequently, they would clap their hands together as if having won the Derby, and reveal all they knew.

One of the most reliable elderly explorer types who came to Langton House was a military man called Dr Grimes. No matter the weather, he was always dressed impeccably in tweeds, a farmer's checked shirt, and a regimental tie. Langton House seemed to draw graciousness from its visitors, but Dr Grimes took courtesy to an entirely new level.

Looking back, I sense he had absolutely no interest in discussing expeditions with a six-year-old but, such was his expertise, he gave the impression that nothing on earth would give him greater pleasure.

Before Dr Grimes visited, I would ask my parents over and over if he was a true expert on the expedition business.

'Of course he is, yes, yes!' my father would exclaim.

'No one's done more expeditions than Dr G,' my mother would add, looking up from her knitting.

'What kind of expeditions does he know about most of all?'

The question would cause both my parents to appear transfixed, as though they had seen angels.

'He's done them all,' my father would say.

'Searched for treasure?'

'Oh, yes, of course.'

'Lost cities?'

'So many, yes!'

'Unknown animals?'

Again, my father would nod frantically.

'That's another one of his specialities.'

'Do you think Dr Grimes minds me talking to him?' I would ask.

'I think he likes it very much,' my mother would say.

'Why?'

'Because I suspect it reminds him of his youth.'

Over the years Dr Grimes visited, he would ask how my equipment was getting on, and would always beg to see any new bits and pieces I had sequestered away in the banana box.

Sometimes I'd show him a few feet of parachute cord I'd found on the ground in the village, or a clutch of bottle caps pressed from a sheet of extra-thick tin.

'Very useful,' Dr Grimes would intone. 'This will be just what you need when you're on the expedition.'

One day, when we had got to know each other better, I hurried over as soon as he'd blustered in through the hallway.

'I think it's time that you start planning some expeditions,' he said.

'*Some expeditions?*'

'Yes.'

'Don't you think I ought to begin with one expedition and see how that goes?' I asked anxiously – after all, I was only eight.

'Oh no... no, no, no,' Dr Grimes responded fast. 'You must always plan several expeditions at once.'

'Why?'

'Because it's the only way to be certain of thinking big!'

'How big should I be thinking?' I probed gingerly.

Dr Grimes beckoned me forward. Sitting in a low armchair in the drawing room, his face was in line with my own.

Stepping forward, I observed him at close quarters, my mind mapping the wrinkles, the broken veins, and the individual strands of silvery bristle that formed his moustache.

Bloodshot blue eyes peering into mine, he responded:

'When you're older you will find something to be true.'

'What, Dr Grimes?'

'That almost everyone you will ever meet will set the bar very low. They don't push themselves because they're frightened.'

'Frightened of what?'

'Frightened of failure!'

My expression was taut, my mouth cold.

'I don't want to fail,' I said.

'Nonsense!' the seasoned explorer boomed. 'If you stop fearing failure and start doing things, you'll ultimately succeed!'

'What expedition should I plan?'

Dr Grimes pulled out a silk handkerchief, blew his nose, grunted, and said:

'One of each I should think.'

'A lost city…?'

'Yes, yes, a good start, and a lost treasure, and a plant and animal that are unknown, and a species of butterfly… and what about meteorites as well?'

Fetching a pen and paper from my father's study, I made a list and held it up. Dr Grimes pulled out a monocle and went through it one item at a time.

'I want you to promise me something,' he said all of a sudden, his bird-like hand snatching my wrist.

'Something about expeditions?'

'Yes.'

'What?'

'People will say you can't find a lost city or a treasure... or that you're too young or too unprepared. Every time they doubt you, make up your mind to prove them wrong – do you understand?'

'Yes, Dr Grimes. Yes, I do.'

Slipping away his glasses case, he blew his nose again, and grunted twice.

'The reason to go on an expedition is not to learn about the place you are traversing,' he said. 'But as a method by which to know yourself. Know yourself inside and out, and you'll be the man you're destined to be.'

## *Seventeen*

ne morning while walking from his home to his field, Nasrudin spotted a clutch of scorpions drowning in a puddle.

Although fearful, he plucked up the courage to stop and rescue them.

Once dried off by the sun, the creatures arced their tails as if about to strike. Undeterred, Nasrudin opened up his knapsack and laid out his lunch before them on the ground.

'Feast, my friends, feast!' he cried. 'And tell your tribe that it was Nasrudin – Protector of

Scorpions – who took pity on you, and saved you from the flood!'

KOLKATA, 1998

By nature I am drawn to extremes.

I like severe heat and freezing cold, towering mountains and pancake-flat plateaux, epic stories, and tales no more than a few lines long. I like journeys that take months to complete, and fast, spontaneous trips that shake you from your comfort zone. I love the countryside – rolling landscapes where there's nothing but nature.

And, just as I love such geography, I love cities, too.

My notion of a city is rarely one that's prim and proper – the kind you encounter in the refined capitals of Europe. Rather, my idea of a city is a sprawling, seething cornucopia of people, invention, noise, filth, riot and uproar. The kind of place that shakes you to the marrow of your bones... a place that sucks you in, stirs you around hard as you steep in it like sheets of leather in a vat of dye, before spewing you out at a time of its choosing.

I love cities because I hate them.

Just as I have a grotesque and macabre fascination for medical curiosities, I find myself gripped by urban life in a way that almost defies description. For me, the allure of a metropolis is all about layers.

However hard I try, I can't ignore detail.

Walk down a street and my mind bombards me with every smell, sound, and sight, pleading with me to reach out and touch the wall I'm brushing against, or to taste the heaps of fruit for sale on makeshift carts. As I notice it all, I see it all together and set apart. I see old and new, soft and hard, light, dark, wild, and restrained.

The more I suck it in, the more my mind races at the ingenuity and the interaction, and the more I want to experience.

Drawn as I am to wonder, it's no surprise that the conurbations of the Indian subcontinent and the Far East offer me special delight. Walk down a stretch of Kolkata pavement, for example, and you are introduced to an all-encompassing hurly burly of life, wit, wisdom, and problem solving.

A few years ago, while doing just that, I came to a ramshackle street-side stall serving tea in tiny, unfired cups. Under an awning stretched out between three upright poles, I noticed a foreigner who looked decidedly out of place. Wide-eyed and appreciative, he seemed to be savouring every moment.

'Bill from Tuscaloosa,' he said, even before I'd sat down on one of the broken old stools.

'Tahir, from all kinds of places,' I replied.

We shook hands, Bill's grip muscular and tight.

'Just arrived,' he said.

'Looks like you found your feet pretty fast.'

'Certainly have.'

'What brought you to India?'

Sneezing hard, Bill asked for another cup of tea.

'Needed a dose of frenzy,' he replied.

'*Frenzy*? And did you find it?'

'Yup.'

'What kind of frenzy?'

'The kind you can't get on the Travel Channel.'

'As in?'

'As in cinema-scope IMAX 3D taste- and smell-o-vision.'

'With full Surround Sound?'

'That's it!' Bill roared. 'You know it!'

'Yes I do. And why Kolkata?'

'Because it's fully loaded, that's why.'

'Not quite with you.'

Bill appeared disappointed, as though I wasn't keeping up.

'Kolkata looks like a city,' he explained. 'It smells like a city, too, and behaves like a city in every way… but in actual fact it isn't a city at all.'

'Really?'

'Yup.'

'Then what is Kolkata if it isn't a city?'

Bill clicked his neck, left right left, and sighed.

'It's an onion,' he said.

'How's that?'

'Because of the layers.'

'*Onion* layers.'

Bill from Tuscaloosa gave me a double thumbs up.

'Now you're getting it!' he yelled.

## *Eighteen*

asrudin's son came home from college with a tattoo on his chest, and showed it off in the teahouse.

The design was of an eagle, with a magnificent beak, plumage, and talons. It was quite the most beautiful tattoo anyone in the village had ever seen.

Green with jealousy at being upstaged by his son, Nasrudin hurried to the nearest tattoo parlour next morning before anyone was awake. Hammering on the door, he promised to pay double the usual price if the work was begun at once.

Wiping the sleep from his eyes, the tattoo artist asked what Nasrudin wanted.

'I'd like a huge roaring tiger – bigger and better than anything you've ever imagined let alone created before! I want him snarling, and leering, and to cover every square inch of my chest!'

'Very well, but it will take time and will be painful.'

'I have time and pain is nothing to a man like me!' Nasrudin exclaimed.

Removing his shirt, he lay down on the workbench and prepared himself. The tattoo artist put on his surgical gloves, plugged in the electric needle, and got down to work.

As soon as the tip of the needle touched Nasrudin's chest, he groaned in pain.

'What part are you drawing?' he screamed.

'The right eye.'

'Well, forget about it,' Nasrudin directed. 'My tiger doesn't have a right eye.'

Again, the artist touched the needle to the customer's skin and, again, Nasrudin howled in pain.

'What are you drawing now?!' he exclaimed.

'The left eye.'

'Well, my tiger doesn't have a left eye!'

'Neither a left nor a right eye?'

'Yes!' Nasrudin bellowed. 'It comes from a land where tigers are blind!'

The artist began drawing the creature's tail.

'Leave out the tail,' Nasrudin moaned, 'because in the land of blind tigers there are no tails!'

On and on it went, until the wise fool had forbidden the artist to draw anything at all. His needle had only made a single pinprick.

Excusing himself with an invented emergency, Nasrudin stumbled away. When he reached the teahouse, he couldn't help but brag about how he'd been at the tattoo studio all day. Clustering around, his friends demanded to see the artwork he'd described so intricately.

Unable to help himself, he ripped off his shirt.

'There it is!' he exclaimed.

'*Where?*'

'There!'

'That little speck?'

'It looks like a flea!' someone cackled, rolling about in laughter.

'It may be a flea,' Nasrudin retorted, puffing out his chest like a prize-fighter, 'but it's a flea on a tiger's back!'


PESHAWAR, 1983

Major Hassan Shah, the indefatigable relation to whom I'd been entrusted, was keen for me to befriend a relative my age on his wife's side of the family.

Not wishing to appear rude, and unable to object, I was introduced, and we hung out during my stay in Peshawar. His name was Abdul-Lateef, and he was in the first year of medical training, at Peshawar University.

One evening, Abdul-Lateef dropped in to see me at Major Hassan Shah's home in the Cantonment. I was sitting on my bed there writing my journal when he appeared at the door.

'There's something I want to tell you,' he said.

'What?'

'A secret.'

I tried to remain calm.

'All right, go ahead.'

'Not here. *He's* listening,' Abdul-Lateef said, straightening his back like an officer.

'OK. Then shall we go into the garden?' I said in a hushed tone.

'No, no. He can even hear out there.'

'Then where?'

'Tomorrow morning, at the university.'

'OK. What time?'

'Eight-thirty.'

'I'll see you there.'

Next morning I reached the medical faculty right on time, having evaded Major Hassan Shah. Prowling back and forth at the front of the house, he was certain something was up.

Abdul-Lateef came out to greet me, then led me to a common room where his breakfast was laid out.

'So, what's the secret?' I asked.

'First eat some breakfast. There's tea, fried eggs and lots of parathas.'

Wrapping an egg in a paratha, I took a bite.

'OK, tell me,' I said as I chewed, 'what's it all about?'

Abdul-Lateef sipped his tea.

'It's a very delicate secret. A very *secret* secret,' he said. 'You won't be able to handle it unless your stomach's full.'

'I'm sure I can deal with it. Go ahead.'

Grimacing, Abdul-Lateef was about to say something, when a group of his fellow students burst into the common room, talking boisterously amongst themselves.

'No good now,' he grumbled under his breath. 'They'll hear.'

'Why not write it on a scrap of paper and give it to me to read?'

'No, no, no… too complicated for me to do that.'

I sighed.

'OK. Well, what shall we do?'

'Let's go there.'

'Where?'

'To the next room.'

Abdul-Lateef grabbed the container with the parathas and the eggs, motioning me to bring the thermos.

Pushing through a set of swing doors, he paced along a corridor, and through yet more swing doors.

Even before we were inside, I felt terribly ill at ease.

Unlike the common room or the corridor, the chamber in which I found myself was windowless and bare. It was lit by neon tube lights, and had no furniture at all. Instead, there was a series of uniform concrete slabs.

On three of them were lying partially dissected human bodies. One was missing half its head. The second had no head. And, the third was opened up down the middle. The stench was so awful I gagged.

Apparently oblivious to the fact we were in the morgue, Abdul-Lateef laid out what was left of breakfast, and urged me to take another egg.

'Mummy made them herself,' he said.

'I'd rather not be in here,' I replied sternly.

'Why not? Are you squeamish?'

'Yes... and especially so at breakfast time!'

Abdul-Lateef's face fell.

'But the secret,' he said. 'I have to tell it to you.'

Unable to stand it another moment, I whipped round and ran back out through the swing doors.

Having packed up the food, Abdul-Lateef followed.

'Morgues aren't my thing,' I said briskly, 'and having breakfast in them is even less my thing.'

'So sorry.'

'I don't want to hurry you, but maybe you should just come out with it – tell me the secret, so we can both get on.'

Abdul-Lateef glanced at his watch.

'Class is about to start now,' he said, cocking a head back towards the morgue.

'Let's meet later then.'

'OK. Five o'clock.'

'Where?'

'At the clock tower near Qissa Khana Bazaar.'

'But it'll be crowded with people.'

'No problem. They won't listening.'

'All right. See you there.'


Built to commemorate Queen Victoria's Diamond Jubilee, the Sir Cunningham Clock had seen better days.

I waited beneath it and, an hour late, Abdul-Lateef trundled up in a rickshaw.

'Very sorry, the stomach dissection took longer than expected.'

'Are you ready to tell me?'

'What?'

'The secret.'

'Yes, yes!'

'Well, I'm listening.'

Abdul-Lateef clenched his fists and shook them up and down.

'It's such a big secret,' he said.

'OK.'

What little patience and interest I'd mustered at the start was long gone.

'It's such a big secret, that I shall tell you half now and half later.'

'Does that make sense?'

'Yes, yes.'

'All right. What's the first half?'

Abdul-Lateef took a pace forward until he was uncomfortably close. Pressing his lips to my ear, he whispered:

'I overheard what Mummy said to Baba.'

'What did she say?'

'No, no, can't tell you that... not yet. It's the second half of the secret.'

'Listen, Abdul-Lateef, I know you're worried by whatever it is, but I'm sure I can handle it if you just tell me.'

'Tomorrow. I'll tell you tomorrow.'

'OK. But I'm not meeting you at the morgue again!'

'OK. Not there.'

'Where?'

'At the church in the Cantonment... no one ever goes there... at five p.m.'

A day later, I slipped away from Major Hassan Shah's eagle-like gaze, and made my way to St John's Church – another vestige of the long-departed British Raj.

As Abdul-Lateef had foreseen, there was no one in sight, except for a gardener and a courting couple skulking in the shadows. Once again, I waited the requisite hour before Abdul-Lateef swanned up in a rickshaw.

'Here we are,' I exclaimed, shaking his hand. 'Ready for the rest of the secret.'

'Oh yes, yes.'

'Please just tell it to me.'

'OK. OK. You promise not to tell anyone?'

'Yes!'

Again, Abdul-Lateef stepped forwards, his lips very close to my ear.

'I overheard Mummy telling Baba,' he recapped.

'*What*? What did you overhear her say?'

'That Abdul-Lateef has a problem. A really "significant" problem!'

'What problem?'

'A problem with secrets,' he said.

asrudin's generosity was a thing of legend, so much so that word of it spread throughout the kingdom and far beyond. His friends would often come and eat fabulous meals, and it wasn't long before friends of friends started to arrive.

At first Nasrudin welcomed the strangers and fed them. Then, friends of friends of friends began turning up. Enthusing about the hospitality they'd received, they told their own friends.

When a group of friends of friends of friends of friends arrived, Nasrudin knew it was time to put his foot down. Inviting the guests in, he led them through into the salon and announced dinner would be served in a moment.

Running through into the kitchen, the wise fool boiled a pot of water, added salt and pepper, and poured it ceremoniously into his largest serving dish.

Staggering through into the salon with it, where the guests awaited, he laid it down and announced,

'This is the specialty of the house!'

Raising the dome from the pot, the host served his guests.

'It's just water!' one of them complained.

'No it is not,' Nasrudin corrected, 'but rather it is the soup of the soup of the soup!'

TOKYO, 1992

No one believed me when I explained I didn't want to teach English.

'I really don't,' I would tell them. 'I've come to Japan for other reasons.'

'But it's a golden age for foreigners here!' they exclaimed one after the next. 'English teachers are treated like royalty, and given huge salaries. Even the stupidest man alive could get a job teaching English in Japan!'

'I may be a fool,' I would reply, 'but I'm not in search of easy cash.'

'Why not?!'

'Because I'm on a mission.'

'What is it?'

'Can't tell you that,' I would sigh. 'All I can say is that it's to do with a man called Kashikoi-bakka.'

For the first three months, I lived at a small hostel in Tokyo's Ikebukuro district, which I paid for in advance. Unlike me, everyone else staying there was an English-teaching foreigner. Hailing from all over the Anglophone world, they were armed with a single uniform skill – the ability to speak English.

It may have been a bonanza time for English teachers, but back then Tokyo was the most expensive city on Earth. A cup of coffee and a sandwich could cost the same as a three-course meal at a top London restaurant.

Steep prices weren't a worry for the English teachers though. More and more of them arrived every day, as word of the gold rush spread further into the Anglophone hinterlands.

One morning I found a heavily built Australian filling the hostel's doorframe.

'G'day,' he said, sticking out an oversized hand, 'the name's Franc.'

Much of Franc's face was obscured in a scruffy red beard – grown, I suspected, not as a fashion statement, but through lack of funds with which to buy razor blades.

'Just got in from Alice,' he said.

'*Alice?*'

'Alice Springs.'

'Alice Springs in the Outback?'

'Yup.'

'Wow.'

'Charged a ticket on Mastercard, and here I am. Heard money's growing on the bonsai trees!'

While Franc chortled at his joke, I nodded.

'Yes. It's boom time.'

'Excellent! So where do I get a job?'

'I'm not the person to ask... I'm not working.'

The Aussie scratched a claw-like thumbnail to the back of his neck.

'Oh,' he said, disappointed. 'Thought any absolute moron could get teaching work in Japan.'

'They can, but this moron isn't interested. You see I'm on a quest.'

'Got ya!' Outback Franc retorted, stumbling through into the reception. Within an hour and a half of arriving, he'd landed a well-paid job teaching English to Japanese housewives.

Each night, the teaching crowd at the hostel used to go to bars, splashing the kind of cash most of them had never known before. As the weeks rolled by, and as my funds were depleted, I was invited less and less.

Eventually I was shunned altogether.

The only person who'd talk to me was Outback Franc from Alice Springs.

'They think you're a weirdo,' he said one night, finding me stretching a single packet of minute-noodles into an evening meal.

'I don't care what people think of me.'

'Why not?'

'Because he who is different is the master of his fate.'

'D'you get that from TV?'

'No, from my aunt.'

'Why don't you get a part-time job,' Franc urged, 'and at least you wouldn't have to eat that crap.'

'That would be selling out. As I told you, I'm on a quest.'

'You need to get some proper tucker into you, mate.'

During the day, when the English teachers were out selling themselves, I worked away at my quest for Kashikoi-bakka. The name had first caught my attention when, in my teens, I'd seen a sketch dating from the Meiji Era. It showed a woodcutter in a geometric-patterned overcoat, the kind worn by the ancient race of Ainu. In one hand was an axe, and in the other was clutched a pen. Beneath it was a caption in Japanese.

An English translation was written on the back.

It said:

'Kashikoi-bakka, imaginer of miracles and wisest fool who ever lived, whose pen is sharper than the keenest blade.'

Over weeks, I trawled through the shelves of the rare-book emporiums in Jinbocho, searching for any mention of Kashikoi-bakka. Then, I moved on to the public libraries, and to the national university. The only mention of the character I could find was in a treatise written by a Christian missionary a hundred and five years before.

A single disparaging line exclaimed:

'The jester figure of the Hairy Ainu, Kashikoi-bakka, is a reflection of why the Ainu are in urgent need of civilization through God's salvation.'

Each week, I grew more and more impoverished. My sorry financial state forced me to constantly refine the skill of spending no money.

By the second month, I had a system.

The first part took advantage of the Japanese obsession with getting things perfect.

Each morning, I'd make a beeline to a high-end bakery near Ikebukuro subway station. Day after day I'd loitered at the front window, drooling over the pastries and cakes – each one more sumptuous than the last.

They were way out of the budget of a fool who refused to sell out.

One morning, while taking a shortcut down an alley lined with low-life yakuza bars, my nostrils caught the mouth-watering scent of baking. Peering in through an open door, I realized it was the back of the exclusive bakery. Just as I passed, a woman in an apron stepped out, with a stack of boxes on a tray. She laid them on a table along with a sign inviting anyone to help themselves.

In a land where only the best is served, imperfect cakes were my Food of Paradise.

Having given thanks to Providence, I would gorge like a lion feasting on a zebra carcass, snarling at anyone passing by.

My stomach filled to capacity, I'd get on with my research. By evening, famished once again, I'd make my way to the basements of Sogo department store. Spread out over two subterranean levels, thousands of extra-special culinary delights were on display. They were the kind of things reserved as honoured gifts rather than a normal purchase. There were square melons in mahogany boxes, chocolates from the Swiss Alps, Kobe beef steaks, and gold-plated tins of the finest beluga caviar.

Naturally, everything on offer was well beyond my means. But that was no impediment at all. For, floating through the halls was a team of impeccably dressed ladies. Heads were crowned with wide-brimmed hats, their lips were painted in an identical shade of pink. Bearing silver trays at shoulder height, they invited the high-end customers to sample their delights.

Allowing hunger to trump my sense of shame, I would pick at the platters discreetly, commenting on each mouthful, muttering superlatives between bites. From time to time I'd pause, ask the price of a bucket of beluga, or enquire on the availability of a bulk order of Serrano ham. Then, slipping into the next hall, the feasting would continue.

In my search for Kashikoi-bakka, I quizzed dozens of scholars, seeking them out in ever-more specialized academic institutes and departments. In a culture where the word 'no' is rarely pronounced, my enquiries led to more red herrings and dead ends than I care to remember.

At times, I felt like Nasrudin – a fool searching for a fool.

After three months, the pre-paid nights at the hostel ran out, and I was thrown into the streets of Ikebukuro as commuters hurried to work. Franc from the Outback found me standing on the street, suitcase in hand, my face a mask of dread.

Unlike me, he was heading off to work.

'Told you to get a job!' he jeered.

'And I told you I won't sell out.'

'So what are you gonna do?'

'Something'll turn up,' I whimpered despondently.

'Think so?'

'Yup – it always does.'

And, it did.

By nightfall, I had a new home.

Taking pity on me, the friend of a friend from England took me in. His name was Robert Twigger and, like me, he was an aspiring writer. Unlike me, he wasn't – in the parlance of Outback Franc – an 'absolute moron'.

155

He had a job.

A good job... a good job teaching English.

More importantly, an apartment was thrown in for free.

The only thing was that Twigger had to pretend he lived there alone. The owner of his English school was a mistrustful character who'd been burned by foreigners dead-set on breaking the rules. I can't quite remember why, but we came up with a ruse in which I claimed to be a Texan cowboy who was staying a couple of days to do research on Kobe beef.

Even by a fool's standards it was a pitiable lie – especially as the school's owner had himself spent time in Texas. For weeks... and then months, we limped on with me hiding out.

Located in the suburb of Azaminio-Yon-Chome, the apartment was small, and looked like it'd been snapped together from a giant Lego set. The tatami mats caused my asthma to flare up terribly. The only spot free from dust was under the table in the kitchen-sitting-room. So I used to lie under it, scribbling notes on the wise fool of the Ainu, and wondering how on earth I'd ever regain my life.

Finding myself far from the bright lights of central Tokyo, my habitual feeding grounds were far away. Generously, Twigger invited me to help myself to his supply of raw gyoza in the fridge. Following his example, I heated the upturned iron and cooked some. They were delicious, although rather underdone.

Not wishing to be a freeloader, I went out to hunt for supplies.

By the time I returned late that evening, Twigger was home. He was drawing on a pipe, the apple-scented smoke enveloping every inch of available space. The crackly sound of Lucienne Boyer's 1920s classic *Parlez-moi d'amour* was playing on the cassette deck. The only tape Twigger owned, he played it on a loop.

I held up a postal sack I'd found outside the local post office.

'What's in it?'

My eyes glinting with anticipation at the meal we would have, I emptied it out on the table.

Six large ceremonial cabbages, the kind grown in Japanese public gardens for their aesthetic beauty. Having been lovingly attended from saplings by an expert gardener, they were in excellent condition. No slug damage, and all the outer leaves had already been trimmed away.

'Got them from the gardens behind the cemetery,' I said. 'There are loads of them!'

Drawing on the briar pipe ruminatively, Twigger didn't say anything. He must have been wondering what kind of a nutcase he'd taken in.

Within half an hour, the plunder had been brewed up into passable, if rather bland, cabbage soup.

'Think I'll have that every night,' I said brightly.

Twigger seemed to be enjoying it, too.

'Not bad,' he muttered, draining the bowl.

'Want some more?'

'You have it.'

'But there's lots!'

'Is there?' Twigger replied downheartedly. 'Are you sure we can't find you a job?'

Over the months I lived beneath the sitting-room table, under the assumed identity of a Texan cowboy, I perfected the recipe for cabbage soup.

I'd once read that British POWs, forced to work on Burma's fabled Railway of Death, kept themselves alive by cooking up a broth from leaves and roots, gathered while toiling during the day. Although starved beyond belief, they always kept a cup of the soup in reserve, using it as stock for the following night's batch of soup.

Taking inspiration from them, I did the same – each night making a fresh batch of soup, seeding it with a cup from the night before. There was no question that the taste was vastly improved, compared with simply starting from scratch.

As we sat at the table one evening, me with my cabbage soup, and Twigger with some ironed gyoza,

I gave thanks to the prisoners-of-war who'd endured the ruthless regime of the Japanese.

'This soup is like a chain of transmission,' I said.

'What d'you mean?'

'This soup of the soup of the soup, is a most remarkable thing.'

'Not bad, but I'm taking a break tonight,' Twigger mumbled awkwardly.

'I don't mean the taste. It's more than that.'

'Don't quite follow.'

'Each night when I brew up a fresh batch, using a cup of the soup from the night before, it's as though I'm benefiting in an almost transcendental way. I know this must sound crazy,' I said, 'but it's as if the soup from last night is teaching the soup from tonight.'

'Teaching it to be soup?' Twigger reasoned.

'Yes! That's it! That's the chain of transmission.'

'Think you just found Kashikoi-bakka!' Twigger exclaimed.

### Twenty

asrudin was passing the house of a rich merchant when he smelled a most delicious meal. Remembering how the man had once borrowed money from him, he knocked in the hope of being invited in. A servant opened the door and asked what Nasrudin wanted.

'I have come to ask your master to repay the loan I made him three years ago.'

'My master is out in the market,' said the servant.

'Is that so?' Nasrudin responded. 'Well, perhaps I could leave something for your master to receive on his return.'

'Of course. What?' the servant enquired.

'A piece of advice,' said Nasrudin. 'It's this: "Only a fool leaves his face in the window when he goes shopping!"'

London, 1996

I have a theory about people which I've never shared before.

The way I see it, society doesn't always develop by evolving in an orderly way. Instead, I think it progresses in fits and starts, depending on who's present in a particular group at a particular time. According to my home-grown hypothesis, inclusive groups develop and eventually perish in entirety.

It explains why, when I was young, there was a surfeit of elderly English gentlemen whose manners and deportment were matched only by their impeccable sense of dress.

My parents had an affection for such gentlemen, and certainly seemed to know a lot of them; for they were always being entertained in the drawing room, or strolling through the gardens of Langton House.

Most had clipped silvery-white moustaches and short-back-and-sides. Invariably, they were dressed in tweed jackets, waistcoats, cravats or regimental ties, and highly polished brogues. Soft-spoken and exceptionally kind, they'd tell me about adventures made in their youth in far-off places whose names had long since changed.

Whenever I asked who the gentlemen were, my parents answered carefully, straining to be discreet. They preferred to tell us what they were known for, rather than explaining who the gentlemen actually were.

'He escaped from Colditz,' my father would say. Or, 'He was smuggled behind enemy lines during the war, disguised as a circus clown.'

In our presence, very few were actually referred to by name. Even then, they were addressed by their title, or surname, and never with the kind of informality that now prevails.

One of the named gentlemen, the author L. F. Rushbrook Williams had, I learned later, been sent to shadow my grandfather on a long journey through the Middle East. He'd followed him for years between the wars, dispatching reports back to Whitehall. Eventually, they became inseparable friends.

Sir John Glubb was another named family friend, as was the celebrated gardener, Russell Page. He was a favourite of my sisters and me.

As bald as he was tall, he was the most softly spoken of them all. Immaculately dressed, he would always arrive bearing gifts.

Boiled sweets for us children.

Flowers for my mother.

And an assortment of unexpected wonders for my father – such as a seven-foot narwhal's tusk.

Coinciding with the moment in which my childhood ended, the elderly gentlemen disappeared. Like the mysterious and immediate annihilation of a species, there were none left.

Even my mother noticed they'd gone.

'Used to be droves of them,' she remarked wistfully, as if describing herds of antelope roaming the savannah.

'Perhaps they'll pop up again one day,' I said.

My mother's brow wrinkled in a frown.

'I fear they're extinct,' she replied.

A handful of years slipped by in which I missed the lost species of old gentlemen very greatly indeed. The only one I knew was my dear friend the explorer, Sir Wilfred Thesiger. But he was still living in northern Kenya with the nomadic Samburu at the time.

Then, over coffee one morning, a writer friend said he wanted to introduce me to a retired diplomat who'd known my grandfather during the war.

Pricking up my ears, I asked:

'Is he a soft-spoken old gentleman?'

'Yes, he is.'

'I want to meet him!' I cried.

On the scale of immaculate soft-spoken gentlemen, Hugh Carless was in a league of his own.

As a young diplomat, he'd been sent as Third Secretary to the British Embassy in Kabul, in 1951, and then as First Secretary to Tehran. It was there he received a telegram from his friend, would-be writer and rag-trade virtuoso, Eric Newby. The message suggested they make the first ascent of Mir Samir in the Hindu Kush together.

The journey resulted in Newby's hilarious book *A Short Walk in the Hindu Kush*. The travelogue ends with the desperately pathetic Carless–Newby party crossing paths with Thesiger, who was hard as nails.

Having spent years in the Foreign Office's Central Asian Service, Carless was dispatched to Latin America – where he was later promoted to ambassador. It seemed an odd placement, after all he was an expert in Asia and knew next to nothing about South America.

He explained the thinking to me years later.

'The men in grey suits always have the same worry,' he said.

'What is it?'

'That the chaps in the field will go native!'

The week after my friend first suggested the introduction, I received a letter from Carless, inviting me to his flat for tea.

Unsure what to expect, I made my way to the splendid building on Bryanston Square, a stone's throw from Marble Arch – a long way from the retired diplomat's former stomping grounds of Central Asia.

Having learned everything I knew about him from Newby's travel book, and from a pithy entry in *Who's Who*, the moment we came face to face was one of pronounced expectation.

Carless was standing at the top of the stairs, as though waiting to receive a visiting dignitary. Although not tall, there was something utterly superlative about him.

The first thing I noticed was his posture.

A thing of wonder, it was well beyond ramrod-straight, and must have been achieved through years of self-discipline and sacrifice. After the posture, I took in the shoes: jet-black Oxfords with a parade-ground shine.

Ascending the stairs in what seemed like slow motion, my line of vision ranged upwards: over grey flannel trousers with a razor-sharp crease, up higher over a Savile Row blazer, a cravat, and finally onto the face.

Eyes deep pools of blue, his cheeks were clean-shaven, and his elongated forehead led down to a perfect short-back-and-sides. But it wasn't the features that I noticed, so much as the way that, in combination with one another, they conjured a sense of utter tranquillity.

Again, I pondered whether such a lack of fear and worry was natural or learned.

I've heard it said that to get elected as US President, a candidate must greet voters one-on-one as though they're meeting the most singular person on Earth... a combination of eye contact, sincerity, and sedateness. That's how Hugh Carless greeted me – not only the first time we met, but always.

As we entered the drawing room, my eyes picked out objects and textures I knew from my travels. I couldn't help but give voice to the delight, as I roamed from damascened brass dish to Oriental tapestry, and from Mughal miniature to lacquered Kajar screen.

'I've lived with all this bric-à-brac for so long, I hardly see it,' Carless said in his soft trademark voice, ushering me to a low, leather armchair.

'But I'm sure you love it all,' I said.

'I do… but not the part of the object you see.'

'How do you mean?'

Carless smiled, the slow, meandering smile of a man who had gained wisdom through travel.

'Everything has two parts,' he replied. 'The first is the part I suspect you see – the thing visitors tend to marvel at or admire.'

'What's the other part?'

'That which is formed from an object's own secret history, and from the story connecting it to what came before.'

Afternoon tea was brought in, and the elaborate ritual of politeness began for which the beverage was invented to display.

We talked about Central Asia, Africa, and the Americas, telling stories and sharing points of etiquette. Taking turns, we described destinations we had both known and loved, realizing our lives had overlapped.

When telling a story, Carless would pause expertly before delivering the punchline, censoring himself in the name of modesty. A diplomat to the core, his entire performance was designed to elevate his guest by lowering his own sense of worth. As the afternoon progressed, I wondered how I would ever be able to bear conversing with anyone out in the real world again.

After a second cup of orange pekoe, I scanned

the room for the twentieth time. Without thinking, I asked if there was an object for which he reserved a special fondness.

'Indeed,' Carless said, his deep blue eyes staring into space.

'May I ask what it is?'

Standing, he drifted in silence to the far side of the room. And, hovering there for a moment, he held a hand towards a metal object, as one might do when introducing two strangers.

I observed it with care.

Two feet change high, it was a simple model of a peacock fashioned in steel, the display at the back intricately etched with a pattern and what looked like the sun.

'This is the most precious object I have ever had the pleasure of knowing,' he said.

'Where's it from?'

'From the Yezidi culture of Iraq.'

'The People of the Peacock Angel?'

'That's right,' Carless replied. 'They were once thought to be devil worshippers, but that was nonsense of course. Theirs is a fine and quite remarkable society.'

'If this is the object, what is its story?'

Carless seemed pleased to have been asked.

'Well,' he said, pondering on how to shape his answer, 'diplomats are taught about the country to which they are being sent, or at least they were when I was a young man. While informative, what they learn is from the outside in, and not from the inside out.

'When I was sent to Tehran in the 'fifties, I looked for ways of knowing Iran in another way. I read its literature, appreciated its marvels in architecture and cuisine, but most of all, I liked to visit the Grand Bazaar.

'It was like something out of the pages of *A Thousand and One Nights*. Caverns packed floor to ceiling with treasure – the kind of things that had been crafted as empires rose, and carried away by the hordes when they fell.'

Hugh Carless fell silent, as though seduced by the memory of a particular day.

'Rustam Ali Mansur was rumoured by some to be king of the smugglers, and by others to be second in wealth only to the Shah,' he went on, turning slightly to face the light. 'I never discovered what was true and what was not. Like everyone else with an interest in knowing Iran in a less than obvious way, I became a customer of the inimitable Rustam Ali Mansur.

'You will need to take advantage of your own imagination to picture the scene of the emporium,' Carless intoned. 'Winged lions sculpted from tremendous blocks of stone in ancient Babylonia. Solid silver bedsteads made for emperors and kings.

Venetian chandeliers, grand pianos, grandfather clocks made for Louis XIV.

'Whenever I visited, I would wear my roughest old hiking clothes. I'd pretend I was a writer on my travels, and that my budget was next to nothing. Many of the other dealers might have shooed me away, but Rustam Ali Mansur had a skill they did not possess. From the moment you entered the emporium, eyes wide at the wonders contained inside, he would – as my American friends say – be "sizing you up".

'In his mind he would have picked out an object for you to buy, without letting on what it was. Like a stage magician executing the perfect illusion, he'd lead you to it in an almost telepathic way.

'One afternoon I slipped out from the embassy, went home to change into my hiking clothes, and took a taxi down to the Grand Bazaar. Weaving through miles of passages, I made my way to Ali Mansur's shop, where I found the dealer waiting for me.

'My visit coincided with a government crackdown on tax. Antiques had been subjected to additional duty, which had caused great problems for many of the *bazaaris*. However, the ingenious Rustam Ali Mansur didn't think like the others.'

'How did he think?' I asked.

'Like a fox.'

Turning back to the peacock, Carless allowed

the side of his hand to brush against it, as though transporting him back to Tehran's Grand Bazaar.

'If an object was presented as a gift, no tax was due,' he said. 'And so, seeing me intrigued by our friend here, the old fox called out to me, "Everything this afternoon is free!"

'Although delighted at the information, I was naturally suspicious. So I asked for clarification. "It's simple," Rustam Ali Mansur said, "take anything you wish – including that peacock – for nothing. However, you should know that connected to every object is a story. A story that is as much the object as it is itself. Being a treasure in its own right, the story does have a nominal price."

'I asked what the story attached to the peacock cost. Rustam Ali Mansur shook his head. "Better to ask first what the story is," he responded, "rather than the price. After all, you may not wish to buy it."

'"But it's actually the peacock I am interested in," I said, "rather than its story." The dealer shook his head again. "With one comes the other, he explained. They are inseparable." Weary of Oriental logic, I asked for the story.

'This is what he told me:

'"Once upon a time, Nasrudin put all his savings into a pen of cut-rate peacocks, or rather into peacock chicks. Every day, he fed them with grain, greedily waiting for the time when he could sell them for their feathers. As you know, peacocks are intelligent birds. They soon worked out the fate destined for them. So, just before reaching maturity, they stopped growing. Nasrudin couldn't understand it. He asked another peacock farmer, then a vet, and after him an astrologer, but none had an answer why the adolescent creatures had not grown, with magnificent plumage. At his wits' end, Nasrudin went to the pen where the birds were kept. Waving his fists at them, he screamed: 'You think I've been raising you for your adult feathers, don't you?! Well, it may interest you to know that it's not the case. I've been raising you for lovely soft down with which to fill my pillow... the kind young peacocks like you possess. So, unless you get moving to the next phase of your development, you'll be cuddling my head as I dream tonight!"'

Hugh Carless passed away in 2011, robbing me of the last soft-spoken gentleman I have had the good fortune to know.

Days before he died, he sent me a typed memoir of his life. Though a wonderful surprise, it was not the last that I received from my impeccable, straight-backed friend.

For, a few weeks after his funeral, the porter at my London club said a large cardboard box had come for me.

A large box filled with polystyrene chips.

Delving both hands in, my fingers touched a metal object. Even before my eyes had seen it, I knew what it was.

The Yezidi Peacock: as much a wonderful story as it was itself.

## Twenty-one

The traffic was so bad in Nasrudin's village there was nowhere to tie up a donkey when out at work. Unsure of what to do, the wise fool took his donkey to a used donkey showroom.

'I'd like to trade my donkey in for another used one,' he said.

'But, sir, your donkey looks perfectly good to me,' said the salesman.

'You're right,' Nasrudin answered. 'He's a fine donkey but I'd like to replace him with one that's already parked.'

LHASA, 2008

Arriving in the Tibetan capital by train as I did, I was the first to admit being impressed that the railway was an engineering feat of its age.

The journey from Beijing West to Lhasa, which

ascended to more than 16,000 feet at the Tanggula Pass, was only made possible by the availability of oxygen masks.

On the platform at Lhasa Railway Station, I put down my bags, and fumbled with my camera.

Even before I had managed to take off the lens cap, a pair of officers strode up.

'No photo!'

'Just want a snap of the train, as a souvenir.'

'Stop!' the guards yelled, their voices blending into one.

Before I could protest, they turned, white-gloved hands motioning at a sign featuring a camera behind prison bars.

'Do not break the rules!' the officers exclaimed.

'I'll do my best,' I said.

Looking back, the weeks I spent in Tibet were all about rules.

I had stepped through the eye of a needle into a magical world quite unlike any other. A place more beautiful than anywhere I'd ever dreamed of experiencing. A realm with mountains and crystal lakes, ancient traditions, monuments, and monasteries.

At the same time, it was a Monty Python twilight zone which might have been amusing if it wasn't so terribly sad.

The sign at the railway station – the camera behind

bars – had obviously been manufactured in bulk, no doubt in a factory down the line in China.

It was everywhere:

Outside schools and public buildings, monasteries, bus stations, offices, and even at an amusement park.

The sign wasn't the problem, so much as the mindset.

Tibetan culture is mischievous and unapologetically fun. Like everyone else in my generation, I'd been weaned on back issues of *National Geographic*, in which laughing Buddhist monks squinted in the bright light of Tibet.

Those old photos tallied with the land I discovered at the end of the tracks. It seemed free from book-thumping preachers, pulpits, and an unyielding sense of doom and dread – the kind meted out in a great many societies in the name of faith.

There was irony, of course, in that the doom and dread was there in abundance all the same... an all-powerful, all-seeing, all-punishing backdrop to life in the shape of the Party.

Rather than the liturgy of a religion, it had rules:

No photography.

No public gatherings.

No protesting.

No dissent.

And, no reincarnation... at least not without permission.

On the third day in Lhasa, I was sitting on the terrace of a café eating a plate of *momo* dumplings, scribbling notes in my journal.

Across the street was a little mosque. Furled tight in barbed wire, the minaret had been requisitioned as a sniper post. At the side of the mosque stood an armoured car, an orderly arrangement of sandbags, and an officer at attention. In his hand was a steel attaché case – the kind containing a time-bomb in *Mission Impossible* films.

A bedraggled American beatnik at the next table noticed me eyeing it. It looked like he'd been sleeping rough.

'Stun grenades,' he said.

'Huh?'

'Stun grenades.'

'Really?'

'Yeah.'

'Why?'

'Revolution.'

'Get the sense this place is locked down too tight for insurrection,' I said.

Lighting a hand-rolled cigarette, the beatnik picked a stray fibre of tobacco from his tongue.

'The best bombs have the thickest casings,' he said.

At that moment, as if an invisible director had called *Action!*, I watched as the might of the Party slammed down.

Two dozen demonstrators stepped out from the backstreets, placards in hand, outrage and anger on their lips.

Like a tarantula ensnaring then devouring its prey, the fledgling protest was instantly quashed, with the same ruthless efficiency responsible for the construction of the railway from Beijing.

Within five minutes, the protestors had been stopped, seized, cuffed, photographed once, then again, and whisked away.

'Bastards!' growled the American.

'Think they'll get beaten?'

'Yeah,' the American said. 'At least they will once their families have been rounded up, and their homes burned down.'

Next day I found myself at an austere government building on the edge of Lhasa. One of those bastions of 'no hope bureaucracy' you get throughout the developing world, it was a shrine to form-filling, rubber stamps, despondent applicants, and administrative red tape.

Like all non-Chinese foreigners visiting Tibet, I needed permission to venture out into the countryside. My travel agent had promised to get the papers in order, but had failed. So, it was left for me to brave the queues and the officials, and to get my paperwork stamped.

For three hours I went through the ritual of pleading then waiting, waiting then pleading, before being shunted through into the 'Hall of Facilitation'.

A throng of Buddhist monks in maroon robes were sitting on the floor, as though they'd been waiting for days. I supposed they had paperwork problems, like me. Each one was clutching a dossier, a photocopy of their identity card pasted to the top. Across from them, a rowdy group of Italians were ordering the officials to stamp their papers.

As I scanned the room, wondering whose example to follow, the beatnik from the day before appeared, a partially filled form in hand.

'We meet again,' he declared, conspiratorially.

I groaned.

'This is my worst nightmare.'

'Think you've got problems? Well, spare a thought for them.'

The American cocked the side of his head at the lamas.

'Protestors?' I whispered.

'Nope.'

'Then, what?'

'Something far more challenging.'

I shrugged.

'What?'

'A new law. A law from the Land of Fools.'

'What law?'

The beatnik breathed in, then exhaled in a sigh.

'They've got to get permission from the State before they can be reincarnated,' he said.

## Twenty-two

ne night when Nasrudin was coming home from the teahouse he spotted something at the side of the road – a huge strongbox. Excited, he opened it up and found a fabulous treasure.

Bursting into laughter, he slapped his thigh, then walked on.

'When will Providence stop trying to test me in such an obvious way?' he mumbled to himself.

BALKH, 2006

Until the aftermath of 9/11, the name 'Afghanistan' was rarely spoken in the West.

Overnight, everything changed.

Newspapers and TV networks were plastered with maps of the war-torn country, along with descriptions of its geography and culture. I remember hearing that the United States was going after Bin Laden in the Tora Bora cave complex with 'bunker-busting' bombs, and reflecting on what my father and grandfather would have made of it all.

For three-quarters of a century, our family had droned on about Afghanistan. In 1927, my grandfather published his first book on the country – *Afghanistan of the Afghans* – in which he did his level best to package a description of the kingdom for the Occidental world. Throughout his life, he published books and articles about his homeland. Having eloped to the Hindu Kush with him, my Scottish-born grandmother followed suit – writing dozens of articles about Afghan culture and folklore, as well as penning two travel books, *My Khyber Marriage* and *Valley of the Giant Buddhas*.

My father continued the mission, writing masses on Afghanistan, as though his life depended on it – doubling and redoubling his efforts when the Russians surged across the border on Christmas Eve 1979. Delving deep into centuries of ancestral folklore and knowhow, he churned out a best-selling novel, *Kara Kush*.

Stretching to twelve hundred pages in manuscript form, the book was a veritable instruction manual on Afghanistan. One morning when I asked him how the book was going, he wagged a finger at me.

'I'm not writing a book,' he said.

'But you're typing away day and night.'

'Yes, but it's not a book that I'm creating.'

'What is it, then?'

'A horse.'

'Huh?'

'A Trojan Horse!'

The way my father saw it, the West had to be informed about the war in Afghanistan, but educated through Oriental thinking. Only then, he would tell us, would people fully understand what was going on.

So, fashioning a Trojan Horse from paragraphs and lines, he packed it with information that would be ingested along with the story.

'When you want to tell a child something,' he said, 'the best way to do it is not by telling it to them straight out. Most of the time they'll listen and then forget, or not listen at all. If you want it to get through, rooted in their subconscious, there's only one way to do it.'

'How, Baba?'

'By giving them a story.'

The story my father spun from the threads of Afghan folklore told of a massive treasure, hidden somewhere in the mountains:

The lost treasure of Ahmed Shah Durrani.

When *Kara Kush* was launched in 1986, it was a runaway success.

My father was pleased – not because he'd turned himself into a best-selling novelist, but because he had succeeded in creating the ultimate Trojan Horse.

Three years later – nine years since its invasion – the Russian military machine withdrew back across the border, having been routed, just as my father maintained it would be right from the start.

By the time US forces began storming Tora Bora with their bunker-busting bombs, my family had single-handedly written more books on Afghanistan than any other in the Western world. My grandfather, grandmother, father, and aunt were responsible for showing the country to the outside world in a way it would understand. Shortly before the 9/11 atrocities, my sister, Saira, made her award-winning documentary, *Beneath the Veil.*

A full five years after the first bunker-busting bombs were dropped at Tora Bora, I arrived in Kabul with my Swedish film crew from Caravan Film.

I had arrived there for a thousand reasons.

At the top of the list was to continue the tradition of showing Afghanistan from the inside out. At the same time, I longed to find Nasrudin in the land of my forefathers, and to observe the country through the lens of the wise fool.

We set ourselves what seemed to be an obvious task: to locate the massive lost treasure of Ahmed Shah – valued at $520 billion.

Landing at Kabul Airport early in 2006, we were enthusiastic, although a little less than usual, having been locked up for sixteen days in a torture jail while doing pre-production in Pakistan.

Medieval to the core, Afghanistan doesn't run along the lines to which most other countries ultimately conform. An enchanted realm of preposterously back-to-front behaviour, it's like nowhere else. On my search for the lost treasure of Ahmed Shah, I was constantly exposed to Nasrudin.

He was everywhere – in caravanserais and teahouses, on buses and in bazaars, walking over mountains and along streams.

Spend time in Afghanistan and you find yourself wishing everywhere else could be like it, at least some of the time. Because, in the Land of Nasrudin anything is possible, except of course the probable.

Criss-crossing the country, I took with me a caged hoopoe. A storyteller in Kabul had informed me that only a man carrying one – the favourite bird of King Solomon – had a hope of finding the treasure of Ahmed Shah. When the hoard was near, he revealed, the hoopoe would sing.

Over weeks, I followed all kinds of clues, working with leads laid down by my father and grandfather – searching frantically for a hollowed-out mountain, where they both hinted the treasure lay.

From the moment I reached Kabul, it dawned on me that mounting a quest for the lost treasure of Ahmed Shah was possibly an act of foolishness worthy of Nasrudin.

At a time at which the Americans and their allies were dropping bunker-busting bombs with reckless abandon, I was roaming the country, caged hoopoe in hand, hunting for a cave system in which the treasure might be hidden.

One of the first destinations on a journey of spectacular danger was Balkh, in northern Afghanistan. It was there that Alexander the Great built his capital, while planning an advance into India… an advance that never came.

By the time I arrived at Balkh, it was a backwater in the shadow of nearby Mazar-i-Sharif. Although gracious, the locals were uneasy at finding a film crew searching for a lost treasure – as though fearing our mission might somehow end in an airstrike.

On our first night, the owner of the *chaikhana* in which we were staying came over with a scrap of paper as I got ready for bed.

'I do not know about the treasure,' he said, 'but my brother-in-law does. When I told him what you are looking for, he wrote down these instructions. If you leave Balkh early, you may reach the place by dusk.'

Taking hold of the scrap, I gave thanks, and heard a voice in my head pronounce a favourite Afghan expression, 'Send the fool another mile!'

Being the fool, I gave the order for the film crew to rise early, so we might leave at dawn.

By dusk the next day, we were far from Balkh.

Despite the distance, I could hear the owner of the teahouse and his extended family hooting with joy at ridding themselves of their perilous guests.

Being so far off the beaten track, I was on edge, and suggested we spend the night at a little village reached by crossing fields on foot.

No people on Earth welcome travellers as Afghans do. A throwback to an ancient time, the hospitality extended is part of a code of honour binding man to man.

The village was far too small and too remote to have a teahouse. So, seeing us approach over the fields, a farmer took us in. His head was crowned in a voluminous turban, his long broad form wrapped up in a sheepskin coat.

Before we knew it, his family were fussing over us. They moved out of their wattle and daub home, insisting we stay there as long as we wished.

That evening, the villagers came together. Slaughtering a sheep, they brought out a carpet usually reserved for weddings, and burned precious paraffin in their lamps.

We presented gifts, then feasted under a full moon and a bewitching canopy of stars. A truly enormous pilau was served, with great chunks of mutton buried in it. As we gorged ourselves, I pondered how best to bring up the quest of the lost treasure.

Every time I framed a sentence enquiring about it in my mind, the farmer would coax me to eat more.

After the meal, the villagers filed away into the darkness, against the strains of a donkey braying as though the end of the world had come.

Ascending a rickety wooden ladder at the side of the adobe building, I climbed up onto the roof. Tilting my head back, I viewed the heavens, the full moon at their heart.

Little by little, my view ranged downwards, taking in a chain of hills lost in shadow. Nestled among them was a small lake, the moon reflecting over its surface in a sheet of silver light.

In the morning, I climbed up onto the roof again, and peered down at the lake. Sapphire blue, it was supremely secretive and mysterious.

When the farmer joined me on the roof, I remarked how fortunate the villagers were to have such a fine lake so close.

'It must be wonderful for fishing,' I said.

To my surprise, the farmer replied that it was not.

'We don't drink its water, or fish in it,' he said.

'Really? Well, I'm sure you swim in it in the summer at least.'

'No, we don't.'

185

'Is it poisoned, or contaminated with a dangerous substance?'

'No.'

'But then, if it's not causing offence to ask, why do you not take advantage of such a fine-looking water source?'

The farmer pressed his hands together.

'There's a reason,' he said, 'a reason which explains what you're asking. It sometimes sounds strange to those who have not heard it before.'

'I'm intrigued,' I replied.

The farmer invited me back down to ground level, where breakfast was waiting along with a handful of villagers. I got the feeling he hoped I would forget about the lake.

'Would you tell me the reason?' I prompted.

The farmer conferred with the others.

'You will not believe us if we tell you,' he said.

'I promise to believe you, even if I do not,' I replied, in a curiously stupid sentence.

Again, the villagers conferred.

'Very well,' the farmer said, his expression grave. 'We will tell you why we do not use the lake.'

I listened intently, and this is what the farmer said:

'When people go into the water, they become the other person who goes in with them. They look the same in every way, but their minds are switched over.'

'Oh,' I said. 'I wouldn't have guessed that.'

The villagers seemed pleased the situation had been explained.

'Now you understand,' the farmer's brother said.

'Yes I do, and then again, no I don't. You see, if someone who goes in the water becomes the person in there with them, why don't you just go in one at a time?'

The farmer nodded.

'The water simply remembers who was in it last. So the person who goes in will become the last person who went in.'

'A delayed reaction?'

'Yes.'

'It doesn't just affect swimming,' a villager called out. 'It even happens when you go fishing, wash there, or fill a bucket with water.'

'How does the water taste?' I asked.

The villagers shook their heads.

'We don't know. None of us have ever drunk it because we will become one another.'

'But how do you know all this?'

The farmer conferred with his brother, and then all the villagers talked together.

'No one told us,' one of them said. 'We've always known it, just as our parents and grandparents did.'

'One last question...' I said. 'What happened to the very first person who went in the water? If they were the first person, surely they weren't swapped with someone else.'

Again, the villagers conferred.

'Even though he's long dead, he must be in a kind of limbo.'

I motioned something to one of our team and he gave a thumbs up.

'Would you mind if we do an experiment?' I asked.

'What kind of experiment?'

'Would you allow me to go down to the lake with my colleague who is sitting over there, and both touch it at the same time?'

The farmer whispered to his brother, and his brother whispered to the others.

'You are welcome, but we warn you of the danger.'

'I will take the risk in the name of science,' I replied.


As the sun rose over the valley, the film crew and I, followed by the villagers, streamed down to the lake.

The body of water was even more striking by day than by night, so much so I was at a loss for words. On the way down to it, we passed children running back and forth to gather water from a far-off stream.

The villagers held back from getting too close, fearful of being splashed. The director of our film crew and I wended our way down to the edge of the lake. Even before we were close we could see the fish darting through the clear water.

The farmer held up a hand.

'You are our honoured guests,' he said. 'Please don't continue, as you will become one another!'

'It's a risk we are prepared to take,' I replied. 'In any case, there's something I haven't told you. We may be brave but even we are not going to dare touch the water without protection.'

Fumbling in my shirt pocket, I pulled out a loop of green nylon parachute cord. The crew's director did the same.

In time with one another, we put them around our necks.

'These cords are amulets which will protect us,' I explained.

'Are you sure?' someone called out.

'Yes, we are absolutely certain.'

With the villagers watching us in trepidation, we took off our shoes and socks, and stepped into the lake.

'Have you become each other?' one of them cried out.

We shook our heads.

'It takes time to happen,' the farmer mumbled knowingly.

'We will wait,' I said.

So we waited and waited, until our feet were wrinkly, and our bodies were frozen to the bone.

After two hours of waiting, the villagers asked again.

'We are still ourselves,' we both said.

'The amulets are strong,' the farmer's brother muttered. 'Where did you get them?'

'From an astrologer in Kabul,' I replied.

On hearing the news the villagers seemed sorrowful. Kabul was too far, and even if any of them went there, none had money with which to buy amulets.

'How many of you live in the village?' I asked, as I dried my feet.

The farmer counted on his fingers.

'There are sixty-three of us, including the children.'

I thanked God.

'That's exactly the number of amulets we have.'

The farmer's brother broke into a grin.

'But do they all have the same power over the lake?' one of the villagers called out.

'Oh, yes, yes… they're all exactly like the one I'm wearing.'

Once back in the village, I raced over the fields, made sixty-three loops as quickly as I could, and was soon back at the farmer's house.

Giving thanks for the hospitality, I turned to the farmer, as the villagers clustered around.

'By the same power that gave our amulets their strength,' I said, 'the astrologer in Kabul foresaw us coming here to your village. He knew there were sixty-three of you, and so he sent that number of amulets.'

I passed over the loops.

'There's a chance that they'll wear out,' I went on, 'or that you will need more when children are born. If that happens, there's a solution. Before we left the astrologer in Kabul, he turned a very long piece of the same material into an amulet.'

I pulled a two-hundred-foot roll of green parachute cord out from my daypack. 'Whenever you need one of the amulets, all you have to do is to make a loop and give it to whoever you like.'

The villagers appeared overcome with joy.

'The astrologer has strong magic,' stated the farmer's brother.

'Yes he does,' I replied. 'So strong in fact, that he added another spell to the amulets. If they're used by everyone in the village they have an extra power.'

'What is it?' asked someone at the back.

'Well, if you all wear the amulets, and go down to the lake every day, and use it for drinking water, fishing and swimming, you'll break the spell of the jinn that guards the lake. If you do so, by the next full moon none of you will need to ever wear amulets again.'

## Twenty-three

**N**asrudin charged into the teahouse in a fit of excitement.

'It happened at last! It happened at last!' he wailed.

'What did?'

'The king spoke to me!'

Everyone gathered around, praising the wise fool for his importance. Before he knew it, customers who never would have given him the time of day were suddenly very friendly.

'You'll need to get a private secretary now that you're important,' suggested one.

'And new clothes fit for someone acquainted with royalty,' offered a second.

'What exactly did His Majesty say to you?' asked a third.

'"Get out of my way you idiot!"' beamed Nasrudin.


YUCATAN, 2017

For as long as I can remember, I've been fascinated by chains of transmission.

The way a single idea – or even an entire body of knowledge – is passed on from one generation to the next, is a reflection of human culture in its truest form.

At the same time, I'm intrigued by examples in which cultural material has been subsumed from one society to another against all odds.

My father devoted his life to showing how stories travel on the wind, seeding themselves in different places in a way that's breathtaking. He would say that stories, and the folklore to which they belong, *are* culture, and that the ability to draw knowledge from such a valuable database is the way a society stays on track.

Although born and raised largely in Europe, I've lived for many years in Morocco. Having been introduced to it as a small child, the kingdom holds a deep and all-encompassing fascination for me. I know of no other realm touched with the same transmission in cultural magic.

As my life has progressed, I've observed from a distance, watching how I myself have been prepared and altered by experience. The seeds planted in me at birth required time and circumstance to germinate... a process borne out through success, failure, danger and delight – but most of all by treading a zigzag path that so often appears to lead nowhere at all.

Anyone who knows me will vouch for how I'm

commanded by a restless soul... a soul that desires to achieve every last ambition right now.

A few years ago, a psychologist friend looked into my eyes at a party, and gave voice to his conclusion.

'It's exhausting being Tahir Shah, isn't it?' he said.

'Yes!' I spluttered. 'But I don't know how not to be the way I am.'

'Try taking time off or relaxing,' my friend suggested.

Alarm descended over my face like a veil.

'If I stop, I'll evaporate,' I said.

Concocted at the crossroads between East and West, with a certain legacy and heritage as pre-programmed wiring, I'm tortured by the inability to sit still.

On long, sleepless nights far away from home I whisper to myself, begging my mind to go to sleep, or at least to pause the incessant stream of ideas, hypotheses, and plans.

However harshly I rail against it, the flow won't stop.

Instead, the more I seek to curb it, the more it gushes, like a magic porridge pot.

From the first lone travels through Africa more than thirty years ago, I've taken refuge in movement. It's my only salvation from the continual terror... terror at not having experienced or created enough.

With movement, my waking mind comforts itself

by making associations between places and ideas – a backdrop that is the lifeblood of travel.

Nothing gives such pleasure as finding a skill in a remote landscape, which I have known elsewhere. In Afghanistan's western city of Herat, I once watched a craftsman working away at a mosaic frieze. The fabulous creation was, I noticed, made with the same hammer grasped in the hands of *zeligiers*, in Morocco's ancient city of Fès.

Immersing myself in the folklore, and in less obvious layers of Moroccan life, I've been prepared to receive configurations of the same elements...

Not in Morocco, but across the ocean.

For five centuries the Iberian Peninsula was dominated by the Arabs, whose legacy continues to be manifested in Spanish and Portuguese culture in all manner of ways.

But there's something that I've found to be equally interesting: the way strains of ancient Arab culture were blown over the Atlantic along with the Conquistadors... a culture which itself had travelled across North Africa from Arabia, having started its journey in the furthest reaches of the East. Taking root, the idiosyncrasies and thinking of the Arabs bloomed, as they combined with the rich soil of the New World.

Throughout my journeys in the Americas, I've

discerned chains of transmission from elsewhere. Preeminent amongst them is a reflection of the wise fool.

Three years ago I spent the summer in Mexico, taking my children, Ariane and Timur, there for the first time. Over weeks we criss-crossed that great country, marvelling at the gloriously delicious stew of life.

One day, while travelling across the Yucatan, Timur asked me whether Nasrudin was found in Mexico.

'I'm sure he is,' I said, 'even if he doesn't have a name.'

Timur screwed up his face.

'How could he exist without a name?'

'By being woven into the fabric of society,' I replied. 'In a way that's hidden in plain sight.'

Three days later we arrived at a tiny town in the middle of the peninsula. Cursing myself at having hired the cheapest rental car, we searched for a garage. Fortunately, we found one easily, and I explained to the mechanic that the car was overheating. He pointed to a clutch of chairs in the shade of a sprawling jacaranda tree.

We went over, ordered cold drinks, and waited for the work to be done.

With no internet reception, and not much going on, time passed slowly.

'Wish there weren't so many flies,' said Ariane.

'Wish there was air conditioning,' said Timur.

'Wish we weren't here,' I said.

Across the street, I could see the mechanic working away under the bonnet, and I could hear him pounding something with a hammer.

'God knows how people deal with life here,' Ariane grumbled.

'I'm sure it's more fun than it looks,' I muttered.

A minute or two later, against the rhythmic din of the hammer pounding, we heard the sound of music. Not music from a radio, but live music.

All three of us squinted through the jacaranda's boughs.

'There!' Timur yelled.

'What is it?'

'It's a one-man band!'

As we watched, a bizarre and unexpected figure came strolling backwards down the street in a fanfare of noise.

On his head was a helmet made from a saucepan, and on his feet were diving flippers. His arms and legs, which looked as though they had been tarred and feathered, were attracting more than their fair share of flies. In one hand he was shaking a home-made tambourine and, in the other, he gripped a set of low-grade panpipes. And, between his lips was a whistle, spewing a crazed cacophony.

As soon as they heard the commotion, people streamed from the shacks in which they lived. The woman who owned the makeshift café rushed over, as did the mechanic fixing my car, as well as the butcher, the cobbler, and a throng of others.

We jumped up, too, and rushed over to the road.

The melancholic atmosphere was instantly lifted. Everyone started laughing, singing, and clapping.

'Who is he?' I asked.

'The idiot!' the man beside me cried out. 'He's the idiot – that's who he is!'

'What does he do?'

'Just what you see,' the café owner said. 'He walks backwards, dressed in that hilarious way, banging pots, or saying the funniest things.'

'You mean jokes?'

'No, not jokes. But funny things.' She thought for a moment. 'Yesterday when it was raining hard, he came out, yelling he was going to swim to China! And, before that, he ran around on all fours, insisting he was a dog.'

'Is he a clown?'

The mechanic, who had heard my question, spiralled a finger at the side of his head.

'He's a madman.'

'How long's he been here?'

'Only a week or two.'

'We love him,' the woman said. 'He's like a member of our family.'

'Does he have a name?'

'"Babak!"'

'*Babak?*'

'Yes, that's right. It's what he shouts out when he's hungry. When he's *babak*.'

'When Babak is babak!' a little boy exclaimed.

'And what does Babak do when he's babak?'

'We just let him go into our homes and help himself to whatever he can find.'

'You trust him?'

'Of course,' said the mechanic. 'He's one of us.'

When Babak was out of sight, everyone got back to what they'd been doing. After another hour of banging, the mechanic whistled from across the street.

I hurried over.

'You'll be fine now, señor,' he said. 'But if you come through on the way back, stop by and I'll double check.'

As we drove on to the coast, all I could think of was Babak.

Timur read my thoughts.

'I can't stop thinking about Babak,' he said.

'Do you think Babak was a wise fool?' Ariane asked.

199

'He didn't look very wise to me.'

'Maybe he was very clever, and was just pretending to be stupid.'

'Nice idea,' I replied. 'But in Babak's case, I think what you see is what you get.'

'I liked him,' Timur said. 'He made everyone happy and he wasn't doing any harm.'

We all agreed the world was better because Babak was in it, and that a few more Babaks would be a good thing.

After almost a week exploring the eastern fringes of the Yucatan, we drove back across the peninsula, luxuriant jungle either side of the road.

'We're near where the car overheated,' I said.

'Let's stop, Baba,' Ariane said.

'Looks as though the engine's fine now.'

'Let's stop not for the car, but for Babak. He might be up to something funny again.'

'All right,' I agreed, 'let's see if Babak is feeling babak.'

Pulling off the main road, we parked where we had done before. The mechanic hurried out and greeted us.

'All good with the engine?'

'Working perfectly,' I replied.

'How's Babak?' Timur asked.

Rather than smiling as we expected, the mechanic scowled.

'Son of a dog!' he yelled.

'What do you mean? Babak was wonderful.'

'He was so funny,' said Ariane.

Picking up his hammer, the mechanic grimaced.

'We trusted him because we thought he was an idiot!'

'Well, he *was* an idiot,' I said, thinking back to how he'd behaved.

'Once he'd gained our trust we let him roam through our houses like members of the family.'

'*So?*'

'So, when we were asleep on Sunday,' the mechanic said, 'Babak went from house to house stealing anything he could find.'

'He was a thief?' I declared in surprise.

'Yes!' said the mechanic. 'The cleverest thief in the Yucatan!'

## Twenty-four

asrudin had reinvented himself as a traveller. Criss-crossing the world, he arrived at a kingdom far from home.

While there he happened to meet an old friend from his own kingdom. They arranged to meet on the weekend to reminisce about old times.

'What day of the week is it today?' the friend asked.

'What a foolish question!' barked Nasrudin. 'You know full well I've just arrived here!'

'So?'

'So I can't be expected to know what days of the week they have in this distant land!'


VENICE, 2008

Without my knowing it at the time we met, Wilhelm van der Meer was a man I'd been searching for my entire life.

Six foot six, and with a mile-wide smile, his name and his height were unmistakably Dutch. His jeans, shoes, and t-shirt were terribly worn, as though he'd been covering a lot of ground.

'I'm so sorry for being so tall,' was the first thing he said to me. 'If we go and sit down you may not notice it so much.'

So we went to a favourite haunt of mine, Caffè Florian, on the covered walkway that runs alongside St Mark's. The most elegant corner of the most opulent city in the world, it was the kind of place that makes you thankful for being alive.

I was by no means the only writer who'd discovered it nor, I suspected, the first to have thanked Providence for guiding me there. The great and the good of literature have sought refuge in its gilded salons for three centuries – among them Byron, Dickens and Proust.

Wilhelm lowered himself onto the narrow banquette. He'd written to me the previous week praising a book I'd written about Ethiopia. Nothing reduces an author's insecurities more than unsolicited praise.

'A coincidence you mentioned you were in Venice. Are you here to see the sights?'

The Dutchman smiled even more expansively than he had done outside, his cheeks pitted with dimples.

'Yes and no,' he reasoned.

'Best way to see the world,' I replied. 'A mixture of work and pleasure.'

Self-consciously, Wilhelm raised a broad hand and smoothed down a mass of straw-blond hair that made him appear even taller than he was.

'When I say I am working,' he said, 'I don't want to give the wrong impression.'

'You've given a good impression so far,' I replied.

'Happy to hear it. Very happy indeed.'

Again, he smoothed down his hair, as though by doing so he might further improve the overall impression.

'So what's your work?' I asked, hoping to move the conversation on.

Sniffing, Wilhelm smiled, the dimples returning to his cheeks.

'It would be true to say I'm a law-breaker,' he said.

'Standing up for your rights?'

'Yes. And then again – no.'

'You speak in riddles,' I said with a smirk, as my mind questioned how I could break free.

But the next thing the Dutchman uttered was the most refreshing nugget of information I had heard in years:

'I break the world's stupidest laws,' he said. 'The kind of laws that would be funny if they weren't so dumb.'

Over pots of tea, and uncomfortable at being forced to perch for so long on the slim banquette, Wilhelm explained his mission – a mission that guffawed in the face of madness.

'In the small town of Blythe, California, I wore cowboy boots,' he said.

'What's wrong with that?'

'By law you have to own at least two cattle to wear boots in Blythe.'

'Did they arrest you?'

Wilhelm shook his head.

'It's not the only law I've broken,' he whispered subversively, dimples even deeper than before.

'What other laws have you contravened?'

My new elongated friend thought for a moment.

'I've fired a water gun in Cambodia, and taken mineral water into Nigeria,' he said. 'I peed in the sea when in Portugal, led a chicken across the road in the state of Georgia, smuggled a durian fruit into my hotel room in Kuala Lumpur, and I've even held a salmon suspiciously in England.'

'How do you hold a salmon "suspiciously"?'

'It's not as easy as you'd imagine,' Wilhelm retorted.

'Any others, or is that it?'

'Oh no... there're lots more.'

'Such as...?'

'Such as flushing the toilet in Switzerland after ten p.m., wearing boxer shorts under a kilt in Edinburgh, camouflage in Tobago, and smuggling gum into Singapore.'

'Any stupid laws you wouldn't break?' I asked.

'Plenty.'

'Like what?'

'Well, I wouldn't kill a sasquatch.'

'You mean a yeti?'

'Yeah.'

'A fictional yeti.'

'Unproven to exist,' Wilhelm corrected.

'Pretty much the same thing.'

'It's a matter of opinion.'

'Agreed,' I said. 'Is that it? What other stupid laws wouldn't you break?'

'Well, there's one that's top of the list.'

'What's that?'

'I wouldn't die in Sarpourenx.'

'Where?'

'In the Pyrénées.'

'What's so bad about dying there?'

'It's against the law.'

'Against the law to die?'

'Yeah. It's called Prohibition of Death.'

'Have you always been a rule-breaker?' I asked.

The Dutchman sipped his tea, no doubt wishing it were something stronger.

'It's not so much about breaking rules,' he answered, 'as about shining a light onto the foolishness of our species. We're idiots,' he said.

'Is that a good thing?'

Wilhelm's face lit up as though he'd witnessed a miracle.

'Yeah!' he exclaimed. 'Stupidity is wonderful. It's what makes us who we are.'

'How do you mean?'

'We laugh at stupid things and stupid people and, as we do so, it has a kind of healing effect. We watch Mr Bean because he's a nutcase, and because he does stuff back-to-front.'

'Like Nasrudin,' I said.

'Who's he?'

'Someone I travel with.'

'Would be nice to meet him.'

'Sounds as though you already have.'

There was a pause in the banter. Having not understood my remark, Wilhelm was too polite to ask what I'd meant.

'Still breaking rules, are you?' I asked, stoking the conversation back into flame.

'Oh yes,' he shot back. 'Very much so.'

'Any recent triumphs?'

'Yes, of course! I frowned in public in Milan last week. Then, yesterday, I built a huge sandcastle on a beach in Eraclea.'

'Let me guess, frowning and sandcastles are against the law?'

'Strictly forbidden,' the Dutchman intoned ominously, pushing his hair down again.

'If I wanted to break the law,' I said, 'where would I start?'

Wilhelm cocked his head to the square.

'Out there.'

'Don't get me wrong,' I said, 'I'm not a complete goody-goody, but I don't want to get banged up.'

'You won't be.'

'Why not?'

'Because we're going to do low-level stuff.'

'*We?*' I echoed, my back warming at the thought of being involved in clandestine activity. 'What are *we* going to do?'

Fishing an enormous hand into a tight trouser pocket, the Dutchman took out a crumpled paper bag.

'What's inside?'

'Breadcrumbs.'

'Breadcrumbs?'

'Yeah. Made them myself.'

'What's our mission?'

'Feeding the birds,' said Wilhelm.

'Doesn't sound very illegal,' I said, a trace of disappointment in my voice.

'It is!'

'Even so, it's not very radical.'

Wilhelm erupted in a dimpled ear-to-ear grin.

'You have to start somewhere,' he said.

## Twenty-five

asrudin was enjoying a long gossip session with his neighbour. They chatted through the afternoon and into the night. Finding themselves in darkness, the neighbour nudged Nasrudin.

'There's a box of candles on your left. Why don't you open it up and light one?'

'What kind of fool do you take me for?' spat Nasrudin. 'How d'you expect me to tell my left from my right in the dark?!'

LANGTON HOUSE, 1973

Whenever he launched a new book, or received a fresh translation, my father put it up on the mantelpiece in his study, a tradition that inspired me to do the same.

Over the years I viewed hundreds of books there, in a kind of gallery of private celebration. Some of the volumes were thick, others were thin, elaborate or were plain, or were in languages I didn't understand. A few of the books were works of art.

Supreme among them was *The Book of the Book*.

I'd missed its original appearance on the mantelpiece because it was published when I was very young. But then in the early 'seventies, it was reissued. As though taking a lap of honour, it was put up above the fireplace once again.

Spotting me sitting in the triangular patch of sunlight outside his study, my father called me in.

'What are you doing there?' he asked.

I shrugged.

'Waiting for something to happen,' I said.

'What?'

'Something interesting.'

'I see,' my father replied. 'Well, you're in luck, because something very interesting has just happened in here and I'm going to show it to you.'

My face lit up.

'Treasure?' I asked. 'You've found treasure?'

'Well…' he reflected for a moment. 'Well, yes, I have found treasure.'

I jumped up and down on the spot.

'Would you show it to me, Baba?'

'I will if you promise me something.'

'I promise.'

'But you haven't heard what it is yet.'

'I promise anyway.'

'Why?'

'Because I'll get to see the treasure.'

'All right. But first you should know something.'

'Yes, Baba?'

'It's that treasure comes in all kinds of shapes and sizes, all colours and textures. It can be heavy like gold, or sparkly like a diamond…'

'Or even shiny like a sack of silver coins.'

'That's right,' my father mused. 'And sometimes, treasure can be treasure because it contains something which is extremely precious.'

'Like a purse full of rubies?'

'Yes, just like that. Or even something you can't see.'

'Something invisible?'

'Yes.'

'What's the treasure you've just found, Baba?' I asked, tiring of being led around in circles.

Reaching up to the mantelpiece, he took down

a thick book with a red binding, onto which a magnificent Arabic calligraphy had been embossed.

'This is the treasure,' he said.

'Is it expensive?' I asked.

'Not especially.'

'Oh.'

'Can you read what it's called?'

Opening it, I read, '*The Book of the Book* by Idries Shah.'

'Is it a book about a book, Baba?'

'Yes, in a way it is.'

'It's a very thick book. How long did it take you to write?'

'Less than an afternoon.'

'Wow!'

My father smiled.

'If you open it in the middle, you'll see why it didn't take long.'

Doing as he suggested, I found the inside blank – all except for about twenty pages of text at the front.

'Why's it all blank, Baba?' I asked, feeling as though I was being tricked.

'Because it's a story about the difference between two things.'

'What two things?'

'Think of it as the difference between a bottle of ink, and the ink inside the bottle.'

'Baba, will you…'

Even before I'd finished the question, he had begun to read *The Book of the Book*.

When I was older, I realized what a furore *The Book of the Book* had caused when first published in 1969.

Fabulously produced, it was an object of real beauty. And, being thick as it was, and having my father's name on the spine as it did, people assumed it would be a deep, metaphysical roller coaster.

As soon as copies found their way into bookshops, the chaos began.

Booksellers shipped the boxes back to the publisher, insisting they'd been sent misprinted copies. Customers who'd bought the book demanded their money back. Reviewers lashed out with vitriol – claiming that Idries Shah was a trickster par excellence.

The answer was, of course, that – while my father delighted in illuminating the foolish side of human nature – he'd conceived *The Book of the Book* as a serious psychological experiment.

Had things been different – and the readers all lapped it up right away – he would have regarded the experiment as a failure. But by being lampooned and ridiculed, he showed how a simple literary device could in an instant highlight the shortcomings of Occidental thought.

This summer is exactly fifty years since *The Book of the Book* was first published. In all that time it hasn't been out of print once, and it continues to be a bestseller in English, and in dozens of other languages the world over.

## Twenty-six

Nasrudin heard the king had sent a high-level delegation through the kingdom in search of a man with a long and distinguished ancestry to be his chief of fisheries. Eager for the position, and as destitute as ever, the wise fool went down to the docks and borrowed a tattered old fishing net from a friend.

With great care, he made himself a waistcoat from part of the net, before going from teahouse to teahouse to plant a story of his family's associations with the sea.

A few days passed, and the delegation arrived at his door, trumpets sounding, buglers heralding.

'We have heard that you are descended from the first fisherman of our kingdom!' the chief of the delegation cried.

'It is true,' Nasrudin admitted bashfully. 'This

waistcoat I wear is fashioned from the first net, the one made by my ancestor – Nasrudin of the Seas!'

Deeply impressed, the delegation reported to the king and, a day or two later, the wise fool was made chief of all fisheries. Soon after, the head of the delegation bumped into Nasrudin on the street.

'I hope you are satisfied with your elevated position,' he said.

'Thank you! Yes! I am pleased and so is my wife... she's stopped nagging me for being such a wretch.'

Before going on his way, the king's representative raised an eyebrow.

'I must ask you something.'

'Of course, anything,' Nasrudin intoned obsequiously.

'You were hired because of that extraordinary waistcoat you wore, the one made from your ancestor's fishing net. But now I'm rather surprised to see that you are not wearing it.'

'No matter,' Nasrudin riposted. 'You see, the net has performed its duty and is no longer required.'

'What duty did it perform?'

'It caught me a prized fish,' said Nasrudin.

# TRAVELS WITH NASRUDIN

Twenty years ago, while learning conjuring in what was then Calcutta, Kolkata, I was ordered by my teacher to embark on a Journey of Observation.

The idea was that I would blaze a zigzag trail anywhere I pleased, and gather information and experiences to provide an upper hand when performing magic tricks. Looking back, it was a pre-eminently Oriental approach, one that baffled those who read *Sorcerer's Apprentice*, the book I subsequently wrote.

To my surprise, some readers suspected that I had invented the course, under the pupillage of the sadistic master, Hakim Feroze. When they write to me, I write back, as I almost always do when approached by people who read my books. More often than not, I found myself explaining that in *Sorcerer's Apprentice* I left out many of the strangest events, for fear that no one would believe them. I've even found myself telling people it was fiction, just to keep them quiet.

I'm not sure why, but my life seems to have been shaped by bizarre encounters and coincidences far more than those of my family or friends. It's something I don't appear to have any power over – a kind of bewitched backdrop against which an animated story is played out. All I can think of is that

I stumble through life with my mind tuned to pick up the frequency of the extraordinary – which enables me to observe things those around me miss.

Unlike many people I encounter, I take on a hundred times more projects, embark on far more journeys, and engage in thousands more correspondences, because my restless soul won't stop.

After *Sorcerer's Apprentice* was launched, I got on with writing books, making documentaries, and engaging in a raft of other projects for which I don't seek the limelight.

One morning an envelope bearing Indian postage stamps arrived via my publisher. It had journeyed sea-mail, and looked as though it had taken a truly circuitous route on its voyage of discovery from the East.

Opening it, I found a letter from Seema, a health worker in Tamil Nadu, in southern India. She reminded me how we'd met at a café in a small town north of Madurai ten years before.

Preoccupied with my Journey of Observation, I'd quizzed her about her life, and – as she recalled – I'd been greatly interested in everything I heard and saw.

While sitting in the café, we'd both observed a beggar being taunted by a group of high school kids. Doing his best to earn a living, the man had made a fabulously elaborate cage from scraps of wire and wood, in which he kept a dozen or so rats. He was inviting passers-by to pay anything they liked, and feed a few grains of food to his rodents in return for good luck.

The kids had been scathing at what they regarded as a health hazard. Jeering at the man, they hurled empty mango-drink cartons at him, bawling for him to take his rats and go far away.

Seema and I had watched sorrowfully as the beggar staggered over to the shade, where he waited on his haunches with the cage – coming out only when the high school kids had gone.

Then he started up again, inviting anyone with a little spare change to feed the rats. Taking pity on him, I strode over and slipped him a large wad of notes – far more than I imagined anyone had ever given him before. Thanking me, he sprinkled some pellets on my palm, and invited me to feed the rats by placing the food into a spring-loaded metal drawer, the size and shape of a matchbox.

Once I'd done as he instructed, a mechanism powered by a hidden clockwork movement came to life. The pellets were delivered to the rodents through a series of tubes, against a sound rather like that of an old-fashioned barrel organ.

By the end of the first side of the letter, a clear mental picture had formed in my mind of Seema, the café, the beggar, the ornate home-made cage, and the rats.

Turning the page, I read:

'I know you are far away, and that you are certainly busy, but I felt it my duty to inform you of a remarkable occurrence – as it may be of interest to you. The occurrence of which I write has changed the life of the beggar we watched from the café that day. As you may remember, I am based in Madurai, but visit the town every few months to check up on our sanitation project. While making my scheduled visit last week, I happened to see him again. What I saw was of great interest to me, as I imagine it would be to you.'

Rather than describe the 'remarkable occurrence', Seema urged me to visit India at my earliest opportunity – perhaps imagining it would be easier for me to accomplish than it actually was.

Writing back, I declared how I hoped to have the chance of visiting again in the future. Posting the letter, I got on with my work.

As is so often the case, I was unable to get the subject out of my mind. The more I pushed it away, the more it crept back in.

Until I'd reached a point at which I couldn't stop second-guessing what had happened to the beggar, the cage, and the rats.

A few weeks passed, in which I finished a new book, and got down to a project devoted to bridging West and East.

But Seema's letter, the beggar and his rats, spun round and round until I could stand it no more. We had planned to visit my in-laws in Mumbai. So, while the rest of the family hung out together, I flew down to Madurai, in the hope of witnessing the 'remarkable occurrence'.

Seema and her husband picked me up at the airport, and we drove straight out into the countryside. As their Maruti trundled north along bumpy roads, zigzagging between petrol tankers and sacred cows, I prodded them both for clues.

'Please be patient,' said Seema.

So, I bit my lip, and reminded myself, in case I needed reminding, how wonderful Tamil Nadu is – awash with lush farmland and forest, and free from the nonsensical pressure that tends to fill my life.

As the town approached, I tried to remember visiting it before, albeit under wholly different circumstances. But there wasn't much solid memory to cling to – just a general haze.

When we'd parked the car, we stopped at the café where Seema and I had met a decade before.

'Oh yes, I remember it well,' I lied.

'That's where the high-schoolers were standing… and the beggar was there,' Seema said, pointing to the ground, glass bangles jingling as she did so.

While straining to appear upbeat, I was beginning to wonder if I had been lured on the kind of wild

219

goose chase to which sensible people give an extra-wide berth.

'So,' I said keenly, 'I'm ready for the secret.'

Seema pointed at the distance, her bangles jingling again.

'Over there.'

The three of us ambled in the direction of a school, following a track until we were on open ground. At the far end was a shallow pool and, beyond it, what looked like a cross between a temple and a palace. Unlike the usual stone palaces you come across in India, this one was far more elaborate.

Again Seema's hand pointed, bangles jingling.

'That's it!'

'What is?'

'Where the beggar lives.'

Travel through India and it's hard not to be amazed by things that might be unlikely or even impossible elsewhere. Founded on a bedrock of unparalleled scope and scale, the subcontinent has no challengers when it comes to pure, unadulterated wonder.

For a travel writer, India's as good as it gets.

And, the beggar in the small town north of Madurai was as impressive a 'remarkable occurrence' as I had seen in a long, long time.

As we approached the palatial building, Seema asked if it reminded me of anything.

'In a strange way, it reminds me of the wire and wood cage in which the beggar kept his rats,' I replied.

Circumventing the pool, we made our way to the door. A retainer welcomed us without asking who we were or why we'd come.

Kicking off our shoes, we went in.

The front part of the building was dominated by a courtyard, the size of a tennis court. Laid with polished stone, there were channels of water zigzagged through. In the far corner, a clutch of cross-legged *pundits* was performing a *puja*, the sound of their prayers echoing round the patio.

At the far end was a low doorway, apparently leading to a shrine. From time to time, devotees would saunter in. Barefoot and stooping, they'd make a beeline for the sanctuary, ring a temple bell, and amble back out.

Before I could ask the retainer about the shrine, the figure we'd seen begging ten years before stepped out from a side door.

Unmistakably the same man, he looked a little older, and was certainly better dressed. The rags were long gone, replaced by a *kurta* and *salwar* in ivory-coloured silk.

Seema and her husband began explaining who we were.

The former beggar, who seemed genuinely

pleased at seeing us, led us through into his private quarters.

Soon, we were sitting in a garden overflowing with exotic plants and trees, while the man delivered a long, formal welcome. To my surprise, he spoke good English, and seemed well-educated.

'My name is Prashant,' he said, his long, thin face kindly, and his mouth dominated by overly protruding front teeth. 'But people usually call me "Chooha-baba".'

'"Chooha-baba"?' I said. 'You mean, "rat-man".'

Prashant grinned.

'It's been my nickname since I was a child.'

Unsure where to start, I jumped in at the deep end.

'Ten years ago I was sitting in a little café out there during a journey through India,' I said. 'I'd got talking to Seema, and was asking her about her life. As we sat there, sipping our tea, we saw you – with an ornate cage full of rats. A group of children were yelling insults at you.'

Chooha-baba didn't reply – not at first anyway.

For a moment, I wondered if we'd confused him with someone else, or if he was embarrassed at being reminded of the event.

'Yes,' he said, after a long silence.

'*Yes?*'

'Yes, I remember that day. I remember those children… and I remember how you came to me and gave me a large amount of money. I can only hope that by feeding my rats you got good luck.'

Although ashamed of myself, I was pleased he remembered.

'I apologize in advance,' I said, 'but I have an enquiring mind. And there's something I am wondering about.'

'What is it?' Chooha-baba asked gently.

'Well, when I saw you ten years ago, it seemed as though you were living a modest life. None of *this*,' I said, peering around the grand courtyard.

Chooha-baba brushed his hands together in thought.

'Most people drift through life,' he replied. 'They do their best to keep to a path that runs across even ground. They prefer not to climb mountains or go down deep into valleys. A life like that is good, of course. At the same time it's robbed of something.'

'Robbed of what?'

'Robbed of the chance to descend to terrible depths and to soar as high as the birds.'

I was about to ask a follow-up question, when Chooha-baba signalled for me to wait.

'I will tell you what happened,' he said. 'Not because it's especially interesting, but because, in a way, it began with you.'

'With *me*?'

'That's right. With you... On that day, when

the children mocked me, and when you gave me so much money, I turned a page in my life. Until then I had been living from day to day. As you saw I was in a sorry state. Born into the Brahmin class, I was fortunate to have been given a good education. But my family lost its wealth and ancestral lands as a result of bad investments. Facing great debts, I was reduced to nothing... to owning a few rats which lived in cages I made for them myself.

'People were very unkind to me. They laughed and called me names. They said I was an idiot. I was sad because even a beggar has a sense of pride. Even though things were bad, I kept going. I knew that sooner or later an opportunity would come along – but that I needed to recognize the opportunity. When people are wealthy they can't think on their feet, or seize opportunities.

'So, on that day when you so kindly gave me money, I sat down in the shade behind the school out there and tried to think of a way to multiply the cash you had given. It was the first time I had more money than I needed for a single day. It was enough to live on for two or three months. I knew it was the right moment to grasp the opportunity. And so that's what I did.'

'But how did you do it?'

Chooha-baba swallowed, front teeth protruding through his lips even when his mouth was closed.

'I used what I already knew,' he replied.

'What was that?'

'Rats.'

'*Rats*?!'

'Yes, rats. You see, here in Tamil Nadu we have plenty of rats. No one likes them, and everyone wishes they were not there.'

'But how did you turn rats into wealth?'

'By guaranteeing people they'd never encounter a rat.'

'Is that possible though?'

Chooha-baba grinned.

'Anything is possible,' he said.

'But how did you do it? By using pesticides?'

'No, no, no! That would not be right. I was born into a Brahmin family and we do not believe in killing.'

'So, if you couldn't kill the rats, what did you do to them?'

'We blessed them, and asked them to bless us,' Chooha-baba said.

'The Karni Matha Temple in Bikaner has thousands of rats,' Seema broke in. 'People go to pray there – because rats feature in the scriptures.'

'Ganesha used to ride on a rat,' Seema's husband added.

'That is correct,' the former beggar replied. 'And it is what gave me my idea. You see, my days of being destitute were unpleasant, but they gave me the opportunity to learn about all kinds of things, especially rats. I learned all about them – what they liked and didn't like; what they were feeling and, most importantly of all, how to catch them.'

'How?'

'As a child I had an interest in making things,' Chooha-baba said. 'When my fellow classmates were out playing games, I would hide myself away, making mechanical objects using cogs from discarded alarm clocks, and things like that. So, when I was living on the streets, I used my knowledge of mechanics to make a cage that was also a maze-trap. People like to say cats are inquisitive, but rats are far more so. They follow a maze if they think it leads to food. What I did was to use their native inquisitiveness against them, trapping them in a humane way – so that they didn't get hurt.

'At first, people laughed at me. They remembered how I had begged for a living, and so they continued with their taunts. They jeered that my traps were made by a clown, and that they belonged in a circus – a rat circus. They said I was a fool for not using poison like everyone else.

'Then one day contractors began to hear of my traps. They were putting up expensive new apartment buildings all around the town, and they found rats plaguing them. They'd tried poison, but it led to rotting rats in pipes and that kind of thing.

'The first contractor ordered one or two traps. He was very happy because he caught four hundred rats in a single night. Word spread, and I soon had to hire other people to help me. Within a few months, I was receiving orders for thousands of my maze-traps, and had a production line in place. Money rolled in.'

'There's something I'm missing,' I said. 'If you don't kill the rats, what do you do with them – release them in the countryside?'

'No, no, no,' Chooha-baba said. 'Do that, and they'd instantly return to the town.'

'So...?'

'So I keep them in special farms on the edge of the town. A local businessman, a devotee of Lord Ganesha, pays to feed them as an act of piety. In that way, there are no significant costs associated with the creatures themselves.'

'But don't they just breed... *like rats?*'

'No, no, no.'

'Why not?'

'Because, when they arrive, we divide them into male and female. The males are all put in one place and the females in another. We make sure that no "wild" rats can ever get in. With time, the rats live their lives, and pass away from natural causes.'

'What's the average age of a rat in Tamil Nadu?' I asked.

'About two years – sometimes more; sometimes less.'

'Do you think you'll ever reach a time when there are no more rats?'

Chooha-baba balked at the question.

'I imagine not,' he answered. 'Because even if Tamil Nadu ran out of rats, a lot more would come over the border from other states.'

'Sounds like a perfect business model,' said Seema.

'What's the secret to your success?' I asked.

Chooha-baba thought hard for a moment and looked into my eyes.

'The secret of anything is respect,' he said.

# PART THREE

# NASRUDIN-NESS

## Twenty-seven

n the dead of night Nasrudin was observed by a neighbour breaking into his own home. The next evening he was seen breaking in a second time, and then a third. Unable to stand it, the neighbour clambered out of bed and hurried to the window where Nasrudin was standing, ladder in hand.

'What kind of an imbecile breaks into his own house?!' he hissed.

'*Shush*!' Nasrudin responded, with a finger to his lips.

'Why?'

'Because my wife says I sleepwalk.'

'*So?*'

'So I'm trying to creep up on myself!' cried Nasrudin.

SHAKISO, 2000

Over the years, I've witnessed some very fine examples of what I like to call 'Zigzag Think' – examples in which people have been catapulted forward by flipping normal behaviour on its head.

The way I see it, that's the essence of Nasrudin: to take a situation in which people do the opposite of what might be expected of them. Throughout my travels, it's a kind of Holy Grail I have searched for, even though on the face of it I may have been on the trail of something else.

A perfect example occurred in Ethiopia when I was hunting for King Solomon's mines. The journey later formed the basis of my book on the subject and, a year or so later, I returned to make a documentary for National Geographic TV on the same subject.

Before starting, I remember boasting to my friends in London how I was going to search for King Solomon's mines. The subject was fine fodder for third-rate cocktail party chitchat – the kind of event I always seemed to be invited to. It went down especially well with the Euro-banker crowd.

'What's your strategy?' a Swedish money-man had asked me at one event, having listened to my plan.

'Well, er, the usual kind of thing,' I muttered, thinking on my feet, a glass of mouthwash white wine in hand. 'I'll make my way to Ethiopia and locate the illegal mines.'

'Why Ethiopia?'

'Because it's a mountainous country with ample gold.'

'What's the significance of the mountains?' the Swede asked, nudging a pair of expensive horn-rims back to the bridge of his nose.

'When mining gold, mountains are a shortcut,' I

explained, having read why in a magazine article that very morning.

'Why?'

'Glad you asked. It's because when mountains are formed, they pull the mother-lode upwards, closer to the surface. So you don't need to tunnel down so much.'

Overhearing our conversation, another Scandinavian sauntered over. An almost identical clone of his Euro-banker friend, he cleared his throat.

'Surely it's not as easy as it seems to actually break into Ethiopia's gold mines, is it?' he asked.

Sipping the mouthwash wine, I struggled for an answer to satisfy the Scandies.

'This kind of project's my forte,' I said, making it up as I went along. 'You see, I'm something of an Africa hand. Studied African dictatorships in the 'eighties.'

The Swede tugged a polka-dot handkerchief out of his blazer's pocket and polished the lenses of his horn-rims. It may have been an involuntary action, but I believe he did it so as to observe my response on the clincher question:

'Where exactly are the illegal gold mines?'

A quest, like the search for King Solomon's mines, is all well and good as a topic of discussion on the cocktail circuit – but when push comes to shove, it's a scary undertaking.

My enthusiasm to locate the mines was tempered by the fact that, although no longer a dictatorship, Ethiopia was very much locked down. Tourists were few and far between, and they rarely left the beaten track – the Lalibela–Axum–Gondar triangle.

Although on a tourist visa like everyone else, my motives were quite different from touring historical sites. And, my luggage was a total giveaway. It was comprised of three British Army kit-bags. They were stuffed with books and papers devoted to gold, as well as a well-hidden satellite phone, military maps of Ethiopia, gold testing kits, and even a metal detector tuned to locate the mother-lode.

Having arrived at my hotel in Addis Ababa at midnight, I woke at four a.m. drenched in sweat. As ever, I'd bitten off far more than I could possibly chew, and chastised myself for doing so.

As I lay there, propped up in bed, the sound of wild dogs howling out in the darkness, I heard a voice.

The voice of my grandfather, Sirdar Ikbal Ali Shah.

'You will succeed, dear Tahir Jan,' he said, 'but not by following usual processes in thinking. Shun the obvious, and tune your mind to pick up another frequency – the frequency that made every discovery and breakthrough in human history possible.'

The voice vanished as quickly as it had arrived.

Three hours later, my quest for King Solomon's mines began.

Retune the mind to receive, and things start bombarding you – like a meteor shower.

The secret is to open up one's bandwidth to the widest possible setting, or else the location of the stepping stones are filtered out.

In my experience, the best way to pick up a trail is to not search for it at all. It's better to embark on a random agenda and observe from a distance where it leads.

Finding the first seed in my quest for King Solomon's mines was a case in point. Addis Ababa had been flooded by heavy winter rain, and the sewers had overflowed. On that first morning I watched a funeral procession wending its way through the streets. There was none of the gloom or hysteria that tends to accompany such a ritual elsewhere. Wrapped in simple cotton shawls, the mourners were almost too graceful to describe.

Unsure where to begin my search, and with the torrential rain striking up again, I got into a taxi. The driver had halted as the cortège passed. Clambering out, he had stood beside his vehicle, hands held together at his waist, head bowed low in respect.

I asked him to take me to the tomb of Emperor Menelik II, at the Saint Gabriel Cathedral. If Nasrudin had been searching for Solomon's mines, I felt as though he would have started there as well.

With the rain lashing down, the driver steered his dilapidated turquoise Lada towards the cathedral. Once we were there, I hurried up the steps.

To my surprise, the driver came too.

Inside, a priest opened up a hatch in the floor, and led the way down into the crypt. Lost in shadows, the scent of burning myrrh heavy in the air, were the monumental granite sarcophagi of Emperor Menelik II, his queen, and Emperor Haile Selassie.

Unlike the others, Selassie's coffin hadn't been interred in a tomb, but in a frail glass-fronted cabinet. A place of pilgrimage for Rastafarians, the emperor's mortal remains were in limbo at the time. Having been removed from beneath the now-deposed President Mengistu's lavatory, they were waiting for reburial.

But that's another story.

Paying my respects to the monarchs of Ethiopia, I felt somehow connected to my quest. After all, they claimed descendance from King Solomon himself.

As I stood there, humbled and, at the same time, fearful of what lay ahead of me, the taxi driver struck up a conversation.

He said his name was Samson, and that the wealth of Ethiopia was being drained by wrongdoers. Within three minutes of chatter, in the crypt of the hallowed church, the word 'gold' was on Samson's lips.

Three minutes after that, I found myself back in Samson's Russian-built Lada, learning how he'd toiled in illegal gold mines of the south... at a place called Shakiso.

At that moment, I promoted Samson from modest taxi driver to unlikely ace in an outlandish and unconventional adventure.

Zigzagging our way through Ethiopia, we eventually arrived at Shakiso.

I still get shivers down my spine thinking of it.

Thousands of men, women, and children toiled there – most were digging with their hands. It was like something from the pages of the Old Testament.

Legions of miners scraping at the mud, in which there were alluvial deposits of gold – gold dust eroded in ancient times from the mother-lode. They'd ferry it down to the river to be panned, in a system developed three thousand years before, in Ancient Egypt.

Life was cheap at Shakiso.

Every week dreadful accidents occurred. Children were buried alive in tunnels. Drunken miners killed each other over a few grains of gold. There was disease and squalor as bad as any I'd seen.

Samson described how the community was arranged, highlighting elements that would certainly have passed me by if he hadn't been there.

Over the days we spent at Shakiso, I met all kinds of characters. Some of them were straight out of *The Treasure of the Sierra Madre*.

The one man different from the rest was Musa Ibrahim.

His gentleness put him out of place at Shakiso. He was well dressed and seemed to be very rich. Some said he was a spy. Others that he'd once found a gold nugget the size of a man's fist. Over the time I spent at Shakiso, I got to know him.

One day, when we were sitting together in the shade, I asked for the secret of his success.

Musa Ibrahim took a slow, reflective sip of his tea, and smiled.

'Look at all those people out there,' he said. 'They're killing themselves for a few specks of gold. Anything they find will be stolen, or squandered on vice. Each day they start afresh, a little poorer than the day before.'

'So you didn't make your money from mining, then?'

Musa Ibrabim let out a muffled squeal of horror.

'Of course not!' he replied. 'From the moment I arrived here I saw the only way forward was to be different from them. You see, the last thing that works is to do the obvious. And, as the obvious thing was to mine gold, I put it out of my head straight away.

'With the little money I had, I bought some equipment and a couple of mules. Renting them to the miners, I reinvested the profits. Very soon, I was offering not only equipment and pack mules, but food, clean drinking water, medicines, and reliable digital scales for weighing gold dust. While the miners have all stayed in limbo, I myself have progressed.'

Before Samson and I left Shakiso, I tracked down Musa Ibrahim for a final chat. He asked if I'd take a letter to his brother in Addis Ababa.

'Yes of course, but I may not reach the capital for two or three weeks. Travelling here's slow as you know.'

'Alas, Ethiopia is the land of unhurried movement,' the wily old businessman replied.

'Thank God for that.'

'But a little speed would change our situation.'

'In a good way?'

'Yes!'

'How?'

'Take milk, churn it round and round, and what do you get?'

'Cheese...?'

'A wonderful food from the simplest of drinks. And all you needed to do was shake things about,' said Musa Ibrahim.

asrudin was regaling the other regulars in the teahouse with stories of his travels.

'I once crossed the Empty Quarter of the Arabian Desert,' he boasted, 'a land of interminable heat, and a dominion peopled by terribly dangerous tribes.'

'Wasn't it very dangerous?' someone asked.

'Yes, very much so. But I, Nasrudin, know not the meaning of fear. You know, on one occasion I caused an entire tribe of Bedouin to run over the baking sands at full speed!'

The customers praised the great explorer for his bravery.

'How on earth did you manage to get the valiant Bedouin to run?' asked the owner of the teahouse. 'For everyone knows how fearless they are.'

'It was simple,' Nasrudin replied. 'I just ran for my life, and they ran after me!'


MADRE DE DIOS, 2002

My journey in search of Paititi, the greatest lost city in the Americas, had gone from bad to worse.

After ten weeks of following dead-end leads, we'd

hit rock bottom, and were camped at the edge of the river, morale at its lowest ebb.

Crouching there, cold, crunching pebbles beneath our boots, we were too exhausted to speak, or even to think. The porters would have killed me, I am certain of it, if any of them had possessed the strength to devise a plan with which to end my life.

Leading the expedition from the front, I'd pushed them as hard as I had pushed myself – marching on day after day, deeper and deeper into the cloud forest.

Long before, we'd all succumbed to dysentery, to septic mosquito bites, and to dengue fever. Trudging through the river for so long had abraded the skin from our feet, making us lame. The only thing keeping the men going was the thought of gorging themselves on what was left of the tapir meat. They didn't seem to care that it was thick with maggots.

They had no interest in actually discovering the ruins. Their hearts had never been in making the journey – and they were only taking part because of the day wage and promise of hot food. For me, on the other hand, the quest for Paititi – the so-called 'House of the Tiger King' – was a chance at immediate and universal recognition.

Find Paititi, and my face would be framed by *Time* magazine's red border. Before I knew it, I'd be featured on the TV networks. After that there'd be the chat show circuit, mini-series, and movie deals.

Interviewed for the thousandth time, I'd tell how we'd hit rock bottom but had pushed through the pain barrier to eventual glory.

During periods of intense misery, I've always found my imagination compensates. A survival mechanism, it kicks in, and projects a backdrop of wonder by which I can keep going. It happened when I was at the wretched prep school where I endured six years of hell. It happened, too, when my film crew and I were locked up in a Pakistani torture jail for sixteen ghastly days and nights.

And, it happened on my search for Paititi.

Each night as we slept in a row beneath a single sheet of plastic, my imagination slogged harder and harder to compensate for the gloom.

In the first weeks, I dreamt of pushing deep into virgin jungle, my mind's eye projecting the beauty of it all. Then, night after night, my dreams progressed. I imagined setting eyes on the lost ruins for the first time. Gripped by an electrifying sense of utter wonder, I would watch myself posing for photos at a great overgrown citadel.

As septic mosquito bites gave way to the delirium of dengue fever, I visualized the pomp of being catapulted from insignificance to the high table. Find a lost city and in the blink of an eye you go from being no one to being the most celebrated adventurer on Earth.

The night before we found ourselves crouched at the edge of the river, I'd dreamt of being received at Buckingham Palace. While I knelt in the throne room, the Queen tapped a cutlass blade to my shoulder in honour of services to exploration.

It may have been the dengue fever, or a general slip into mania, resulting from deplorable conditions. The more time I spent in deep jungle, the more I seemed to have become Nasrudin.

Camping there at the edge of the river, as the team slept, I found myself turning the mission around my head. As I reasoned it, the journey thus far had been horrific, but necessary. Not because it had taken us to within an arm's length of potentially finding Paititi, but because it had lured my imagination to the ultimate quixotic no man's land.

Having reached such hallowed ground, I could simply close my eyes and visualize finding Paititi, and being fêted for it. Lying there, soaked through and aching, I thought back to my father and his fixation with Afghanistan.

Through the wending course of our childhoods, he'd ranted on and on about the homeland of our ancestors. While other children were taught practical lessons, most of our youth was devoted to hearing stories - stories which, like patches on a quilt, formed something greater than the sum of their parts.

The stories would invariably feature an element

of Afghanistan, even if in passing. The hero may have been from Bukhara, but he'd perhaps have studied in Kabul – providing my father with a chance to describe the melons there, the valleys of spring flowers, or the sight of swallows darting through the air at dusk.

Every so often we'd be so enthused by tall tales of Afghanistan that we expressed an impassioned desire to set foot there ourselves. On hearing such pleas from his children, our father didn't react well.

Instead of embracing us, he would scowl with indignation, and yell:

'Why oh why would you want to go to Afghanistan?!'

'Because it's the land of our ancestors, and you speak about nothing else.'

'But you have misunderstood,' he'd say. 'I've given you something far better than the land of your forefathers. I've given you Afghanistan in story form. An Afghanistan that's far better than the real thing.'

'How could it be, Baba?' we would ask.

'Because even if you are separated from it, it will always be there in your heart.'

The same was true for Paititi.

Why look for it, when my imagination had already created it – or at least a form of it – in spectacular detail?

Chuckling to myself, I thought of Nasrudin,

and how he might have searched for Paititi. It was obvious, of course...

The greatest lost-city-hunter of his age, Nasrudin was celebrated for hunting rather than actually finding. His descriptions of adventure were so entertaining no one seemed bothered he never discovered the location of Paititi, or anywhere else.

On one of his many expeditions to the jungle, Nasrudin's nephew, a would-be adventurer, tagged along. Against a great fanfare, the quest began, scouring a small area of jungle remarkably close to a road.

Weeks passed, in which Nasrudin regaled his men with tales of his heroic triumphs. The team seemed delighted by how the search was going. Everyone, that is, except Nasrudin's nephew. He was the only one who appeared to have studied the map. Plucking up courage, he approached his uncle one evening as the porters feasted in the firelight.

'Why are we searching here, uncle?' the boy asked, map in hand. 'When all the evidence points at the ruins being over there in deep cloud forest.'

'You may have youth, but you do not have experience,' the veteran adventurer riposted. 'An inexperienced trailblazer such as yourself may question my methods, but you'd be wrong. This tract of jungle may not contain the ruins, but it's easily accessible, with good hunting, and fresh water as well. It's absolutely perfect!'

'Perfect in what way?' the nephew asked.

'Perfect as a place to search for Paititi!' bellowed Nasrudin.

## Twenty-nine

earing that the king was holding a banquet for everyone in the kingdom, Nasrudin hurried to the palace in the hope of getting to the front of the line. With no time to go home and change, he arrived in his work clothes, straight from his job cleaning out the sewers.

Standing by the monarch's pledge to feed everyone no matter of their status, the master of ceremonies led Nasrudin to the end of the hall, as far from the king's table as possible.

With thousands of mouths to feed, and having been positioned miles from the kitchen, the wise fool feared he'd never be fed. So, weighing up the situation in his mind, he slunk out through a back door, rushed home, and opened up a huge wicker hamper left there by an actor friend.

Selecting the costume of an emperor, Nasrudin

adorned himself in a magnificent cloak of the finest silk, golden sandals, strands of gems, and a colossal turban. Suitably dressed, he returned to the palace.

As soon as the master of ceremonies spotted a visiting dignitary at the banquet hall's door, he rushed over and escorted him to the king's own table. Thrilled at having an emperor at his gathering, the monarch ordered that an extra-special dish be served to his respected guest.

Moments later the platter was borne over to Nasrudin. Thanking his host for such refined hospitality, the wise fool grabbed a lump of meat and rubbed it into his cloak.

The monarch and his family looked on in bewilderment. Assuming the ritual of rubbing food into one's clothing to be an act of rarefied etiquette reserved for emperors, they all did the same.

Only when they were all covered in food did the king enquire as to the origins of the elevated tradition.

'I'm just feeding the cloak as a reward,' Nasrudin explained.

'Fascinating!' the king boomed. 'A reward for what?'

'A reward for getting its owner a prime seat at this important gathering!'

Casablanca, 2009

Our housekeeper, Zohra had heard me tell Ariane and Timur stories of Nasrudin a thousand times.

She had dusted the books by my father of the wise fool's exploits, too, as well as the many framed Nasrudin illustrations hanging from walls all over the house. Quite understandably, she'd never linked the name 'Nasrudin' to 'Joha' – the appellation by which he's known in Morocco.

One afternoon, as she fussed about in the kitchen, it suddenly clicked.

'Oooooooo-eeeeeee-aaaaaaaah!' she howled in a shrill exclamation of pleasure.

I scurried through from the library, where I was supposed to be writing a book.

'*Joha!*' Zohra howled. '*Il est la même que votre Nasrudin!*'

From that moment, we were all subjected to the formidable treasure of Joha tales locked up in Zohra's head.

She told Joha stories when she was cleaning the kitchen, and washing the floors, making the beds, or cooking *tajine*. She recounted them as well when out on the terrace hanging up the laundry, ironing, bathing the children, or chaperoning them to school.

Sometimes I'd try and tell a Nasrudin story, but Zohra despised competition, especially when it was manifested in the form of what she regarded as a second-rate Afghan impostor.

'There is only one Joha!' she declared one morning at breakfast. 'And the version you are telling is not right. It's wrong, wrong, wrong!'

'But they're one and the same,' I explained. 'Because Nasrudin – I mean *Joha* – is known from where we are sitting here in Casablanca, all the way to India!'

Zohra grimaced.

'A version of him is known outside Morocco,' she countered. 'Yet, in the same way that you can get *La Vache Qui Rit* cheese in other countries, real *La Vache Qui Rit* is only found here in Morocco.'

'Actually, *La Vache Qui Rit* is French,' I countered.

'That's not right!' Zohra huffed. 'Everyone knows that real *La Vache Qui Rit* is Moroccan, just as they know Joha is from Morrocco!'

'OK!' I puffed, rising to the bait. 'Where in Morocco does Joha come from, then?'

'*Tsk! Tsk! Tsk!*' Zohra snorted.

'Don't you know?'

'Yes, I know! Of course I know, monsieur!'

'Then tell me the name of the place where Joha comes from.'

Zohra slanted her head to the side in deep thought.

'I was told the name once,' she replied. 'By my grandmother... the one who passed on all the stories.'

'Then tell it to me and I'll shut up.'

All of a sudden Zohra clapped her hands together triumphantly.

'I've remembered!' she wailed. 'Joha's from Sidi Ifni!'

'How do I know you didn't just say the first name that came into your head?'

'Because everyone in Sidi Ifni wears their clothes back-to-front.'

'I've been to Sidi Ifni,' I said, 'and I didn't see anyone dressed like that.'

Zohra blushed, then frowned.

'Of course you didn't!'

'Why not?'

'Because you didn't recognize they were dressed back-to-front.'

'Huh?'

Zohra beamed at her power of deduction.

'You didn't see the people of Sidi Ifni were dressed back-to-front,' she proclaimed, 'because you thought Joha was called Nasrudin!'

# *Thirty*

very night, Nasrudin threw handfuls of salt into the flowerbed around his house in a curious ritual. As months passed, he added new layers of behaviour.

First, he clapped his hands between throwing each handful of salt. Then, he danced about between claps. After that he jumped up and down between dancing around and clapping.

Watching from across the street, Nasrudin's long-suffering neighbour couldn't understand what was going on. He assumed the wise fool had finally cracked. But, willing to give him the benefit of the doubt, he went over at the end of the evening ritual and enquired what was going on.

'Simple,' Nasrudin said, 'I'm keeping the tigers away.'

'But my dear neighbour, there are no tigers in these parts.'

Nasrudin narrowed his eyes subversively.

'Effective, isn't it?!' he cried.


LANGTON HOUSE 1972

In the early part of my childhood, I assumed everyone lived in big white houses, had fathers who never stopped typing or talking, and gardens where seasoned old classicists were out digging ditches, or where novelists were drying herbs in potting sheds.

Langton House was a magical island where we lived with a yellow Labrador, a second-hand tortoise, and oh so many cats. Our mother, who was half-Parsi and half-English, was the cat-lover, and the knitter.

She knitted everything – even my dressing gown.

While my mother knitted, my father typed.

Rising long before dawn, he would clatter away at an old dependable Triumph manual. Later he splashed out on an IBM 'golf ball' electric – the true love of his life. When he was typing, no one dared disturb him, even though the door to his study was always propped open with a chunk of quartz mined in the High Atlas Mountains of Morocco.

From an early age, I used to sit outside the open door in the triangular patch of sunlight, streaming in through an arched window giving onto the rose garden. At least one Siamese would be found curled up in the light. I would sit cross-legged beside it, listening to my father's index fingers hammering away. From time to time he would pause to relight a Montecristo, or roll a fresh sheet of Croxley Script into his beloved machine.

Every couple of hours he'd stop, grab a wad of pages, and stalk through the house, hunting for an audience.

Our mother, who'd typically be counting stitches or spinning wool, was a reluctant listener. At any rate, she'd no doubt have heard the material in an earlier draft.

While my father liked any audience, he preferred ears that were fresh. Such ears tended to be found in the kitchens, or up in the playroom – ears belonging to the throng of housekeepers, nannies, handymen, and hangers-on – all of whom were woven into the fabric of life at Langton House.

On the rare occasions my father found no one to charm with his freshest material, he would venture out of the front door. Hurrying past a ditch dug by Robert Graves, and along a gravel path, he'd slink into the first cottage, Montecristo smoke streaming behind like a vapour trail.

In the office there his ever-loyal secretary, Helena, kept guard. Although born 'Joan', in her youth she'd studied as a pupil of the Russian mystic George Gurdjieff. He knew her as 'Blonde No. 24'; he encouraged his disciples to select names for themselves as part of a quest for their own identity.

On Helena's desk multiple telephones were arranged that rarely stopped ringing. All through the day postmen dragged in sackfuls of letters, mailed to Langton House from all corners of the earth. Couriers would frequently arrive, too, bearing urgent telegrams.

And, then, there were the fans.

Drawn to Langton House like moths to a flame, they were often in search of a guru – even though my father's published work urged everyone to shun gurus and to think for themselves.

As the secretary, it fell to Helena to handle the phone calls, incoming mail, and to deal with the uninvited, who turned up in their droves. Details of them, and everything else, were typed out on small slips of recycled paper by Helena a.k.a. Gurdjieff's Blonde No. 24.

Ferried into the main house, they were left in a certain spot on a bookshelf, and eventually reached my father's attention – between bouts of typing, talking, or delivering test-readings of his work.

One evening, as we sat down to dinner, a slip of paper was brought in and placed in the requisite spot.

It read: *Australian family just arrived from Sydney. Came overland. Took them two years. Parents and three small girls. Am feeding them in the Elephant.*

The Elephant was a stone stable block converted into a refectory, in which whoever was around would eat together. Those present at the dinners on Saturday nights will, I am sure, remember them as rare moments of their lives.

As would almost everyone else, the Australian

family were soon listening to my father's fresh material, and were digging ditches, mowing lawns, and drying lavender like everyone else.

The food served in the Elephant was almost always forgettable, except when Monsieur Remi Lacoux conjured a handful of unremarkable ingredients into a feast. Courteous, elderly, and impeccable, he was a chef at Fortnum and Mason's Restaurant.

He once told me that, as a young apprentice, he had been asked to make an enormous cake for the 1929 launch of the R101 airship. As the cake was being brought into the room, it was dropped – breaking in two. Next day, the R101 itself crashed. Split down the middle, it burst into flames, killing almost all the passengers and crew.

All the while, a constant stream of people turned up. As a small child I had no idea who most of them were. At Langton House everyone was someone and no one at the same time.

Drawn from a cross-section of humanity, they were all different from one another. It was only later I realized that I'd spent endless evenings chatting to ballerinas, poets, novelists, film directors, philanthropists, and even to Colditz escapees.

As I got older, I began to see how they were linked together. My father's work and way of thinking was the hub, a shared connecting point – centred through a back-to-front thinking. Although they hadn't originally known each other, those who turned up at Langton House year after year were connected to one another through Nasrudin.

One Saturday evening, my father was chatting to Avi, a Yemeni Jew for whom he had great affection, who was sitting on his right. Having spent a life in the East End rag trade, he was a fabulous storyteller. My father asked how life was treating him. Tugging off the peaked sailor cap he always wore, Avi rubbed a hand over his head.

'Not so good, Shah,' he replied forlornly.

'Sorry to hear it. What's the problem?'

'It's the council. They're giving me trouble for my cart. I don't have a permit and the wheel's fallen off and so they're gonna throw the book at me.'

My father thought for a moment, frowned, and relit his cigar. Sitting on his left was another friend, a Queen's Bench barrister, David Fairbanks.

He turned to the lawyer.

'Don't suppose you can help our friend, Avi, could you?' he asked.

An imposing member of the establishment, Fairbanks gave a grunt and got on with his meal.

The next week, Avi stood before the judge meekly, peaked cap in hand. Preparing to pass sentence, the judge demanded to know whether he had legal representation. At that moment, an imposing figure in the flowing black robes of court stepped from the shadows.

'David Fairbanks QC,' he thundered. 'I shall be representing this man!'

On the many evenings when my father spoke at the Elephant, I assumed what he was saying was utterly random and unplanned. Only later, long after his death, did I realize that it was part of his testing. Like a chef checking whether he had the ingredients right, he would expose the audience to his latest thoughts and ideas.

Forming part of his archive, the notes he kept detailed who was present, what was said and – most important of all – what impact the material appeared to have in a given situation.

Whether his audience was the nanny at Langton House, or a group of world-ranking scientists, my father observed the precise effect of anything he did or said with clinical attention. As he so liked to say, 'We were given two ears and only one mouth for a reason.'

## Thirty-one

Nasrudin won first prize in a competition for fools. To his absolute delight the reward was to cross the ocean in an aeroplane. Unable to contain his excitement, he was first on board.

The plane took off and, once it had reached the cruising altitude, lunch was served.

As Nasrudin munched his way through the meal, the captain's voice came over the intercom.

'I regret to inform you one of the engines has stopped working,' he said. 'Fear not, we have four engines and so we'll be fine. There will, however, be a delay of thirty minutes.'

Shortly afterwards, Nasrudin looked out of the window and noticed a second engine had stopped.

Again, the captain came on the intercom.

'Sorry to inform you all that a starboard engine has just conked out. Fear not, though, we will make it, although we'll be delayed by an hour.'

Cursing the world of modern technology, Nasrudin found himself missing his dependable old donkey. He was about to fall asleep, when the captain's voice came over the intercom again.

'Apologies, folks!' he boomed. 'But the third engine has died on us. Terrible luck, but there's nothing to worry about – we still have a remaining engine to get us across the ocean. But the lack of three engines means we'll be two hours late.'

Frowning angrily, Nasrudin accosted the flight attendant.

'I do hope the fourth engine doesn't stop working,' he grumbled. 'Or else we'll be up here all day!'


San Francisco, 1991

When I've got to know famous people, I've found it difficult to square their public persona with the way they really are.

When I was young at Langton House, Doris Lessing was one of so many who turned up at weekends. She liked to work in the herb garden most of all, and was often found there making potpourri.

Doris didn't stick out in any way at all.

She dressed in an understated way, drove a battered old Volkswagen, and conversed quietly. Her favourite subjects were gardening, Africa, storytelling, and cats. She always struck me as someone who relished life at Langton House because when there she could be herself.

I liked spending time with Doris because she was sensible. Not in an obvious way, but in a way that might be called 'profound'.

When Doris told you something, you knew full-well it had been uttered after careful thought. More often than not, I got the sense that her mind was always grinding away, and that in conversation she tossed in handfuls of ideas and conclusions prepared earlier. Never once can I remember Doris saying something which she hadn't mused on long and hard.

As I grew older, I discovered Doris had a life outside Langton House. Of course she did. The mind of a child makes sense of what it sees and knows, and that's what mine strained to do. Gaps in what I knew were simply filled in with invention – which is why the way children think is the default setting of us all.

In my teens, I would often get a lift up to London with Doris, when she was on her way back to West Hampstead. We would talk about Africa, and travelling, about stories, and Nasrudin.

On one journey, as we jolted forward through nose-to-tail traffic in south London, Doris ended a long silence with the words:

'You know, I was at your naming ceremony.'

'Where was it?'

'At Coombe Springs, a few months before your parents moved to Langton House. I remember the date. It was March 21st, 1967 – when Safia and you were four months old.'

'On Nauruz, Afghan New Year?'

'Yes, that's right.'

'Who else was there?'

'A long list of luminaries,' Doris replied, her eyes widening at the memory. 'Russell Page and Robert

Graves, and dozens of others – all of them quite extraordinary in their own right.'

'Do you remember anything from the ceremony?'

Doris fell silent, her mind scrolling back through the years.

'Yes, I do,' she said. 'Your father wore a magnificent robe over his shoulders, presented to him by King Ibn Saud. He quoted passages from the *Rubaiyat of Omar Khayyam*, and from Rumi's *Masnavi*. Prayers were spoken, and thanks for your life were given. You were both named, and then something remarkable happened.'

'What?'

'Your father touched a hand to your forehead and announced you would be protected throughout your life by your sense of humour – the kind contained in the wisdom of Mulla Nasrudin.'

'My suit of armour,' I mumbled. 'The one he said would always shield me from danger and injustice.'

Like me, Doris savoured conversation, following the thread of an idea, teasing it out, and seeing where it led.

A voracious reader, she had a vast knowledge ready and waiting to be harnessed. An inspiration in a deep down way, she expected others to work as hard as she herself did.

'The secret of success is applying oneself,' she once told me. 'Not in a mediocre way, but as though your life depended upon it. Most people fear hard work, or are too lazy for it. I feel for them, because they have no idea of the joy it brings.'

From time to time, we'd meet somewhere unexpectedly, and take up right away where we had left off.

On a handful of occasions I saw Doris out in the bear-pit of superstardom. At best it was uncomfortable to witness, and at worst it was like having one's teeth pulled. I watched as the quiet woman I knew and loved was overwhelmed by seething, frenzied crowds of fans.

One memory springs to mind.

We happened to be in San Francisco at the same time. I was on my way to Tokyo, and she was speaking at a literary event.

Many hundreds of people from the Bay Area and far beyond had packed into the huge auditorium. Most were clutching well-thumbed copies of their favourite Lessing novels. Some wore t-shirts that blared:

'I LOVE DORIS EVEN MORE THAN YOU!'

I was bustled into the green room, where Doris was sitting alone with a cup of tea. As soon as she saw me, her eyes lit up.

'Take me somewhere with you,' she said.

'You mean, outside, to a café – somewhere like that?'

'No time.'

'So where?'

'Let's go somewhere in our imagination,' she said. So we did.

We chatted about the scent of the first rain on African soil, and how people in Harare dress up to go to Sunday church. We laughed about the foolishness of publishers, and how the same object or idea can seem different along the journey of one's life.

Then, sipping her tea, Doris said:

'You will be a great writer, but only if you remember not to be like them.'

'*Them*?'

'The others.'

'Which others?'

'The ones who write for the wrong reasons.'

'What reasons?'

'For publicity and fame, for attention and glory.'

'Why do *you* write?' I asked.

'Because I can't stop. It's a fountain inside me, a fountain that can't be turned off. Or at least, I haven't yet found a way to control it. So it gushes and gushes. Like something out of the *Arabian Nights*, I summon it, and have shaped it over time. If I stopped writing, the fountain's water would get higher and higher, and would drown me.'

'But would you ever want to stop writing?'

'Don't think so. You see, it gives me great pleasure.'

'How?'

'By allowing me to take a lump of clay and shape it. I do it out of curiosity as much as anything else. Taking a handful of characters, I put them into a situation, and watch how they react.'

I fluttered a hand towards the auditorium.

'What about all that?'

Doris huffed in boredom.

'I write for myself,' she answered. 'I don't do it for anyone else. I suggest you grasp the bull by the horns and dive in. Keep writing, even when you're down. Don't wait for people to praise you. Hone your style, and observe yourself from above as you move ahead. Experiment with ideas, and in the way you present them. Of course, use an audience as your sounding board, but remember who you're writing for.'

'For myself?'

'Yes! That's it. For you, and no one else. Just as your father and grandfather did. To keep on track you have to write, write, write – and not listen to anyone who holds you back. Put out work the way you want it to be, and not because you're getting a big fat advance for it. Advances are all well and good for paying the gas bill, but they're blood money – blood money paid by the Imbecile Order.'

'*Imbecile Order*...?'

'The Imbecile Order of Publishers!'

Again, Doris huffed.

'They can all go to hell!' she growled. 'Find me any other vocation in which the so-called "professionals" are as incapable as they are in the publishing business. Most of them don't have a clue. They're all Bertie Wooster!'

'Maybe they're secretly Nasrudin,' I chipped in.

Doris balked.

'I wish it were so,' she replied. 'At least then they'd be wise fools.'

## Thirty-two

Nasrudin had made it into old age, a feat regarded as impressive for a fool as foolish as himself. Having reached the age of a hundred, he was given a free consultation with a psychologist.

'Anything you'd like to report to me?' the doctor asked.

Nasrudin thought long and hard, then said:

'The problem with age is that I keep forgetting things.'

The psychologist scribbled on his notepad.
'When did it start?'
'When did what start?' asked Nasrudin.

LONDON, 1994

Although brought up with teaching stories from an
Oriental tradition, and with the kind of back-to-front
thinking promulgated by Nasrudin, my sisters and I
rarely heard the word 'Sufi' spoken by our father's
lips.

As he saw it, the Occidental world was far too
concerned with the container and not the content.
It was something he never failed to notice and point
out. I remember him holding up a jar of pickles in the
kitchen when we were children.

'Look at this magnificent jar!' he exclaimed. 'It's
the most beautiful thing I've ever seen! Such a pretty
pattern moulded into the glass, and such an elegant
label. It belongs in an art gallery.'

'How are the pickles though?' I asked.

'*Disgusting*! The worst I've ever tasted. And, as
you know, I have a fondness for good pickles.' My
father paused. 'What a pity they didn't care less about
the container, and a little more about the content.'

For my father, the same was true of Sufism as it
was with pickles.

'All people care about is that which has no

relevance,' he said as we wandered through London's Bermondsey Market early one morning, on the trail of Islamic antiques. 'I've never really understood why they don't grasp the thing of real value, when it's right there in front of them.'

'Perhaps they don't see it,' I said.

Slowly, my father's gaze pulled from the middle distance and onto my face.

'If I could succeed at anything in my life,' he said, 'it would be to unhook the essence of this work from the mass of packaging that surrounds it. In book after book I reach out, my hand holding a gift of real treasure. But everyone seems oblivious to what I'm offering. I'm trying to pass on a precious gem, but all they want is the velvet-lined presentation box in which it sits.'

A few months later, I asked him why he rarely spoke of Sufis in conversation.

'The answer to that is not so much a reflection of me,' he said, 'but of the people with whom I am conversing. It's as though I were talking of a secret society, or magic. The mere mention of it gets people here in the West worked up into a hysteria.'

'But why?'

'Because these ideas are regarded as new and exciting, even though they've been hiding in plain sight for centuries.'

My father stared into space for a minute or two,

as he often did while wondering how best to express an idea.

'Your entire life has been surrounded by me publishing books on Eastern thought,' he said. 'You've been witness to it all, and have seen people turning up day after day, rather than staying at home and reading what I write. You've seen those who actually buy the books, sending sacks of nonsensical letters, detailing improvements for the paper they're printed on. I'd have hoped that the readers of my books would be ready to move on by now.'

'On to what?'

'On to the more advanced levels of thinking.'

'Aren't they?'

'*No*! Most definitely not! And it saddens me. After all, I've prepared this material in the most painstaking and deliberate way, shaping it to fit the society and time in which we live. I've spent thirty years analysing how best to introduce these ideas so that they can be received, and in launching them.'

Again, my father fell silent.

'All I can hope is that one day they'll stop worrying about the etymological derivation of the word "Sufi",' he said, 'and instead harness their time by considering the doors that Sufi thinking could open.'

'*The Book of the Book*,' I said.

'Yes. *The Book of the Book*.'

My father sighed.

'I won't be around forever,' he said. 'So I leave it to you three children to carry on. As they say in Persian – *Pidar natawanad, Pisar tamam kunad,* "If the father cannot, the son may bring it to conclusion."'

### Thirty-three

The entire village had put on their best clothes and were streaming out in the direction of the cemetery.

'You'd better hurry up, Nasrudin!' yelled an old man who was staggering ahead at top speed.

'Why?'

'Because it's the mayor's funeral!'

'Don't see why I should bother to be on time for his funeral.'

'Why not?'

'Well, I don't expect he'll bother to come to mine!'

Kosovo, 1998

In the years since my father's death, I've come across endless examples of container being mistaken for content.

You get it with everything of course – from jars

269

of pickles to electronics, and from luxury clothing to sumptuous coffee table books.

In my experience, nothing is quite so misconstrued as Nasrudin.

The wise fool of Oriental folklore is an intellectual device by which preconceived thought can be challenged, and then altered. Nasrudin is what my father liked to call a 'Trojan Horse' – a method to effect intellectual change.

Although this is clear for everyone to appreciate, a great many people – most of them in the Occidental world – continue to concern themselves with the container.

Check online and you'll find tens of thousands of pages deliberating on where Nasrudin was from, in which year he was born and when he died; whether he was a judge, a merchant, or a wandering dervish; or whether he had daughters or sons.

A quick Google search is how I came across the world's foremost expert on the life of Nasrudin. He lived in Kosovo, and I'll call him Professor Ahmeti.

I had travelled to Kosovo with Erol Gurian, an old photographer friend whom I'd originally met at a cryonic suspension centre in Arizona. Over the years we'd reported on all kinds of subjects, from a Bible-based weight loss programme in the Deep South, to the widows who cleared landmines in northern Cambodia.

Having taken a great interest in Kosovo, Erol invited me to accompany him there shortly after the end of the civil war. We arrived in late January. The bitter winter climate was brutal, but nothing when compared to the terrors of the recent war.

Over the weeks we travelled around the province – which was yet to gain its independence. In that time, we took photographs taken on Erol's previous visits into schools, showed them to children, and asked them to comment. The project resulted in some of the most unlikely encounters of my life.

Fascinating as they were, the kids' observations were overshadowed by my meeting with Professor Ahmeti.

Schooled in the literature of the USSR, the academic was soft-spoken, precise, and exactly how I expected him to be.

From the moment I had emailed him, he'd behaved as I predicted – not because I was any great visionary, but because I am my father's son. Thirty years of listening had prepared me for what to expect.

Professor Ahmeti was waiting for me in a coffee shop in the small town of Prizren, his navy trench-coat and trilby on an empty chair beside him. He must have been sixty, but looked much older, the war having taken a terrible toll on almost everyone I met in Kosovo.

Standing to greet me, Ahmeti cupped my right hand in both of his.

I apologized for being a little late, but the professor waved my apologies away as if swishing away a fly.

'The lateness of one only increases the anticipation of the other,' he said.

Taking our seats, we exchanged pleasantries, and began a conversation I never imagined I would have.

A conversation devoted to the life of Nasrudin.

From the professor's first remark on the subject, I knew it was a mistake to have arranged the meeting.

Ahmeti was kind, thoughtful, and exceptionally eloquent, but I'd been programmed to disapprove of him in a base and fundamental way.

His idea of right was my idea of wrong. And, just as I had been raised to receive the contents of the Trojan Horse, he had been schooled in a tradition that celebrated the magnificence of the horse for the horse's sake.

I began by asking Professor Ahmeti about his research into Nasrudin.

Like an automaton whose lever had been pulled, he snapped to action, regaling me with facts, figures, and deductions reached over decades of scholarship.

He told me that the man I knew as 'Nasrudin' had been born in about 1205, in what is now Azerbaijan – and at well over six foot five, he was a giant of his time. Schooled in Islamic law, he'd travelled to Afghanistan, then to Turkey – where he had eventually perished in about 1276.

As I sipped my coffee, Professor Ahmeti fumbled in his satchel and produced several pieces of evidence. The first was a family tree, tracing Nasrudin's genealogy back to Adam and Eve, and on through many generations to the family of the professor's own wife. The second item, preserved in a gilded wooden box, was a tiny square of cloth.

'I see you marvel at it, wondering what it is,' Ahmeti whispered.

'What is it?'

'A fragment of Nasrudin's dervish robe.'

'Impressive,' I said, imagining how enraged my father would have been at having his time wasted by such nonsense. 'May I ask how you came by it?'

Professor Ahmeti pressed his palms together as though about to pray.

'I am a humble lecturer,' he averred, 'and have no access to the kind of money some people possess. But I have the benefit of something that most other people do not – a secret.'

I leaned forward expectantly, hoping to hear what it was.

'What?'

'I can't tell you.'

'Oh. OK. Can I ask why not?'

'Because if I tell you, it will no longer be a secret.'

'Fair enough,' I said.

'But I can tell you this: the effect of the secret is that, from time to time, I find myself in the company of "certain" people.'

'What kind of people?'

'People who have experienced "certain" aspects of life.'

I expected the professor to say they were Sufis.

But he didn't.

'The people who gave me the fragment from Nasrudin's cloak were a group of woodcutters,' he said.

'You mean woodcutters in a metaphoric sense?'

Professor Ahmeti clicked his tongue.

'No, no... *actual* woodcutters. I came to know that they lived in a forest where they sawed wood into planks to build houses. We used to meet quite often near Prizren. At one such meeting, they presented me with this relic... a little piece of Nasrudin's robe.'

Staring into the academic's eyes, I did something terribly wrong.

I burst out laughing.

Not because what he'd said was funny, but rather as he seemed to have missed the point.

The Arabic root 'NSHR', meaning 'to saw', is used by Sufis as a kind of key – a key by which fresh thinking may be reached. For Sufis, the act of sawing represents creation – creating something new from something else. Loaded with other associations, the code word is steeped in interwoven layers of meaning – at least to the initiated it is.

Apologizing to the professor, I explained how my laughter was a result of remembering a story – a story featuring Nasrudin as a woodcutter.

'The jokes are funny,' Ahmeti replied. 'But I feel people who laugh at them are missing the true significance of Nasrudin.'

'*Really?*' I said, doing my best to hide my dismay.

'Yes!'

'As a man of great learning, what would you say is the true significance of Nasrudin?' I asked.

Professor Ahmeti pressed his hands together a second time.

'Nasrudin ought to be remembered as a historical figure who was very tall for the time in which he lived,' he said.


### Thirty-four

Nasrudin was a famous smuggler. Each morning he would cross the border in one direction, and each evening he would return from the other side. He brought nothing of value with him, and the saddlebags on his donkey remained empty.

Year after year, the customs officials checked the saddlebags, but couldn't find any contraband. Even though they found nothing, Nasrudin grew richer and richer.

Within a few years, he became so wealthy that he retired altogether and relocated to a distant kingdom. Having moved into a sprawling mansion, he lived there in the lap of luxury.

One day in a café he happened to meet a customs official from the border he used to cross. Having exchanged pleasantries, the border guard – long since retired – asked Nasrudin what he had been smuggling.

'However hard we tried, we never worked it out,' he said.

The wise fool sipped his tea, smiled to himself, and whispered:

'Donkeys, I was smuggling donkeys.'


IGUAZU FALLS, 1988
An abiding interest of mine – tripoints, the spot where three national borders come together – are fascinating for all sorts of reasons.

Geographically, the various sides of the border tend to be similar in terms of their landscape. Culturally, they're often contradictory – in language, dress, etiquette, economic prosperity, and political outlook.

One side of the border may be so relaxed you get waved through, while on the other side you find yourself being strip-searched.

On travels in Africa, Asia, and Latin America, I perfected the art of crossing borders by not sticking out. I've never got anything to hide of course, but the key thing seasoned customs officers are on the lookout for is always innocence.

During rough journeys through the 'eighties and 'nineties, I endured some truly terrifying experiences crossing borders – particularly in West Africa. Gold and diamond smuggling at the time was taking place on an epidemic scale. Vast fortunes could be made by crossing at a tripoint – for they were super-saturated in desperate citizens, smugglers, and officials.

Although drawn to these quirks of international history, I was less interested in crossing borders than observing life on the individual sides of the frontier.

Over the years, I've watched a rare breed of swashbuckler thriving at tripoints.

King of them all was a character called Héctor, a swaggering slip of a man, whom I first saw hiding in the bushes near the Iguazu Falls dressed from head to toe in Burberry check.

Known as 'Triple Frontera' in Spanish, and 'Tríplice Fronteira' in Portuguese, it's the point at which Brazil, Argentina, and Paraguay meet in a three-way river border.

The bush in which Héctor was skulking was on the Brazilian side of the frontier. Noticing that I'd spotted him, he leapt out of the bush and perched at the end of the bench on which I was sitting.

'You want Rolex, señor?'

'No thank you.'

'Cartier?'

'No.'

'Tiffany?'

'Nothing... no... I'd rather be left alone to write my journal.'

There was silence, so pronounced that I could hear the roar of the falls. Inspired, I continued with scribbling my notes.

But the voice came again:

'American?'

'No.'

'Australian? Yeah, you Australian. From land down under!'

'I'm not an Aussie,' I riposted.

'Manchester United! You, Man-U-man.'

'Listen, I really don't want to be rude, but can you please leave me alone to write?'

'I am Héctor, and my father is Héctor, too.'

'Hello, Héctor. Now, as I said I have to work.'

'You going to Paraguay?'

'I haven't decided.'

'Paraguay is good. Chicas very pretty in Paraguay. Better than over there...'

'Where?'

'In Argentina... like that,' said Héctor, jabbing up the bottom of his nose.

'*Snobs?*'

'*Sí!* Argentina chicas are snob. Snob and rude.'

'And where are you from?'

Héctor thought for a moment, as though unsure what to answer.

'In Brazil I say I am from Paraguay. In Paraguay I say I am from Argentina. And in Argentina I say I am from Brazil.'

'We're in Brazil, so you're from...'

'Paraguay. Yes, Paraguay is good.'

'And what do you do?'

Héctor balked at the question.

'I mean, d'you have work... you know, a job?'

'I cross the border for my job.'

'When?'

'Every day. Sometimes twenty times.'

'Twenty times a day?'

'*Sí. Muy cansado.*'

'Are you a smuggler?' I asked. '*Contrabanista?*'

'I am a "border-crosser".'

'Sounds like the same as a smuggler,' I said accusingly.

'*No contrabanista*... "Border-crosser".'

'And which border are you crossing next?'

'I go to Argentina.'

'When?'

'Now.'

'See you around, then.'

Thanking me for my conversation, Héctor hurried away in the direction of the frontier, leaving me to my notes.

Two hours later, I was still sitting there, wondering whether to go across to Argentina or to Paraguay – where the Russian State Circus was supposedly performing.

All of a sudden, I heard a familiar voice.

'Man-U-man!'

I looked up.

It was Héctor. He wasn't dressed in Burberry any longer – but in an expensive-looking black leather outfit. We chatted for a few minutes. Then I made my way down to the border with Paraguay, while my swaggering friend hurried back to the bushes in which I'd first seen him.

A couple of hours later, I was standing on the other side of the frontier, waiting for a bus to Asunción.

Héctor strode up. The shiny black outfit was gone, replaced by a cashmere coat and denim jeans.

'You certainly get around,' I said.

'Told you, Man-U-man! I am "border-crosser"!'

'I'm happy for you,' I replied. 'But it doesn't seem much of a life – crossing the frontier all day long.'

'Good life,' Héctor corrected.

'Can't imagine you're selling many Rolexes,' I said.

'*No* Rolexes.'

'Well, clothes, then… Suppose that's what you're smuggling, isn't it?'

'*No*, señor.'

'Then what is it that you're smuggling over the border?'

Héctor shrugged.

'*Pasaportes*, señor,' he said.


## Thirty-five

aking a shortcut home from the teahouse one night, Nasrudin found himself in a cemetery. While others would have hurried back in the direction they had come, the wise fool struggled ahead, weaving his way between the graves.

Spooked by a large rat, he tripped, and found

himself propelled into a newly dug grave. Lying there, he assumed that in an inexplicable way, he'd died and been buried. Considering his wretched condition, he made out the heralding of trumpets in the distance.

As he listened, the sound grew louder and louder. Imagining it to be the pandemonium of life in limbo, Nasrudin leapt up, hurried out of the cemetery, and collided into the ranks of the Royal Guard, who were on their way back from patrol.

Caught under the camels' feet, and lashed with the horsemen's whips, he managed to break free and lumber home.

His wife demanded to know why he was so late and so ragged with dirt.

'Dear wife...' he explained. 'A strange thing took place on my way home from the teahouse. Although uncertain how it came to pass, I died and found myself buried in the cemetery.'

'What was it like being dead?'

'Remarkable!' Nasrudin shouted. 'And not altogether unpleasant.'

'Really?'

'Yes! Not unless you get under the feet of the camels. Do that and the horsemen whip you. But otherwise it seemed quite nice.'

RYE, 1993

Spike Milligan has been a hero of mine for as long as I can remember – for his offbeat sense of humour, and for the fact that, tangentially, his life has touched facets of my own.

Along with Peter Sellers and Harry Secombe, he was one of the original 'Goons' – a 1950s radio sensation that paved the way for a new generation of comedy.

Without the Goons there would have been no Monty Python.

And, without Spike, there would have been no Goons.

Born in British India, Spike Milligan had spent a great deal of his youth in Poona (later renamed 'Pune') – the city where my mother lived for the first seven years of her life. Reading about Spike's youth, I always liked to imagine him passing my mother on the street... she in an unwieldy 1920s perambulator pushed by a governess, and he in shorts and sandals, ice cream in hand.

They both arrived in England at roughly the same time, the journey having been made by ship. Knowing nothing until then but blistering heat, they were similarly horrified and amazed at the English speciality – cold winter grey.

At the time of my mother's birth in the 'twenties,

among the greatest slurs one person could level at another was being 'Anglo-Indian'. To be placed in that category you were lost in limbo – despised both by the British Raj, and by the indigenous Indians.

In the summer of 1925, a young Parsi named Fredoon Kabraji arrived in the little village of Islip, five miles north of Oxford. Well-spoken and fair-skinned, and already a published poet, he'd travelled from India with one ambition – to meet his hero, the poet and classicist, Robert Graves.

Four years earlier, Graves had moved to World's End Cottage at the edge of the village, in search of somewhere quiet to write, to bring up his children, and to forget the horrors of the Great War.

On finding the Parsi poet on his doorstep, he graciously afforded him time and conversation. As it was a summer day, Graves suggested they sit out in the garden, and discuss their current work.

A fastidious man, whose life was a search for understanding a world he found baffling, Kabraji noticed Eleanor Wilkinson, a pretty young woman picking apples on the other side of the fence. Before he knew it, Graves had introduced them. And, a few weeks later, Fredoon and Elanor were married, before travelling to eastwards to India.

Born in Poona, my mother and her two brothers first travelled to England by ship in 1935, heading straight to Islip to stay with the Wilkinsons. Graves had published his memoir of the Great War, *Goodbye to All That*, in 1929. In the same year, he and his young family moved to Deià – the rugged mountain village in Mallorca that remained his home until his death.

Hoping to break in to Hampstead's intellectual scene, my grandfather found rooms down the hill in Chalk Farm. My mother used to recount how her parents seemed oblivious of the slide into a second war. As it turned out, they arrived from India just in time for the Blitz.

The nightly bombardments must have been terrifying. But, in recounting the deaths, the destruction, and the routine of seeking shelter in the Underground, my mother was remarkably matter-of-fact.

Like everyone else, her thoughts were on the soldiers at the front.

Far away from Chalk Farm and the Blitz, Spike Milligan was doing his best to survive Monte Cassino, where my own relative Major Hassan Shah was clawing his way over bodies in the blood-drenched scramble up the hill. Again, I always wonder if they set eyes on each other, or if Spike called out to him in Hindi.

In the years after the War, Spike rose to prominence in a land desperate to find humour again. A celebrity in his own right, he was fêted. In the same moment of history, Robert Graves was being championed – no longer a humble poet, but the foremost classicist of his time.

Unlikely friends on the surface, Graves and Milligan had both known futility and pain in abundance. Striking up a friendship, they shared thoughts and recollections in a remarkable correspondence, selections of which were later published in *Dear Robert, Dear Spike.*

A couple of months after the birth of my sister Safia and me, Graves mentioned us in a letter to Spike:

*I may be over in a few weeks to help two young Afghan Arabs named Tahir Shah Sayid and his twin sister with a name so beautiful that I forget it. He's the nearest to Mahomet in a straight line, of any Arab baby in existence. Isn't Tahir a splendid name?*

*I can hear 'Tahir, Tahir'*
*Loud and clear*
*Shouted all the way from Kabul*
*Without the least trouble.*

It was years before I first met Spike.

He was living at Carpenter's Meadow, a large family home near Rye with sweeping views over the Brede Valley. I was led onto the sea of white fitted carpet by Shelagh, Spike's wife.

'Shall I take my shoes off?' I whispered.

Before an answer had been given, Spike opened one eye, then the other. He sat up fast, as though a gun had been jabbed into the small of his back.

'*Namaste!*' he called out, with a look of sincere pleasure, mixed with profound confusion.

I introduced myself.

'I'm here to talk to you about Nasrudin.'

The veteran Goon blinked slowly. Then, as though his concentration was already waning, he said:

'I hate this house!'

'Oh,' I responded.

'Hate it more than you could ever know!'

Putting down my well-travelled canvas bag, I took in the room, and then the view.

'Lots of space,' I said enthusiastically.

'But what's space without beauty?' he responded dreamily.

'I'm a sucker for Georgian buildings,' I said, 'and this house is quite Georgian.'

'No it isn't. It's cinder-block and cement. And even Mad King George didn't use them.'

I was hoping to move on to talking about the wise fool, but however hard I tried, Spike steered the conversation back to his nemesis – the house in which he lived.

'Can I ask you something?' I said, after going round in circles for a good long while.

'*Bolo, sahib*! Speak!'

'Well, if you hate the house so passionately...'

'I hate it!' Spike broke in.

'Yes, well, if you hate it that much, why don't you sell it and move somewhere else?'

Spike Milligan leaned back in his chair, as if savouring the question. Then, having brooded on how to reply, he answered:

'For the same reason that Guy de Maupassant had lunch up the Eiffel Tower every day.'

I flinched.

'Excuse me?'

'Guy de Maupassant... the French novelist.'

'I don't see the connection.'

'Even though de Maupassant despised Monsieur Eiffel's tower, he'd eat lunch there every day. Knowing how he reviled the construction more than anything else, people asked why he didn't patronize another restaurant.'

Spike leaned forwards again, preparing to deliver the death-blow.

'I go to the Eiffel Tower for my lunch,' he said, breaking into the accent of Inspector Clouseau, 'because it is the only place in Paris where I cannot see the Eiffel Tower!'

'I see,' I said, in a substandard reply.

'My connection with this house is the same,' Spike mused. 'Even though I despise it, there's a comfort about living here. It may seem back-to-front to some, but to me it makes perfect sense... because it's the only place in the world where I can be certain of never setting eyes on this bloody house!'

## Thirty-six

Nasrudin's neighbour was widely regarded as the most miserly man in the village and, to make matters worse, he hated the wise fool. Most of the time Nasrudin had no occasion to meet his neighbour. But then, one day, his mother-in-law announced she would be visiting.

'We shall have to cook a big pilau to welcome her,' Nasrudin's wife insisted.

'Quite impossible!' Nasrudin countered. 'We don't have a pot large enough with which to honour her.'

'Our neighbour has a huge pot!' Nasrudin's wife exclaimed. 'Go over and borrow it from him!'

'But he's so miserly he'll never lend it, not even if I make all kinds of promises in return.'

Snarling, Nasrudin's wife opened the door and shoved her husband in the direction of the neighbour's house.

Fearfully, the wise fool rapped on the door, and explained the situation.

'My mother-in-law is like a fire-breathing dragon,' he said. 'If we don't cook a huge pilau to honour her, she'll roast me with her tongue!'

'No!' yelled the neighbour. 'My large pot is very valuable. It was bought in a faraway kingdom and is the most precious thing I possess!'

Nasrudin pleaded and pleaded, and offered all kinds of favours as he knew he would have to do. Finally, and reluctantly, the greedy miserly neighbour gave in.

'I'll lend it to you for a single evening,' he said. 'And I expect it to be returned to me cleaner than clean. If it's dented in any way, I shall come and get revenge!'

Cowering, and gushing thanks, Nasrudin returned home with the pot. That evening, the most enormous pilau was served and the dragon queen mother-in-law appeared pleased.

First thing next morning, Nasrudin hurried back to his neighbour's home. Having returned the pot, he smiled engagingly.

'Something very peculiar took place last night,' he said.

'What?' the neighbour scowled mistrustfully.

'Well, once the evil mother-in-law had feasted, and after I had cleaned your magnificent pot, returning it to a state as though it were new, the pot gave birth.'

'*What*?!' the neighbour screeched. 'How could a pot give birth?!'

'Well, to tell you the truth,' Nasrudin mumbled, 'I was very shocked by it myself. But, it was a wonderful and magical moment. And, as the big pot is yours, I can only assume this lovely little baby pot is rightfully yours as well.'

Fumbling in his robe, Nasrudin pulled out a little pot. Though not large, it was very well formed.

At seeing such a fine object, the greedy neighbour snatched it and the big pot, and slammed the door.

Several weeks elapsed, and word reached Nasrudin that his dreaded mother-in-law was going to visit once again. Even before his wife had instructed him to do so, Nasrudin trudged over to the neighbour and asked politely whether the big pot could be loaned out once again.

Remembering the previous occasion, and the unexpected gift of an exquisite little pot, the neighbour was only too pleased to be of assistance.

Next day, Nasrudin's neighbour waited for a knock at his door, but it didn't come. Another day passed, and still the pot was not returned.

Enraged, the miserly neighbour stormed over to Nasrudin's house and pounded on the door.

'Where's my pot?!' he thundered.

Nasrudin seemed to be in a sombre mood.

'Hello friend,' he said. 'I apologize that I am not in better spirits.'

'Where's my pot?!' the neighbour demanded once again.

'Well,' Nasrudin expressed woefully, 'we have established have we not that pots can be born, live a lifespan, and die?'

'Yes! Yes!' the neighbour responded, expecting another little pot as a gift.

'Alas,' Nasrudin uttered, breaking into a flood of tears, 'at precisely ten o'clock last night, your magnificent pot dropped dead!'


LANGTON HOUSE, 1974

On nights when I cannot sleep, a recurring memory tends to slip onto the stage of my mind:

A towering man with a shock of white hair digging a ditch with a shovel at the front of Langton House. Shirtless, his oyster-grey skin glistening with sweat, he seemed ancient.

But the ditch-digging man is only half the memory.

The second half is of a crusty Latin teacher arriving at the front door to give me extra tuition. He appeared befuddled and confused, as though he'd been struck hard on the head.

'Must be seeing things!' he blustered.

'Excuse me, sir?'

'That man out there... he looks like Robert Graves!'

I blushed, swallowed hard, and replied dismissively:

'Oh, no, sir, he's just one of my father's friends.'

For much of my life, that memory has hung in my mind – like the moment in a film in which the protagonist is almost found out. Thinking about it now, I suppose the seasoned ditch-digger had sloped away by the time the Latin teacher left. If he'd still been out there, my tutor would have realized it was indeed the renowned classicist, Robert Graves.

As far as I knew, there was nothing unusual in Graves digging a ditch at the side of the rose garden. He often took on all sorts of menial work, as did everyone else who visited at weekends.

If the Latin master had gone through into the herb garden, he'd have found Doris Lessing drying pots of lavender. Or, if he had troubled himself to wander through into the old stable block, he would have discovered Walter Gotell – villainous 'General Gogol' in the early James Bond films. Or, in one of the cottages on the estate, he would have come across WWII radar-pioneer 'Coppy' Laws, tinkering with the fuse boxes; or Glubb Pasha chatting to J. D. Salinger on the lawn over a cup of milky tea.

Langton House looked onto the village green. Behind it, a great rambling expanse stretched out – cottages and stables, potting sheds, greenhouses, and fifty acres of woodland and fields.

It was a child's dreamworld.

Founder of the Boy Scouts, Robert Baden-Powell had grown up there, too. He must have spent his time stomping through the brambles and the bracken in the bluebell woods just like me. I imagine Baden-Powell's childhood was rather more conventional than my own.

My father was born in what was then British India, at the hill station of Simla, in the summer of 1924. He died from a heart attack, towards the end of 1996. In the years between those two dates he lived a life unusual by any standards. He's known for the scores of books he wrote, on Eastern mysticism, philosophy and traditional psychology, and for championing the wise fool of Arab folklore.

My earliest memories are of him telling us stories of Nasrudin's topsy-turvy world. In many ways, the wise fool was the perfect instructive device – an embodiment of everything our father was trying to pass on. He regarded Nasrudin as a catalyst, a way of pre-empting new thinking, so as to allow certain ideas and experiences to be absorbed.

He used to say Nasrudin worked like a delicious peach did – the succulent flesh like the entertainment in a story. By devouring the fruit, the thing of real value – the stone – has a chance to be passed on. In the same way, buried in the heart of a tale, the secret value is planted in the head of a listener during the telling of what is perceived to be a mere entertainment.

Nasrudin stories are what they are because the wise fool acts in a way contrary to convention. Stepping into a trap as they listen, the audience recoils as they grasp that conventional thought is the fool, and that the imbecilic thinking is genius.

Over the twenty or so years since my father left us, I've found myself thinking about him, and the effect he had on people.

He couldn't *not* have an effect.

Never one to be a passenger carried downstream by the flow, he thrived on challenging the way people are conditioned – urging them to break free from automatic processes.

In that way, his existence was the epitome of all things Nasrudin – a life that won him enemies as well as friends. For it pitched him against the establishment – a system he railed at for being calcified and entrenched.

One of his obituaries said he 'didn't suffer fools gladly', which was wrong. He loved fools – who he said were doors leading to new and inspired thinking.

What he hated were the arrogant.

Over the two and a half decades we lived at Langton House, I would watch them do their damnedest to impress my father. Sometimes it was by boasting how they'd been wined and dined by royalty, or how they had been selected for a prize. What he despised was not that the person in question had experienced privilege, but that they were using it as a foil to elevate themselves.

One evening over a communal dinner, I watched as a young man liked by us all was obliterated by my father's tongue in the most spectacular way. Thirty years later the man asked if I remembered the night.

'As though it were yesterday,' I replied.

'Then tell me why he savaged me like that, and in such a public way. It took me years to get over it... and on some level I don't think I ever have.'

'He savaged you because he wanted to knock you out of the rut you were slotted into,' I responded. 'As he saw it, the affliction called for a drastic treatment.'

'What treatment?'

'Massive force delivered unexpectedly in the presence of a sizeable audience,' I said.

asrudin travelled across an ocean and a sea, and found himself in a land in which everyone regarded a particular number – 786 – as having magical and mysterious significance.

A travelling fool had at one time tramped through the kingdom, calling out:

'786! It's the meaning to everything!'

'What do you mean?' the people had asked.

'Well, the number 786 possesses certain qualities that are evident only to the wise. Use the number as much as possible in your lives, and you will all be blessed!'

At first, the people laughed at the fool. But then, little by little, they began to stop questioning as they'd originally done, and put their faith in the number.

They used it on everything. Some embroidered it into their clothing. Others had it tattooed on their arms and legs, or even called their children 786.

By the time Nasrudin arrived in the country, it had become known as the 'Kingdom of 786'.

He couldn't help noticing that everything was numbered and named 786 – from the buildings to the children in the school, and even the local football team.

'We're blessed,' the mayor said to Nasrudin smugly, 'because we have the number 786 in our lives.'

'Fascinating,' the traveller replied. 'What does the number represent?'

The mayor mumbled something unintelligible.

'I didn't quite hear what you said,' answered Nasrudin.

Blushing at the thought of being made a fool, the mayor intoned:

'786 is a special number reached by a wise man's mysterious divination.'

'What a funny coincidence,' Nasrudin responded. 'Because I once knew a fool who travelled from kingdom to kingdom, exclaiming "786! 786!"'

'What of it?' snarled the mayor.

'Well,' Nasrudin mused, 'the fool I knew who was obsessed with the number 786, and who insisted it had a metaphysical meaning, was not good with numbers, and he had a terrible memory.'

'What's that got to do with it?' retorted the mayor.

'Well,' said Nasrudin, 'he only got fixated on 786 in the first place because I'd asked him to telephone me.'

'What's your telephone number, then?' the mayor asked, frowning.

'Land of Fools 786, of course!' grinned Nasrudin.

## MARRAKECH, 2014

A great many foreigners have moved to Marrakech in recent years, lured there by what my father called 'The Mysterious East'.

My parents used to take us to the Red City as children, as a way of teaching us about Afghanistan. Thinking about it now, those journeys were very much in line with the ways of Nasrudin.

As we were growing up, Afghanistan was far too dangerous a destination, so we were presented with the next best thing – Morocco.

Our estate car zigzagged over the kingdom's mountain passes, trundling through its deserts, having set off from Langton House weeks before. Vinyl suitcases strapped to the roof, with our gardener at the wheel, and with my father holding court beside him in the front – dishing out wit and wisdom to the captive audience.

'Morocco is cut from the same cultural cloth as your homeland,' he would expound. 'As you see for yourself, there are mountains and deserts, proud tribal traditions, Islamic culture, and rugged history – all of it poised at a crossroads, just like Afghanistan.'

One of us would ask what the most important part of the mix was – the mountains or the deserts, or the tribes? We asked not because we were especially interested in the answer, but because it was guaranteed to lead to what we liked best of all.

'Rather like *mutton do pyaza*, it's a challenge to isolate one thing that stands above another.' My father would think for a moment, his eyes tracing the line forming the distant desert horizon. 'Stories are a reflection of everything.'

'*Stories*, Baba?'

'Yes!' my father would gush. 'Stories!'

'Which stories?'

'The stories of the *Thousand and One Nights*!'

A moment later, the misery of being crumpled up in the back of the Ford estate would be replaced by a tale of heroism, lost love, and jinns.

As my father saw it, Marrakech was a sanitized, accessible form of The Mysterious East. Back in the 'seventies, the Red City was reached by a long and uncomfortable journey over the desert. To arrive there was to have earned it.

These days, budget flights shuttle legions of hen- and stag-parties back and forth to Marrakech, along with the well-heeled jet set, who live it up in palatial homes out in the Palmeraie.

Over the years we have lived in Casablanca, the Red City provided a quick jolt of Morocco's mysterious hinterland whenever we found ourselves tiring of the coast.

Since my first visits to the great central square of Jma al Fna, the so-called 'Place of Execution', Marrakech has changed beyond all recognition. Most likely, my father would be horrified by the phoniness of it all. Then again, I think he'd have marvelled at the way Marrakech has proved itself as the master of reinvention.

Over the years, I've made firm friendships, both with Moroccans and with foreigners living there. I've watched as their lives ebb and flow on the tide of international tourism. And, I've found myself observing a deeper layer… something that's hard for me to express in words.

I'll call it 'Nasrudin-ness'.

It's a kind of thinking that gets inside the heads of certain people at various times. A state of mind, Nasrudin-ness is not something taught in school, generally passed on by parents, or learnt from books. Rather, it's an inside-out-back-to-front-ness, a kind of inverted take on the human condition.

Having been exposed to it since birth, many Orientals possess it. Some delight in it. Others do all they can to suppress it. More still live with it without knowing it's inside them at all.

Unlike those who have been brought up with this revolutionary way of thinking, most Occidentals are knocked off kilter when they first brush up against the back-to-front world. I've made a study of them reacting, observing them from the sidelines.

I have seen how foreigners assume Moroccans are trying to put them down or, to use an Anglo-ism, 'are out to get them'. Railing against the inverted form of common sense, they frequently flounder, and have to be bustled onto the first budget flight back to the grey zone.

Once in a while, however, you come across a foreigner who's embraced Nasrudin-ness lock, stock, and barrel.

When I first met Sidi Mustapha, he had just arrived in Marrakech, having moved to the city from a mill-town in Yorkshire.

Back then, he was known as 'Philip'. Dressed in a leather bomber jacket and jeans, he looked like the most normal man in the world – which is exactly what he was.

Reserved and self-effacing, he was exceptionally quiet – so much so that my friends in Marrakech pointed him out.

'He's a weirdo,' said one, spotting him in a café.

'I'd give him a wide berth,' grunted another.

'Maybe he just needs time to find his feet,' I replied.

I asked where he was living.

'In the Mellah – he's bought a house.'

A month or two later, when I turned up in Marrakech again, I happened to be sitting in the same café with the same friends as before. I had forgotten about our previous conversation, so it took me a moment or two to know what my friend meant, when she exclaimed:

'He's gone native!'

'Who has?'

'Philip from Yorkshire.'

'Who?'

'*Him!*'

I followed the line of my friend's finger, and spotted the back of what looked like a Moroccan man. He was wearing a *jelaba* and sandals, the fingers of his right hand counting through the beads of a rosary. As I was leaving, I saw that it was indeed the man from before.

Another couple of months slipped by and, when I visited Marrakech again, my friends showered me with tales of Philip the Yorkshireman.

'He's insisting that everyone call him "Sidi Mustapha",' a friend explained.

'Has he converted?'

'No, don't think so. Says he just likes the name.'

'He's supposedly living the life of a dervish,' another friend informed me.

'He's walking everywhere, doing things as they might have been done centuries ago,' said another.

'Really does sound as though he's converted,' I replied.

Later, I heard from someone else how Sidi Mustapha had decided to build a palace on the outskirts of Marrakech.

Suppressing the urge to question why a supposed dervish would want a palace, I returned to my home in Casablanca.

A few more weeks slipped by, and I was back in the Red City once again – on the trail of brass lamps. One of my friends suggested I ask Sidi Mustapha.

'He knows all about lamps,' she said.

'Does he?'

'Yes.'

'How d'you know?'

'Because he was seen buying loads of them in the medina.'

'Why so many?'

'For the palace he's building,' said my friend.

So, not quite sure if it was the right thing to do, I approached him that afternoon in the café we both frequented.

This time he was wearing a different *jelaba*. Patches had been sewn crudely all over it, denoting his standing as a dervish.

'I've read your book,' he said, once I had introduced myself.

'Which one?'

'*The Caliph's House.*'

'Like it?' I asked enquiringly.

'Not bad,' the undercover Yorkshireman responded in such a way that I felt the book had missed the mark.

'I hear you're the man to ask about brass lamps,' I said.

Sidi Mustapha's fingers counted the rosary beads all the faster.

'I've bought a lot of them,' he confirmed.

'Heard you're building a palace.'

'Yes. The Palace of the Four Winds.'

'I heard you're a dervish.'

'I'm doing my best.'

'Great,' I said. 'That's a lot to have sunk your teeth into.'

'A man must do something,' replied Sidi Mustapha.

The next time I visited Marrakech, I drove out to the edge of the Agafay Desert, where the Palace of the Four Winds was going to stand.

As rocky as it was beautiful, the landscape was like something out of a child's fantasy.

Sidi Mustapha toured the vast site with me. As we criss-crossed it, he explained where the main building would be constructed, and then described how the gardens would be a representation of Paradise. After that, he explained how the furniture was being made to measure for the palace.

'When's the team going to start building?' I asked.

'*Team?*'

'You know, the workers. The guys who're going to do it all.'

'There isn't a team.'

'But... but... but who's going to build the palace and make the furniture?'

'I am,' replied Sidi Mustapha.

As though having stepped into a time tunnel, I flapped about, waiting desperately for the man from Yorkshire to break into laughter and slap me on the back.

But he didn't.

Looking at me, he smiled.

'I will do it little by little,' he said.

'*Little by little?* That's great... at least with most things,' I responded in alarm. 'But surely building palaces in the Agafay Desert needs more than little by little?'

Fearing I'd spoken out of turn, I rallied my enthusiasm and exclaimed how incredibly wonderful it would all be once it was done.

'Maybe if you wish very hard, it'll be like in the story of Maruf the Cobbler,' I said. 'He dreamed of a vast treasure caravan coming towards him through the desert. Such was his belief, it actually arrived.'

'Maruf the Cobbler was published in *Caravan of Dreams* by Idries Shah,' said Sidi Mustapha.

I nodded.

'That's right.'

'Have you read it?'

'Yes,' I said. 'My father dedicated it to us all.'

The Yorkshireman's face blushed redder than any other face I have ever seen. It went so red I wondered whether it would ever return to its usual pale hue.

'Why didn't you tell me?' he spluttered, hyperventilating.

'Tell you what?'

'That your father was Idries Shah of *Caravan of Dreams*?!'

'Because it's not relevant,' I replied.

In silence, Sidi Mustapha grasped my hand and led me towards a large home-made shed at the edge of the property.

Reaching it, he slipped inside and rooted around.

A moment or two later, he emerged with an extremely ornate wooden chair, upholstered in emerald green.

'I would be proud for the son of Idries Shah to sit on this,' he said.

'Thank you,' I replied, sitting down.

The Yorkshireman paced around the chair.

'Aren't you going to sit as well?'

'No, no...'

'Are you sure?'

'Yes. In any case I can't – you see, that's the only chair I have made so far.'

'It's lovely, and very comfortable,' I replied.

'Took weeks to make.'

'Gosh,' I said, my mind trying to work out how long the entire palace would take to complete.

'Excellent craftsmanship...' I mumbled. 'Can't remember seeing such a fine chair in Marrakech.'

'It's actually a *throne*,' Sidi Mustapha clarified.

'Is it?'

'Yes. But not any ordinary throne!'

'Then what kind of throne is it?'

'It's the throne of the Palace of the Four Winds!'

## Thirty-eight

imes were very hard in the Land of Fools, so much so that fools were going out of business all the time. Never one to be successful in commercial activities, Nasrudin spent his last silver piece on a box of pretty glass beads, sold to him by another fool.

'They're magic beads,' the seller revealed.

'Will they make me rich?' Nasrudin asked.

'Richer than in your wildest dreams.'

Taking the beads home, the wise fool showed them to his wife, and felt her hand slap the side of his head for being such an imbecile.

'Here in the Land of Fools you're not going to find anyone who wants beads!' she yelled.

'You'd be surprised,' Nasrudin answered.

Cutting a hundred strands of twine, he threaded a single glass bead onto each piece and went out to sit under a sprawling banyan tree. Sooner rather than later, a fool turned up and asked what he was doing.

'I'm giving away these sacred talismans.'

'Where d'you get them?'

'From a wise man on the slopes of a distant mountain,' Nasrudin replied.

'How much do they cost?'

'They're not for sale.'

'Why not?'

'Because some things – like wisdom and these talismans – don't have a price.'

'Please, please give me one then!' begged the fool. 'Because I want to be protected.'

Nasrudin rolled his eyes.

'I'll give you one if you promise me something.'

'Of course, anything!'

'Promise me you won't breathe a word of it to anyone, and that you'll keep the talisman hidden at all times.'

'I promise! I promise!' exclaimed the fool.

Nasrudin picked out one of the talismans, tied it around the fool's neck, and sent him away. Within an hour a line of fools was snaking from the banyan tree to the horizon. Every fool in town wanted a free talisman.

When all the fools had been given one they clustered around, and gave thanks to Nasrudin.

'He's given us something we could never buy!' yelled someone in the crowd.

'He's our saviour!' declared another.

'He's certainly no fool!' said the fool who'd sold Nasrudin the beads in the first place.


JODHPUR, 1989

My informant was a wall-eyed paan-seller named Malik Khan, whose stall was lost in the shadows of the old city of Hyderabad.

Never stopping for an instant, he created little packages of paan for regular customers who sought him out in droves during the course of the day. As soon as he spotted a familiar face pushing through the surge of people out in the street, he'd start working on their usual combination.

Over the weeks I spent in Hyderabad, Malik Khan became an invaluable source of information. I'd first stumbled up to his stall for directions and, the next thing I knew, we were acquaintances – chitchatting through the long, sultry afternoons.

Working up to it, I mentioned the name 'Nasrudin', expecting Malik Khan to shrug, or to reveal how the wise fool had been a paan-seller from Hyderabad.

On hearing the name, he said something I was not expecting to hear.

'Nasrudin was Thuggee,' he said.

'*Thuggee*?'

'Thuggee.'

'Thuggee as in "thugs"… the cult of stranglers who terrorized India for centuries?'

Wrapping a dollop of his secret paan mix in a betel leaf, Malik Khan spat out onto the street.

'Same, same.'

'Must be a different Nasrudin,' I replied. 'The one I'm talking about was a wise fool.'

'Thuggee were fools.'

'I am sure they were. They went around strangling people.'

'Thuggee wise as well.'

'How d'you know?'

'Asif told me.'

'*Asif-who*?'

311

'Asif the weaver.'

'Weaver – as in blankets?'

'Carpets. Asif Shah, weaver of carpets.'

'Where is this man, Asif Shah?'

'In next street,' said Malik Khan.

Ten minutes later, I was sitting in a cramped carpet shop, looms clattering at the back, a square of folded paan in my hand as a token offering.

The Thuggee cult was a great interest of mine and I was excited by the lead. I'd read all the nineteenth-century accounts of how the Indian subcontinent had been terrorized by the stranglers for centuries. Picking off unsuspecting travellers, they sometimes followed a wealthy target for months, inveigling servants and hangers-on, before working their way into a position of trust.

Choking their victims with a knotted kerchief, the Thugs, a cult devoted to the goddess Kali, were masters of their craft – which was as skilled as it was ruthless.

Learning I'd been sent by the wall-eyed paan-seller, Asif Shah bustled me in, invited me to sit, and gave thanks for his favourite paan which had been sent as a gift of introduction by Malik Khan.

No matter the circumstances, a foreigner finding himself in a carpet shop from Casablanca to Kolkata tends to result in an obligation to make purchases.

'I have *not* come to buy a carpet,' I said in a firm voice.

Asif Shah the carpet-seller didn't flinch.

'No problem, sir.'

'Instead, I've come to ask you something.'

'Very good, sir.'

'Malik Khan says you believe Nasrudin – the wise fool – was a Thug.'

'Strangler. He was strangler.'

'A strangler with a knotted handkerchief – preying on innocent travellers?'

'Yes. Like that.'

'Can I ask how you know this?'

The carpet-seller stuffed the square of paan into his mouth, and began to chew. His teeth and gums were strained blood read, and he was unable to speak. He held up a hand, indicating an urgent need for a lengthy pause in the conversation.

As everyone knows, paan-chewing cannot be rushed.

Irritated that Asif Shah hadn't waited before getting to work on the paan, I was about to mumble excuses and leave, when another man entered the shop. Dressed in a three-piece suit, he possessed an air of sophistication. In perfect English he introduced himself as Asim Shah, the carpet-seller's brother.

'Is it a family business?'

'Yes and no.'

'Do you know whether Nasrudin was a Thug?'

Asim Shah looked at me, then at his brother, who was still busy chewing the paan.

'Of course he was!' he said. 'Nasrudin was the greatest Thug ever to have lived – even greater than Thug Behram. During British times the mere mention of his name sent travellers into convulsions. It was said he could disguise himself as anyone he wished, and that he'd perfected a method of strangulation so perfect he could end a life with a knotted cummerbund in less time than it takes to tell.'

'Was he ever captured?'

Asif Shah inhaled sharply at the question, his eyes widening as though he'd witnessed it himself.

'The British were fearful of travelling anywhere, because Nasrudin would be waiting for them. They couldn't understand how one man killed so many innocent travellers all over India – it was as though he was everywhere at once. Unable to bear it any longer, they set all their forces on capturing the amazing Nasrudin.

'Even though they hunted him, still he went on strangling. Hundreds more victims lost their lives before they finally ensnared him. It's said that the British paraded Nasrudin around in chains, taunting him, and that they celebrated for forty days and nights.'

'Did they execute him?'

'No, no, no!' Asim Shah replied. 'By doing so they would have made a martyr of Nasrudin. So, they threw him into their most dreadful prison, and left him there to rot. News of his capture spread. The great and the good far away in London heard that Nasrudin was languishing in a jail. And, as you no doubt know, Queen Victoria herself was fond of India – even though she never ventured here herself.'

'She had an Indian manservant,' I said.

'That is correct. She even learned to write Urdu. Less known, however, is that the queen was interested in Thuggee. Against the suggestions of her court, she ordered for the King of the Thugs to be brought to her.

'Many weeks later, the message reached the jail in which Nasrudin was languishing. He was brought out and, beaten one last time for good measure, was dispatched to England.'

'Did he get to see Queen Victoria?'

Asim Shah clicked his tongue, indicating that I would have to listen and wait.

'Having arrived at the docks in Southampton, the King of the Thugs was washed down and dressed in clean clothes. Then, chained for being the criminal he was, he was brought before the Empress of India.

'It is said that Queen Victoria observed him with exceptional care and attention, before addressing him with respect.'

'Because he was King of the Thugs?'

'Perhaps.'

'What did she say to him?'

'She asked whether he might use the skills gathered in strangulation in a less destructive way.'

'Did he agree?'

'By the end of the audience, Nasrudin had promised to use his eye for detail and his talent in tying knots – skills that had made him such a fine strangler – for a less injurious vocation.'

'Knotting nooses for hangings?'

'No, knotting carpets for the Raj.'

'Ah,' I said, casting an eye around the carpet shop. 'So how did it go?'

Asim Shah straightened his tie, and glanced at his brother who was still chewing at the paan.

'Nasrudin took to carpet-making like a duck to water,' he said. 'Not only could he knot carpets faster and more perfectly than anyone else alive, but he came up with patterns that were out of this world. He oversaw the creation of one of the largest carpets ever made, every single knot done by Thuggee prisoners. It was presented to Queen Victoria in the twilight years of her reign, and is still found at Windsor Castle.'

'Was she pleased with it?'

'Why not?!' bellowed Asim Shah.

'You mean she was?'

'Exceptionally so! She ordered for Nasrudin to be made a free man.'

'Did he return to India?'

'Yes and no.'

'*Meaning*...?'

'Yes, he did return to India, but not for as long as you may have imagined. You see, Queen Victoria – who so adored all things Indian – wanted a jester for her court. She had heard that all the European monarchs had Indian jesters and she wanted one too. So she said to Nasrudin: "Go and find me a fool to stay with me in court and to make me laugh!"'

'Did Nasrudin agree?'

'Oh, yes, yes! He was sent back to India on a special ship, dressed in the finest robes. No longer a Thug, he was received as a hero. For months and months he criss-crossed India, searching for a fool sufficiently stupid for Queen Victoria's Court. He found a great many fools, but none of them were right.'

'Why not?'

'Most had diseases, and others were very foolish – but only some of the time.'

'So what happened?'

'Well, one day, the Viceroy summoned Nasrudin and demanded to know if he had found the most foolish man alive for the job of jester.

'Bowing deeply, Nasrudin informed the emissary that indeed he had located the perfect candidate, but that he was too busy to accept the position.

'Horrified anyone would turn the monarch down, the Viceroy enquired why the fool could not travel to court at once.

'Again, the wise fool bowed deep. "Because he's too busy searching for fools to take the job!" exclaimed Nasrudin.'

'That's a great story!' I said.

'Thank you.'

'Is all of it true?'

'Not a word of it,' replied Asim Shah.


### Thirty-nine

Nasrudin's donkey brayed all night, keeping the neighbours awake. Furious at getting no sleep, a posse from his street descended on the wise fool's home, demanding in one voice for the animal to be taken out to a distant pasture.

'Quite impossible!' Nasrudin announced.

'Why not?'

'Because without my donkey there would be no night.'

'What d'you mean?' the neighbours asked.

'I know it may sound strange, just as it did to me when I first heard it, but my donkey is special.'

'*Special*... in what way?'

'Special in that his braying reminds the moon to keep moving through the sky.'

'That's ridiculous!' someone yelled.

'No more ridiculous than telling a poor animal like that to stop being afraid of the dark!' Nasrudin bawled.


M'HAMID, 2004

While in the dunes of southern Morocco on the trail of a story, I was offered a West African fetish made from half a coconut.

Although not the best quality work, there was something pleasing about it, something that reminded me of a raw night I once passed in Kalimantan.

I've always had an interest in African fetishes, and this one was as curious to me as any other I had seen.

Caked in grime and smelling of magic, the eyes were plugged with cowrie shells, the mouth sealed with a dried black bean.

The price was not unreasonable and so I bought it right there and then.

For three nights I slept with the fetish under my pillow.

I'm not sure why, but somehow it seemed to be the right thing to do.

And, each night, I dreamt of an amazing journey, through rainbow lands, bewitched by all manner of people and things.

On the fourth night, I rushed to my tent extra early so as to slip into the dream once again.

But the dream didn't come.

Jerking a hand under the pillow, I fished around for the fetish.

It was gone.

So I slipped on my shoes, went outside, and quizzed the guides.

Heads shook left to right, then right to left.

Dejectedly, I tramped back into the tent and zipped myself up in the sleeping bag.

Alas, there were no dreams that night.

The next morning I heard shrill cries. Running out, I asked what was going on.

'Mustapha went blind in the night,' moaned one of the guides, jerking a hand towards his troubled friend.

I strode over, whispering consolation.

The guide rubbed a thumb to his left eye hard.

'Can't see in it,' he mumbled.

I was about to say something, when I saw the curved lines of a familiar object face down in his lap.

The fetish.

*My* fetish.

'I've seen *that* before,' I said menacingly.

The thumb stopped rubbing and, in one movement, its hand slipped down, grasping the coconut tight.

'It's mine!' Mustapha exclaimed.

In the circumstances, I wasn't going to argue too much. Half of one's sight in return for a modest theft seemed a heavy price. So, wishing the guide well, I went back to gather up my gear.

As I packed my bedroll, I noticed something on the ground, just lying there.

A crescent of hard, white shell.

A cowrie shell.

Before leaving the camp, I shuffled over to where the injured man was sitting. This time he was holding the fetish up to his face.

Its left eye was missing.

'This belongs to you,' I said, reaching out, 'or, rather, it belongs to your friend.'

## *Forty*

Nasrudin had been asked to take a tray piled high with expensive crystal glasses to his mother-in-law. So anxious was he at being yelled at by the woman he regarded as a dragon, that his hands began to shake, causing him to drop the tray.

Seeing a pile of broken glass, a crowd gathered.

'Damn you all!' Nasrudin bellowed. 'Haven't you ever seen a fool before?!'

CASABLANCA, 2010

I have always adored boxes.

It's because they shield secrets from the wandering eye. There's an anticipation about them – a sense of extraordinary possibility. Burmese lacquer boxes are my greatest passion. While living in Morocco, I have collected Berber strong boxes from the Sahara as well.

The collection isn't large, but it gives me astonishing pleasure to be the guardian of these objects for a while. Like Matryoshka dolls, they come in various sizes – large, larger, medium, smaller than medium, smaller still, and petite.

To my delight there were five waiting for me in the shadows of Bab Lakhemis on one particular visit. They are adorned always with curious motifs cut out of sheet steel. As I understand it, they come from Mauritania, although in Morocco everyone calls them 'Berber' boxes.

I like to imagine that these, and all the other boxes

in my collection, once contained treasure – whether it was in the form of gold coins, magical incantations, or wisdom scribbled on a few inches of weather-worn papyrus.

Magic, secrets, and treasure are always very much on my mind...

When I returned to our home in Casablanca, after the summer from a visit to Buenos Aires, there was an unexpected knock at the door. I opened it to find a close Moroccan friend waiting to be received.

He seemed anxious, or even perturbed.

When we had greeted, he introduced me to a slightly built figure dressed in desert robes. My friend said the man was a surprise for me.

We drank tea together, the three of us, exchanged pleasantries, as I wondered about the surprise, and what he would entail. Such surprises tend to end the same, in an eager supplication for funds.

A long silence came and went.

With it gone, my friend explained: the man was a magician, a *sehur*, who had come to exorcise a Jinn. Neither Dar Khalifa nor I were unused to exorcists or to the talk of Jinn. It was a coincidence, as I was working on a novel that delved into that realm.

My friend said that the magician would be living with us, and that his needs were modest. There was no other way for him to do his work. All he required was a little food prepared by the maid, a small space to unfurl his bedroll, and candles to burn both day and night.

Not wishing to upset my friend, I obliged the *sehur* with his needs.

Through days and weeks he wove his spells, having locked himself in my library. Early on, I was given a fold of paper to keep under my pillow, and another to be worn in a pouch, pressed against my heart.

From time to time there were cries from behind the library door, or crazed laughter, chanting, or even the muffled sounds of sobbing.

As days passed, I hoped that I might be able to retake control of my beloved library.

Then, just as I returned from Marrakech with the fresh crop of treasure, the *sehur* opened the library door, and beckoned me to sit with him.

He claimed to have made a long and careful study of my misfortune – problems with neighbours and with jinn. It was, he said, put down to something that had taken place in the *riad*, the garden outside the library half a century before.

A gardener had worked at Dar Khalifa for many years and was liked and trusted. One day, while hoeing the ground, he dug up the end of a heavy iron chain. Wondering what it was doing there, he excavated it, link by link, until it led him to a trap door deep in the ground.

The gardener had opened the door, and found a tunnel. Stone steps descending into the ground. Fighting away his fear, he had crept down the steps and, after twists and turns, had arrived in a vault.

A treasure vault.

There were sackfuls of gold coins and gems the size of his fist; urns and lamps studded with rubies and diamonds; crystal bottles filled with rare perfumes, and miles and miles of silk.

Realizing that he had to tread with care, the gardener took no more than a handful of treasure, before returning to the garden. Over years, he continued his work at Dar Khalifa, slipping down into the vault each night, to take a little more of the secret wealth.

When, at last, the treasure vault had been emptied, the gardener faked his own death, and was never seen again.

This was all explained to me by the magician – a surprise presented by my friend.

While this is the story, it wasn't the reason for my problems. Problems my generous friend insisted burdened my life.

The reason for the problems was, he said, a Jinn. For, unknown to the gardener, a Jinn was guarding the treasure vault. Having been charged with the sole responsibility for centuries, he had taken his large single eye off the treasure, and had fallen into a deep and inexplicable hibernation.

On waking up, as he had recently done, the Jinn was horrified to find the treasure gone. Hence, his rage – a rage directed at me.

The *sehur* exorcised the Jinn, furled up his bedroll, and slunk away into the night. Remarkably, there was no request for payment.

When his shadow was far from the shantytown that circled Dar Khalifa, I took a glass of sweet mint tea with Abdullah, the guardian. He had worked at the house for more than a decade, and was a trusted friend.

Between sips, I asked him about the tale of the gardener, the treasure, and the Jinn.

Abdullah looked me very hard in the eye.

Without blinking, he said:

'It is true.'

'What is?'

'All of it.'

'Are you sure?'

Abdullah nodded once, then again.

'I know it is true,' he said.

'How?'

'Because I saw it in a dream,' he said.

## Forty-one

asrudin's best friend wanted to borrow the wise fool's bicycle. But, remembering the filthy state it had been returned in the previous time, Nasrudin refused.

'I'm using it to dry cabbages,' he said, thinking on his feet.

'That sounds very difficult,' the friend replied.

'Not as difficult as you may think,' Nasrudin retorted.

'Really?'

'Yes.'

'How so?'

'All kinds of difficulties are overcome by a man who does not wish to lend a bicycle,' said Nasrudin.

TUNBRIDGE WELLS, 1976

We all carry happy memories from childhood.

Cycling fast down country lanes.

Iced lemonade on baking summer afternoons.

Laughing so hard you thought you'd pass out.

Sharing secrets with a best friend.

We carry a second set of memories, too: memories of pain, punishment, injustice, and of unspeakable cruelty.

Aged eight, I was sent to Rose Hill Preparatory School for Boys, in the nearby town of Tunbridge Wells. A throwback to the Victorian Age, its abiding claim to fame was that Robert Baden-Powell – founder of the Boy Scouts – had studied there as a child.

From the first day, the masters revealed that choice nugget of Boy Scout trivia again and again. I often wondered why they were so hung up on it. After all, Baden-Powell had lived at Langton House where we lived, and I slept in his old bedroom every night. But it never struck me as being suitably interesting to ever mention.

I arrived at Rose Hill a hundred and eleven years after the founder of the Boy Scouts had. He may have been long gone, but the regime he would have known had endured – a subculture of Latin, and yet more Latin, learning by rote, caning, detention, and cruelty for cruelty's sake.

The uniform was a grey flannel shirt, corduroy shorts, striped pink and grey tie, socks with garters, rose-crested flat cap, and grey blazer bearing another pink rose.

For six years I made the short journey each morning from Langton House to Rose Hill. In that time I learned to endure what might seem unendurable by current standards.

In the second half of the 'seventies, boys' prep schools were feeding grounds where perverted and sadistic masters ran wild, against a backdrop of sustained and unspeakable terror.

Try as I might, I can't bury Rose Hill.

It's always there, waiting for me to observe it through a lens tempered by experience and time. Once in a while, I'll overhear a story of cruelty, or catch a shocking scene in a film, and I'm right back in the changing room before games.

At the end of the first two years, I'd been punished more times than I could remember – for being messy, clumsy, or for withdrawing into my shell. On the rare occasions I did say anything, I was beaten for speaking out of turn.

I can't remember a single thing any of the masters were trying to teach. All I can recall were board rubbers, chalk, and even Bibles, being hurled at me in class. And, of course, being forced to shower naked all together after games – in the lined-up presence of the geriatric staff, their monocles steaming up as they watched.

Then, one day, everything changed.

At the far end of the long, hot summer of 1976, I was once again trussed up in pink and grey, fed hurriedly on cornflakes, and ferried up the steep hill to school.

I remember filing into the gym for assembly that first day of autumn term, for the interminable hymns, scripture readings, Latin prayers, and roll call.

A new teacher was sitting on the stage. Unlike the geriatrics, he was dressed in a tweed jacket, and was leaning forward on his haunches, like a bulldog. In his thirties, his face was dominated by thick-rimmed glasses, and a 'seventies handlebar moustache.

Once finished with all other business, the headmaster introduced the new recruit, and explained he would be teacher to Form Three.

I looked up. Form Three – that was *my* year.

The headmaster explained how Mr Moore had come from Rhodesia in deepest, darkest Africa, and how he was going to be teaching history and geography.

Within ten minutes of setting eyes on the new arrival, I was seated before him in class. On the first morning, he punished me merely for looking at him. And there began the reign of terror that makes it impossible for my memories of Rose Hill to ever fade away.

Singling me out day after day and term after term, he feasted on my many shortcomings – knocking me down instead of leaning down to pull me up.

Looking back, I've asked myself over and over why that one master decided to make my young life such a living hell. As a white Rhodesian who continually railed against African 'barbarism', I suppose my ethnicity was partly to blame.

But why Mr Moore tormented me, while leaving almost everyone else alone, isn't what interests me.

Nor is the question of why my parents were quite so oblivious to the fact something was terribly wrong.

Instead, what interests me is the way Mr Moore made me who I am.

Each night, I'd slink home into Langton House, go up to my room, sit on my bed, and rock back and forth in silent self-misery.

A long while slipped by in which I grew increasingly despondent, until I couldn't bear it any longer. Then, as if triggered, something quite magical occurred.

A natural self-preservation mechanism kicked in.

A mechanism seeded in my father's stories of Nasrudin.

I don't know when or how the stream of tales was turned on. What I do know is that it coursed through me in the way that light tears through a fibre optic cable, spewing out from the end.

Filling me head to toe with dazzling energy, the stories reminded me that the world was not configured from crusty old men with monocles, or tweed-jacketed sadists like Mr Moore, but rather from something far more essential:

Stories. Fables. Myths. Anecdotes.

Supreme among them were the tales of Nasrudin. While some stories provided relief in a temporary way, Nasrudin healed from within.

Robert Twigger, who saved me from the streets of Tokyo, wrote a hilarious book about studying aikido with the Tokyo Riot Police called *Angry White Pyjamas*. In it, he describes how, when subjected to constant injury, knees repair themselves 'from the inside out'. Given time, a sheet of coarse leather grows under the wound, rather than on the outside.

I can only assume that, like Twigger's knees healing from the inside out, the stream of tales was triggered by a primeval method of survival.

From the moment it began, the story-stream caused me to see the world around me in a fresh way. Sucking me in, it rewired my consciousness from the inside out.

As it did so I slipped deeper into Nasrudin's enchanted realm.

Once there, I took firm hold of the most powerful piece of armour my father's tales had passed on.

The power of imagination.

## Forty-two

While fording a river near his village, Nasrudin spotted a silver chalice bobbing up and down in the water. Plucking it from the current, he held it up in the air, admiring the fine workmanship.

'I can sell it and make a fortune,' he cackled to himself.

But, just as he was about to stuff it into his satchel, he noticed the chalice contained some water from the river.

Peering into it, he spied a man's face.

'I am so sorry my dear fellow!' he pleaded. 'It never occurred to me that such a fine object might already have an owner!'

Without giving it another thought, Nasrudin hurled the chalice back into the river.

## Madre de Dios, 2002

During the quest for the lost Inca city of Paititi, the so-called 'House of the Tiger King', I spent sixteen weeks in the Madre de Dios cloud forest.

From the outset, the expedition was far too large. It comprised dozens of porters, an entire film crew, assorted tribesmen, as well as mountains of equipment. With such a large team to feed, and so much gear to lug upriver, we needed extra porters to carry all the food necessary to feed them... the mother of all vicious circles.

Those sixteen weeks introduced me to misery on an unknown scale. Thrown in at the deep end, I grappled to learn the ins and outs of assembling a team, and keeping them together – even when they were at the point of mutiny.

While leading the ragtag procession into ever-deeper jungle, I came to understand the elements of good leadership – even though I was not myself an especially good example of implementing best practice.

The first thing I learned was never to select two people with the same skill set. A team's strength lies in its diversity. Each member of the team should have a different background and different skills. This means that, when unified as a group they bring different flavours to the stew.

Early on, I learned the importance of rewarding hard work and good ideas with praise and – much more importantly – with mountains of hot food. On a jungle expedition the leader ought to lead from the front, and never eat until the porters have refilled their plates a second time.

Hot food is a great motivator in the jungle.

Hot food, and dry clothes.

Through the months we progressed up the swirling, churning waters of the Madre de Dios River, I came to appreciate the value of the ultimate motivating force:

Stories.


When hiring the porters back in the village where the river was wide, a puny young man called Giovanni had stepped forward.

All the other men were built like trees, and so

Giovanni didn't seem like an obvious choice. With two tons of food and equipment to be hauled upriver, we needed brawn.

I was about to turn Giovanni away, when one of the men yelled out that he could tell stories like no man alive.

As soon as I heard that, I hired him right away.

Through the dark windswept nights of many weeks, Giovanni told a tale that went on and on. It was a tale of demons and cannibal tribes, of magical kingdoms, buried treasure, and mermaid princesses whose hair was plaited from strands of pure gold.

Each night, once the men had eaten, and had dried and bandaged their feet, the tale would begin where it had left off the night before.

Like a master storyteller recounting the next instalment of *A Thousand and One Nights*, Giovanni would tailor the evening's episode to the conditions in which we found ourselves.

On nights with especially ferocious weather, or when we had hauled the rubber boats and rafts up rapids, the story would be filled with even more action and dreamlike description than usual.

Giovanni had the ability to gauge what his audience needed – like a doctor devising the perfect treatment. A rare and quite astonishing skill, it's one I've never forgotten.

Of all the magic in his long twisting saga, one

element has stuck in my mind more than any other: the way he breathed an emotional quality into the tale.

Like a gold thread woven into a tapestry, it gave an intoxicating value – appealing to something primeval in all who received it.

As in the tale that Giovanni spun in the jungle each night – the emotional paradigm seeped in through the listener's ears and into their soul. The tale became part of them. Or, rather, the poignant connection became part of them.

The porters came to rely on the prospect of Giovanni's storytelling as a way to get through the hardship of the day. While hauling the Zodiacs and the home-made rafts upriver, their thoughts dwelt not on their aching muscles, or injured feet, but on the next instalment of Giovanni's tale.

In the twelfth week we reached a kind of plateau – not in the geography of the jungle, but in our ability to go on. Utterly exhausted, the men were like a military corps unable to continue. They were on the verge of mutiny, and I didn't know what to do.

At dusk one night, I took Giovanni aside and said to him:

'We both know I'm a terrible leader and that the men hate me... but they *love* you. You're the one person who can rally their spirits. Is there anything you can do to get them moving again?'

Giovanni sighed, as though I were asking for a miracle.

'They want to kill you,' he said. 'They're talking about it openly.'

'I know! I can see it on their faces.'

'This is a dangerous situation,' the storyteller said.

'I'm begging you to help me!'

'There is something,' Giovanni said.

'What?'

'Something that may help.'

'Yes?'

'*Sí.*'

'Please don't suggest more food – we can't spare any more rations.'

'Not food.'

'Then…?'

'Something more delicious than food.'

'What?'

'A story.'

'But you tell stories every night.'

'There's another story – a special one.'

'A better one?'

'A story I've been keeping.'

'Keeping for what?'

'For an emergency.'

As someone who's searched for treasure, lost cities, and even for King Solomon's mines, there are moments in which I feel jaded by it all. In my adventures, every possible excuse, fragment of advice, stray idea, and spoken observation, has reached my ears.

But I'd never once heard of a story being kept for an emergency. It was like breaking the glass to reach a hammer with which to smash a train window in the event of a crash. I asked Giovanni what tale could save us from the jungle, and ourselves.

'The Story of Henrique de Cabarone.'

'*Henrique de...*?'

'Cabarone.'

'Who's he?'

Giovanni the storyteller bit his lower lip anxiously.

'You are Henrique de Cabarone, señor.'

'*Me*?'

'*Sí* señor.'

'How could a tale about me – or Henrique de Cabarone – save the expedition from impending disaster?'

The storyteller rolled his eyes.

'By making the men laugh,' Giovanni said.

The Story of Henrique de Cabarone was one of the strangest stories I've ever heard – not because it contained jokes. It was what the British call 'funny peculiar' rather than 'funny haha' – and was a curious and oblique observation of our own journey.

A bumbling adventurer not unlike a jungle version

of Don Quixote might be, Henrique de Cabarone had strains of Mr Bean, too, and a great big dollop of me.

The quest was described not by the protagonist, but by a colony of fleas living on his body. They took it in turns to chart the misguided exploits of the explorer and his pointless quest for a lost city – detailing how he was pursuing the quest not for science or history, but for a desperate and insatiable need for praise.

The fleas recounted how, whenever a camera was held up, he'd dive into the shot and feign trials and tribulations in the name of exploration. When he came across tribes, he would give them copies of his published books, even though he knew full well they couldn't read. His luggage overflowed with luxuries and unnecessary equipment – from a jacket and tie, to crampons and even ice picks. On the rare occasions he wasn't moaning at the hardship, he was writing up his journal – waxing lyrical about his natural talent at leading men.

Once Henrique de Cabarone had been described in glorious and fanciful detail, his adventures began. While blustering upriver in search of the Inca stronghold, he was seduced by mermaids incarnated as pink river dolphins, captured by cannibals, and carried to a distant land on the wings of a giant bird. Not a mere fool, he was an utter imbecile, the kind one might cross the road to avoid in normal circumstances.

At the same time, he was a swashbuckling adventurer who, although inept, was a bizarre master of his own destiny.

Word by word, the story drifted from Giovanni's mouth to the ears of the porters, and had an extraordinary effect. Laughing so hard, the men rolled back and forth howling like upturned beetles. Their aches, pains, petty squabbles, and the intense longing for home, were melted by the warmth of laughter.

Henrique de Cabarone may have begun as a reflection of a despised and wretched foreigner, but he concluded as a gateway into a new dominion.

By the time the story was over, Giovanni was lauded and cheered, and I was presented with a window of respite before the men reached the brink of mutiny once again.

The morning after the Story of Henrique de Cabarone, I woke earlier than the others, went down to the river, and immersed myself as though taking part in some sacred ritual.

Drying myself off, I sat on the bank, the dawn air thick with dragonflies. Spotting Giovanni approach, I thanked him for saving me.

'I didn't do anything,' he said.

'But you did – with your brilliant Señor Henrique de Cabarone!'

'That wasn't me. It was *you*.'

'A little bit of me,' I said bashfully.

The storyteller peered down at the water, his thoughts carried away with the flow.

'Most people go through life imagining they're someone they are not,' he said. 'They are so desperate to be someone else, they don't see themselves for who they are.'

It was a perceptive comment for so early in the morning.

'Do you think I'm misguided... that I should never have set out to find Paititi?'

Giovanni didn't answer, not at first.

I assumed he hadn't heard my question.

Then, his focus still trained on the river's surface, he said:

'You had no choice.'

'But I did.'

'No, no, señor, you did not.'

'How so?'

'Because searching for the lost city of Paititi is your destiny,' Giovanni said.

### Forty-three

own on his luck, Nasrudin borrowed a cloak from a friend and sought an audience with the king. After

TAHIR SHAH

many hours of waiting, the monarch called him
forward.

Bowing and scraping, the wise fool made his
way obsequiously to the throne and kissed the
king's hand.

'Providence has been unkind to me, Your
Majesty!' he moaned.

'Yet again?'

'Yes, Your Greatness!'

'What happened to all the money I gave you
last time, and the time before that?'

'Spent on frivolity, but I promise I have learnt
the error of my ways.'

'And what do you want this time?'

'Ten gold coins, Majesty.'

'That's a small fortune!'

'I know, Your Magnificence, but it's the price
of what I require to re-establish myself.'

'And what is it you "require" to re-establish
yourself?'

'An elephant, Your Gloriousness!'

'How on earth would a man like you manage
to provide food for a mighty creature like that?'

Nasrudin smiled demurely, his expression
masking anger.

'If it pleases Your Munificence, I have come
here in search of funding rather than advice,' he
said.

# TRAVELS WITH NASRUDIN

Like all of us, my life is plagued by what they call in the media 'digital noise'.

From the moment I wake up in the morning, until the time I rest my head at night, my world is bombarded with messages. They arrive through Twitter, Tumblr, Facebook and Instagram, from WhatsApp, FaceTime, Skype, Signal, and via numerous email accounts. On any given day I receive about four hundred messages. Most are from readers of my work. A few are from people I've encountered on the twisting journey of my life. A great many more hail from an altogether different realm....

Messages that slip through from the Treasure Zone.

On a particularly grey winter morning a couple of years ago, I was sitting up in bed with an espresso wondering how I'd get through a day of storm-clouds and cold hard rain, when my laptop beeped – signalling the call to battle.

In desperate need of something to raise my spirits, I scanned the email inbox, and sifted through the usual onslaught of bills, more bills, invitations and pleas for advice and help.

I was about to close the computer and get back to my espresso, when something caught my eye. By disclosing what it was I'm in danger of lifting the lid on my ingenuous nature. I prefer to call it an optimistic nature – an overwhelming need for a strain of easily-within-reach fabulousness.

And that is exactly what the message from Patrick Walumba promised.

The title read:

'Fifty Gold Bars Awaiting You, Sir!'

Sipping my espresso, I allowed my finger to drag the cursor down to the message.

*Click.*

Patrick Walumba's gilded lifeline opened up:

'Sir, I am a humble farmer from the poor country of Ghana in West Africa. While ploughing fields near my home town of Damongo in the north three months ago it was very hot. So I rested my donkey under a baobab tree, and took rest from the sun. Crouching on the ground, I thanked God for all I have in the world, and all the joy He has bestowed upon me. Even though it was so hot, I prepared to get back to the work – as there was still so much ground to furrow.

'Just as I was about to lead my donkey, Harriet, out of the shade, I tripped over what I thought was a root. Looking down, I noticed it was not a root, but something made from iron. Curious, I scratched away at the object with my hands and saw it was in actual fact an iron handle set into a stone slab.

'As you can imagine, I was surprised. And I was excited. Looking around to check no one else was watching, I used a sharp stone to dig away at the slab. Then, with all my strength, I pulled. There was no chance of raising it. So, I tied a length of rope to the handle, and attached the end to Harriet. A minute or two later, the stone slab was pulled off!

'Peering down into the hole, I saw there was a chamber, with rough stone steps going down. Although very dark, I could see something shining down there... something that looked to my eyes like gold!

'Again, checking no one was watching, I tethered Harriet to the baobab tree, and made my way to the hole. I must be honest, I was very frightened. I feared a snake might be ready to strike me. Or perhaps it was a trick, I thought – and someone was waiting to trap me in there forever.

'But, plucking up courage, I descended the steps one by one. As, my eyes got used to the darkness, I paced down onto the floor of what looked like a natural cave. The baobab's roots covered the walls. And the floor was covered in human bones. Hundreds of them. But they did not seize my attention as you might imagine. The reason is because at the far end of the chamber, there lay a pile of gold bricks. Glinting in the shaft of light that coursed down into the hole, they looked like an apparition.

'For a long time I stood before them, as though witnessing a miracle of God. I didn't know what to do. Something inside me was telling me to run back to the surface, close the hole, and to forget about it. After all, there was a danger of submitting to greed. And greed was sure to lead to disaster for me and my family.

'But then I heard a voice. The voice of an angel. It said to me: "Patrick Walumba you are a humble farmer, and a man who is trusted by God. It's not your destiny to be wealthy, but it is your destiny to help those in need. My master is the Lord, and he is relying on you to do what is right. You must take all the gold from this cave, and distribute it to people in the world whose need is great. Do you understand?"

'Falling to my knees, I gave thanks to the Almighty. Then, led in prayer by the angel, I promised to follow the instructions, even though my mission was sure to be dangerous and hard. Over days and weeks, I removed the golden bars from the cave, making sure no one saw what I was doing. So fearful was I that news of the discovery would get out, I told no one. Not even my wife, or my five precious children. The secret was known to me and the angel.

'Once all five hundred gold bars were out of the cavern, and hidden in various places in the local area, I set about working out a way to do as the blessed angel had instructed – the mission of distributing the wealth to those who needed the money to fulfil their dreams.

'As I have said, I am a humble farmer, and although I can read and write, I was not fortunate to receive a good education. For this reason, I took time to educate myself. I learned about the world, studying by night. I read books about gold, about poverty and wealth. Then, little by little, I learned how to use a computer.

'Once I was familiar with the internet, I spent months searching for good people – the kind who could use prosperity to the benefit of all mankind. And that, sir, is how I came across you.

'My research has told me you have a pure heart, and that you will understand the importance of the mission I have been set. I trust you very deeply, and ask that you place your trust in me.

'I want to give you fifty of the gold bars. They are of a standard size and weight, and are located in a hiding place at my village. I realize this may seem a strange request, but I am ready to pass on the fifty gold bars to you. All I ask in return is that you send me some basic information so that we can proceed. I will need your full name, your bank account number, your account password, and security details. I also need your telephone number, and ask that you send me $100 by Western Union in Ghana, to prove your interest. I am your faithful servant, Patrick Titanic Walumba.'

Draining my espresso, I thanked Providence for sending me a cause by which I might fend off the winter blues.

Clicking 'Reply', I wrote:

'Dear Patrick Titanic Walumba, it was with absolute delight and joy that I woke this morning to your message. I am a struggling author, in need of nothing more than fifty bars of pure gold. Although I don't know how you selected me from the millions of others who are surely more worthy, I'd very much like to take you up on your offer. Before I provide the information you require, I would like to meet you face-to-face, so that you can gain full trust in me. For, as I understand it, nothing is so important in life than trust. Please let me know where to meet you and when.'

Rousing myself from bed, I went through to the bathroom, soaked in a tub for a while, got dressed, paid some bills, and moaned about the rain. In truth, I'd already forgotten about my generous friend from Ghana.

Until, that is, my email account went '*bing*!'

Sensing Patrick Walumba's febrile state of mind, I read:

'Dear Shah, the angel brought us together... and

as a devoted servant of the Lord, I place my trust in you. There is nothing I would not do for you, and would never ask for anything in return. You are my brother. There is no need to waste your valuable time with a meeting. Ghana is far away, and I would never want to put you to the discomfort or the expense of travelling here. So, send the information I require, and I will send the gold bars to you by Federal Express.'

The rain was lashing down outside, the winter sky ink-grey. But the last thing on my mind was the weather. For I had a tonic that could revive the spirits of a dying man.

Clicking 'Reply' once again, I wrote:

'My dear friend Patrick Titanic Walumba, I thank the universe for sending you to me, and promise to be honest and honourable. While I have total faith in you, I fear the internet is not safe. For this reason, I think it best that I provide the information to you directly. Tell me where to meet you, and when, and I shall be there.'

An hour later, my new philanthropic friend responded:

'Dear Shah, again I say there's no need for you to come here to meet me. Please send your bank account details, and the relevant information, and I shall send the gold bars. I am polishing them at this very moment, and packaging them up for you. I think you will be pleased because they are shining very brightly.'

An hour later, I did something many people would not have done. I bought a ticket to Ghana leaving that same afternoon.

Then, smugly, I replied:

'Dear Patrick Titanic Walumba, I will be arriving in Accra this evening, and will bring the information you require with me. I shall also bring $25,000 in cash as a gift of friendship. This will be presented by me to you when we meet.'

Five minutes later I received a reply:

'Hello Shah! Yes! I shall meet you in Accra tomorrow morning at 9 o'clock outside the Holy Trinity Cathedral!'

Checking on Google Maps, I noticed that Damongo – where Patrick the farmer ploughed his fields – was more than ten hours' drive from the Ghanaian capital. Assuming he would not have enough time to make the journey, I drew the point to Patrick's attention.

Instantly, he replied:

'Do not fear my beloved friend Shah, I will travel through the night, and reach Accra well within time. I shall bring a bag for the $25,000 gift of friendship. It will be useful to know in advance what size of banknotes you will be bringing.'

I replied:

'$100 bills. See you tomorrow. Excited. Tahir Shah.'

Taking the direct flight from Casablanca down to Accra was simplicity itself. It was so easy that I asked myself why I didn't zip down to West Africa more often. A rarity for the region, Ghana speaks English – a legacy of its British colonial rule, which ended in 1957... before calls for independence reached other African lands.

Standing outside the Holy Trinity Cathedral, I reflected that Ghana's former colonial appellation – Gold Coast – was appropriate for the business of my journey. All manner of questions raced through my head. They included:

What was I thinking?

Was I insane?

Would I be lured to the backstreets and robbed?

Would I be shot/knifed/strangled to death?

How would I get through life by wasting so much time?

Was there a chance that Patrick Titanic Walumba would keep his word?

If I were actually given fifty bars of gold, how would I get it out of the country?

My mind turned to logistics. Gold isn't an easy metal to lug about – a problem glossed over by almost all heist films. Adventures scouring Ethiopia for the mines of biblical 'Ophir' – the land from which King

Solomon supposedly acquired his gold – had taught me that the yellow metal is much heavier than you'd expect.

Back in Ethiopia, I'd blagged my way through military-style security into Legadembi – the only legal gold mine in the country. The highlight of that journey had been watching molten gold being poured into ingots, and being photographed with as much of it as I could handle.

I admit I'm not as tough as the brawny South Africans running the gold mine, but even when gritting my teeth I wasn't able to hold more than four bars. So, the thought of fifty bars was a worry.

Cautioning myself, I agreed to cross that bridge once I got to it.

First things first.

As my mind rolled through potential scenarios, I heard a pair of small feet shuffling fast through the dust behind me.

I turned.

'Shah?' asked a wispy young man of about nineteen, wearing black-framed plastic glasses, t-shirt and jeans.

He looked like a college kid. And, when he stuck out a hand for me to shake, my mind reported that it was soft as silk. Not the hand of a farmer.

'Are you Patrick Titanic Walumba?' I asked expectantly.

The young man nodded hard, before sliding the bridge of his glasses back up his nose.

'There was no need to come to Accra,' he said. 'We could have completed the business by email.'

'How was your journey from the north?' I asked.

Walumba frowned.

'What?'

'From Damongo?'

'Oh, it was very nice. Oh yes, a very nice journey. Such beautiful countryside.'

'But wasn't it too dark to see anything, as you drove through the night?'

Patrick thought before answering.

'Ghana has a very bright moon,' he said.

'So, what's the plan? You know, for the handover?'

'I need your bank details and the information I asked for in my email. And the money you promised as well.'

'The gift of friendship?'

Patrick Titanic Walumba grinned from ear to ear.

'$25,000,' he said.

'OK. So… I give you the details which prove I am who I say I am, and give you the money, and in return, you give me fifty gold bars, the bars you discovered in the cave up in Damongo?'

Patrick nodded again.

'Yes.'

'Can I just double check when the gold will be given to me?' I said.

'As soon as I have your details and the gift of friendship.'

'It sounds easy.'

'Oh yes, yes, Shah, it is very easy. In fact it is easier than easy.'

'Like the sound of easier than easy,' I said.

Patrick Titanic Walumba sneezed, blew his nose on his t-shirt, and pulled a pen from his jeans pocket.

'I will write down your bank account number,' he said.

'Of course… but maybe we should meet later and finish it. You don't have the gold, and I don't have the dollars… so let's meet later when we have it all.'

'The gold is heavy,' Patrick said.

'Yes, I've handled bullion before,' I said, 'and I know what a hassle it is. A hassle, but a fun hassle all the same.'

'We can meet later.'

'What time?'

'At five o'clock.'

'Here?'

'Yes.'

'I'll bring the dollars and you'll bring the gold, right?'

'Right.'

'Then you'll take the bus back to Harriet, and I'll take my flight back home.'

'*Harriet?*'

'Isn't that the name of your donkey at your farm?'

A veil of confusion descended like a shutter over Patrick's face.

'Yes, Ha-rr-ie-t,' he stammered. 'My donkey. She is a good one. Very kind.'

'Had her long?'

'Who?'

'Harriet?'

'Um, er… yes. Long.'

'I love donkeys,' I said. 'They're almost as special to me as mules.'

At five o'clock we reconvened at the cathedral – me with a sealed padded envelope in hand, and Patrick Titanic Walumba with two wooden boxes carried to the spot by two more young men.

Like the supposed farmer, they were dressed in t-shirts and jeans, and had an air of geekiness about them, as though they wouldn't have known a farm, or even a treasure cave, if they found it in their soup.

'These are my friends,' said Patrick.

'Are they farmers as well?'

'Um, er, yes, farmers. From Damongo.'

'I hear it's wonderful up there in the north,' I said.

'I've got a few days before my flight leaves, so I think I'll travel back up there with you all, and see it for myself.'

Patrick and his friends exchanged frantic glances.

'Rain,' said one.

'Flooding,' another added.

'Bandits,' Patrick chipped in.

'Oh, dear. Then another time, when the rain and the bandits aren't such a problem.'

'Yes, another time,' the three agreed in unison.

I waved the thick padded envelope which had some numbers written on the front.

'Here's the money, and my bank details are written on it as you can see – proof of who I am.'

'Proof,' said one of the men. 'That is good.'

Weighing the envelope in my hand, I looked at the young men.

'Your trust means so much to me,' I said. 'Because trust is what the world is built on. Love and trust... but mostly trust.'

'Trust!' the three exclaimed in a chorus.

'As I trust you three as much as you trust me,' I said, 'I'm not even going to open the crates, because I know to do so would be insulting – just as opening this envelope to check it would be insulting to me.'

Six eyes drilled into mine, as though trying to discern what was going through my head.

'When you put the crates into my taxi over there, I'll give you the envelope.'

Patrick's friends staggered over to the taxi, stowed the wooden crates in the back, and nodded. Then, shaking the farmer from Damongo firmly by the hand, I thanked him for his sense of philanthropy, and presented him with the padded envelope.

'We deserve each other,' I said. 'Because you are just as wise and as foolish as me.'

### Forty-four

In the dead of night, Nasrudin heard a group of thieves break into his house, and start rummaging through his meagre possessions.

In fear, he hid under the bed.

On seeing the bed empty, the thieves assumed no one was home. One of them lit a candle, opened the cupboards and checked under the bed.

'Hello!' exclaimed Nasrudin awkwardly, on being discovered.

'What are you doing under the bed?' asked one of the thieves.

'Hiding from shame at not having better possessions to steal!' he said.

LANGTON HOUSE, 1983

Hailing from an Afghan family with its lineage rooted in the Hindu Kush, my father had been raised on stories, just as we were, and as my own children have been.

They weren't any ordinary tales, however, but stories from a matrix of Oriental teaching – the system of philosophical thought championed by Sufis.

These days there's an awful lot of misinformation surrounding Sufis. Google the word 'Sufi' and you get a hotchpotch of music, whirling, dance moves, random quotations from Rumi, and so much more. My father spent his life distilling the essence of Sufi thought, separating it from distracting overtones, and preparing it in a way he believed it would be best absorbed.

Astonished that in the West people seemed to yearn for a guru figure, he would shout out how the secret to life was taking responsibility for yourself. I remember how thrilled he was with Monty Python's *Life of Brian*, erupting in joy when Brian exclaimed: 'You don't need to follow me! You don't need to follow anyone!'

But the more my father spurned the role of the guru, the more people arrived, and the more mail they sent. Obsessing about him, in the way Brian's disciples had done about Brian, they hung on anything he did or said.

The intense effect he had on people wasn't restricted to those who read his books. It happened with almost everyone who encountered him, as though he could peer deep into who they were, rather than into whom they were pretending to be.

An example of this is when he learnt to drive.

My father came from an Oriental line that for centuries had spawned warriors and mystical luminaries. That was all well and good in the East. The line having transferred to the West, strains of behaviour that came so naturally may have been mistaken at times for delusions of grandeur.

In the 'thirties, my grandfather, the Sirdar Ikbal Ali Shah, dropped in at a Rolls-Royce showroom in Mayfair to check the current models on behalf of his friend, the Maharaja of Jaipur.

A fawning salesman swanned up and enquired whether my grandfather would wish to take the latest Tourer for a spin. Turning to him, my grandfather riposted with loathing,

'Are you deliberately trying to insult me?'

No member of my family had ever learned to drive. They'd always been driven. But then, in 1978, my mother passed a driving test at the age of fifty. So as not to be outdone, my father dropped everything and took lessons – hundreds and hundreds of them.

His instructor was a long-suffering gentleman from Tunbridge Wells, whose name was Mr Butcher.

Eventually, my father took his test, passed, and never once drove again.

Years slipped by.

Then, one evening, Blonde No. 24 brought in a scrap of paper with a typed message:

*Mr Butcher the driving instructor is on his deathbed. Not expected to survive the night. His wife just telephoned. She says he is calling for a former pupil to be there at his end... Idries Shah.*

Instantly, my father leapt up, was driven to the hospital, and reached dear Mr Butcher moments before he expired. Next morning I asked him about it. He replied,

'Always remember that in life the most exceptional individuals cross one's path in the most unlikely of ways.'

People were drawn to my father partly because of his natural charisma, and partly because he was a master at challenging the way they were taught to think. He believed that the West could shake itself from chronic cerebral slumber, by questioning the world around it in a root and branch kind of way.

Throughout our childhood, he would rail against the futility of school, while championing a different method of learning – learning through experience.

He would encourage us to talk to everyone we met – not superficially, but with method – the kind that delved deep into who and why they were.

'Learn from living three-dimensional people who pass you in life,' he would say, 'rather than from flat second-hand representations you read about in books. Ask them questions, root about in their wealth of experience, and then apply what you've learnt to your own life.'

Another thing he repeated time and again, was that in the West people were often starved of attention. In his opinion, family and friend structures in the Occidental world fell short of what they might be. The result was that a great many people one encountered in daily life could be 'switched on' by being deluged in attention. Watch politicians on the campaign trail, and you see it right away.

Most of the time my father provided attention showers to help the person in front of him. Like seasonal rain in a wilderness, he believed you had to raise the water table before you could start growing crops on desert land.

'The kind of people who are in chronic need of attention,' he once told me, 'are the kind who get sucked into cults – because their needs are fulfilled. They're so desperate to belong, and to be listened to, that they resign themselves to the group. It's a terrible thing – which is why we need to show people how to think for themselves.'

When my father died, I received hundreds of letters from people expressing how he had affected

361

them in an overwhelming way. Some explained he'd helped them in paying debts, or getting back on track after problems with drink or drugs.

Of all the letters, the most poignant was a single anonymous line.

It read simply:

'Your father listened to me.'

## Forty-five

Nasrudin had taken a job as a night watchman. It was very badly paid, but he was in desperate need of the money. His wife had been scolding him for weeks, yelling that he was lazy and good for nothing.

After the first night on the job, Nasrudin arrived home exhausted. His wife fussed about, ordering him to hand over his pay. Having done so, he went upstairs to get some well-earned sleep.

As his wife counted the coins, she heard a loud *thump*!

'What was that terrible noise?!' she bawled.

'Nothing my dear. Just my coat falling to the floor.'

'Didn't sound like a coat to me! Sounded much worse!'

'That's because I was inside it at the time!' called Nasrudin.


ALICE SPRINGS, 2018

News of my arrival had swept through Alice at lightning speed, not because I'm especially well-known in Australia, but because of the length of my Wikipedia page.

Breaking the journey by train from Darwin, I planned to spend a few days doing research for a book on Afghanistan. At first glance, the link between the fiery core of the great antipodean landmass and the landlocked realm of my ancestors was not immediately apparent. But, having completed my initial research, the pilgrimage to the Outback made complete sense.

As soon as I stepped off the fabulous 'Ghan' – the train that runs north–south from Darwin to Adelaide – and onto the platform at Alice Springs, I felt my eyeballs being cooked like poached eggs. Almost unable to breathe, I was ferried to a modest hotel I'd booked online by a fretful cab driver called 'Chak'.

'Toasty today,' was all I could manage.

'Yer, this is a right one.'

'Think I'll take a cold bath.'

'You wouldn't wanna do that, mate,' answered Chak.

'Why not?'

''Cos you'll get a dose of walla-walla!'

'What's that?'

'When you start bleeding through your privates!'

'Is it?'

'Yeah.'

'Haven't heard of that one before.'

'First time in Alice?'

'Yes it is.'

'Best thing's to stay out of the heat,' said Chak.

When I'd checked in at the hotel, the manager swept out from his office, lurched for my hand, and shook it very roughly indeed.

'Great to finally meet you!' he roared, as if he really meant it.

'Pleased to be here.'

'Hell of a number!'

'Excuse me?'

'Yer number! It's marvellous. Pages and pages. Thought they'd never end!'

'I'm not following you,' I said.

'The wife's the expert of course, and she says she's not seen so many pages since that other writer.'

'*Huh*?'

'The one who writes the horror books as thick as doorstops.'

'Stephen King?'

'Yeah. That one. He's got more pages, but you've still got time, right?!'

I'd only been out of the train's air conditioning for half an hour but I could feel the heat getting to me.

'Need to lie down for a little while,' I said. 'I would have taken a cold bath but I hear that's not such a good idea. So I think I'll just lie down.'

The manager twitched his head left to right.

'The walla-walla,' he whispered darkly. 'Anyway, there's no time for bathing or shut-eye.'

'Why not? I'm not in a rush.'

''Cos he'll be 'ere at four-thirty.'

'Who will?'

'*He* will. The big cheese. The main man.'

'*Who*?'

The manager recoiled as though I were an absolute imbecile.

'Not joining up the dots, are you?'

'Well, I'm rather hot. That's why I need to rest.'

'The editor wants to splash you over the local rag!'

'But why?'

''Cos you're newsworthy.'

'Am I?'

''Course you are!'
'How so?'
'Because you're a celeb on Google!'

Taking refuge in my room, I hung a 'Do Not Disturb' sign on the handle, and stretched out on the bed.

As soon as I closed my eyes, a fist pounded at the door.

Annoyed, I got up, opened it, and found a fleshy man standing in the corridor. Bald, and curiously forlorn, his face was jaundiced.

'Pete. That's me!' he yelled, thrusting out his hand.

'But I'm lying down. Think I've got heat stroke.'

'Won't take a jiff.'

'What won't?'

'The angle.'

'Angle?'

Pete whipped out his phone and held up my Wikipedia page.

'Royalty, you are.'

'Hardly,' I said.

With no other choice, I followed Pete through to the lounge and explained why I was in Alice Springs:

'Between the 1880s and 1930s,' I said, 'about thirty thousand camels and camelteers were brought to the Outback from Afghanistan and India. They criss-crossed the desert in caravans known as…'

'"The Ghan",' said Pete. 'Same as the train that now runs the route.'

'That's right. And I'm here in Australia trying to find out about those forgotten camelteers. It's a lost fragment of history.'

Pete wasn't listening. Or, if he was, he wasn't interested.

'So,' he said, summing up, 'how's the entry changed yer life?'

I turned the question over in my mind.

'It hasn't,' I said. 'I write books and do other stuff, and sometimes people cover it, and sometimes they don't. Most of the interesting stuff I've done isn't even mentioned on Wikipedia.'

'Pah!' spat Pete.

'It's true. You see, I'm not interested in what people write about me, and am certainly not bothered about my Wikipedia page. All I care about is doing interesting work that pleases me.'

'Yer, you've gotta say that, haven't you?'

'Not really, no.'

'Well, how'd you feel if tomorrow the page was deleted?'

All I could think about was getting back to my room.

'Wouldn't really care either way.'

Pete reached over and jabbed me in the ribs.

'Knew you'd say that!' he grinned.

On my first full day in Alice, I took a bag of washing to a laundromat, and spent the afternoon there while the machines churned away at it.

For the first hour I was there alone; then an elderly Aboriginal woman came in. From the moment I set eyes on her, I was moved in a strange, inside-out kind of a way. But I couldn't work out why.

She was wearing a neat flower-print dress, with a full-length apron drawn over it, and a string of red glass beads around her neck. Although relatively dark, her complexion and features weren't like those of other Aboriginals I'd seen hanging about the street corners in Alice Springs. Her face was distinguished, her nose aquiline, and her hands blessed with the most beautifully long tapered fingers.

We got chatting. The woman, whose name was Marjorie, told me about her life.

'I was born in the bush,' she said. 'Never planned to move to town. Hated it here when I first came.'

'Why did you come to Alice, then?'

'A minister was passing,' she said. 'He picked me out and said – "She'll do."'

'What did that mean?'

'That he'd give me an education. So I went with him and his wife. Hadn't worn shoes before. Hadn't ever held a spoon or a fork. I hadn't even slept in a room with glass in the windows.'

'Did you speak English?'

Marjorie erupted into fits of laughter.

'Course not!'

'How old were you?'

'Must have been eleven, or twelve.'

'Weren't you frightened?'

'Not frightened,' Marjorie reflected, staring into the washing machine's window as its drum rolled round and around. 'Wouldn't say that. But I was anxious.'

'At leaving your family?'

'No.'

'Then anxious of what?'

'Of leaving the sky I had known,' she said.

Meeting people is what travel is about, and I've been blessed to encounter far more than my fair share of extraordinary people.

But rarely have I ever had the pleasure of conversing with someone quite so spellbinding as Marjorie.

Although not wishing to break the flow of the conversation, I explained why I'd come to Alice – lured by a quest to learn more of the Afghan camelteers.

Marjorie looked down at the scuffed lino beneath her flip-flops.

'I don't talk about that,' she said.

'About what?'

'About my grandfather's line.'

'Will you tell me about them?' I asked, guessing it was a thread to gently tug.

'They were Afghans,' Marjorie mumbled, as though the word were too shocking to speak.

'Afghans who were with the Ghan?'

'Yes.'

'You're going to think me odd for mentioning this,' I remarked. 'And please believe me I say it in flattery – but you remind me very much of my favourite aunt.'

'How?'

'Same nose, same smile, same hands. But more than that. It's as though you were long-lost sisters.'

Marjorie glowed with delight.

'You've just made a silly old woman dance inside,' she said.

### Forty-six

Nasrudin was a hoarder, while his wife had almost no possessions at all. While he filled their small lodgings with junk, she cursed him, threatening to throw it all out. With time, there was so little space inside the house that the couple were forced to sleep out on the roof.

As they prepared themselves for bed, Nasrudin's wife scolded him for the thousandth time for being such a hoarder.

As if rising to the bait, the wise fool shook a fist at the heavens.

'Why are you cursing God?' she asked. 'It'll do no good!'

'It's not the Almighty I am cursing, but rather the stars.'

'Have you finally gone mad?'

'Quite the opposite,' Nasrudin replied. 'You see there are so many of them up there ready for the taking, but we have so little space left in the house!'

LANGTON HOUSE, 1974

From early childhood my sisters and I were encouraged to start collections.

Looking back, it was a pursuit inspired by my parents' own youth. Trawl through eBay and you'll find thousands of albums containing everything from postage stamps to bookmarks, and from beer mats to luggage labels. Assembled over the precious years of childhood, the yellowed pages are a testament to youthful diligence.

One Christmas, we were given albums by our eccentric and favourite aunt, Amina.

'I'm going to collect pictures of butterflies,' said Safia.

'I'm going to collect foreign banknotes,' said Saira.

'I'm going to collect people,' I said.

And that's just what I did.

While my sisters worked away at their more practical collections, I filled my album with material of a quite different nature. Although hindered by truly terrible handwriting, I collected descriptions of people I knew.

At first, the people I detailed were Mrs Ellard, the housekeeper, our beloved nanny Pauline, George the handyman, and my father's secretary, Helena. Then, I branched out to take in the village's regular cast – Mrs Knock at the post office, where we bought sweets with our pocket money; Mr Lovett the butcher; and the prim lady with no lips behind the counter at the bakery.

After a few weeks I got into my stride. Whenever anyone stepped in through the front door, I would observe them from my position at the top of the stairs. Like an eagle perched on a high vantage point I watched intently, noting down details that seemed important to me – such as what they were dressed in, and whether they moved slowly or quickly. Sometimes I would try and find out who the visitors were. More often than not I was shooed away and told to go up to the playroom. In such cases I gave them a codename instead.

A sample entry read:

*Poncho-man: Beard. Long hair. Happy. Blue poncho. First time I have seen him. Smells of expensive cheese. Maybe from Mexico. Seemed in a hurry to talk to Baba. Study door closed when he arrived. Tea served by Mrs Ellard. Laughed when door to study opened. Waved to me sitting on the stairs. Shouted 'Hola!' Hope he comes back.*

As the years passed, my people collection went from strength to strength, as I made note of almost everyone who came down on the weekends. Most of the visitors were not well known, and many of those who were had been given invented names.

One afternoon I sat on the floor of the small sitting room with my people collection. Behind me, my mother was knitting, her lips counting stitches.

'One day you'll be able to sell that for a lot, darling,' she said.

I gasped at the comment.

'Couldn't sell it!' I exclaimed, clutching the album to my chest.

'You've got some famous people in there.'

'But they're not for sale.'

'Not even for a million pounds?'

'No! Not even for a *billion* pounds!'

My mother looked down at me, her hands knitting on autopilot.

'I am pleased to hear it,' she said. 'Because some things should never be bought or sold.'

The next week I took the album to my prep school with the intention of expanding some of the entries during break. I'd never planned to write notes on any of the teachers. They were such a rotten bunch I didn't want them in my beloved collection. But a sudden urge to collect caused me to break my own rule.

At the end of prep we were dismissed with some nonsensical phrase in Latin, by an ex-army-monocle-tweed-clad master. As I took the album out from my desk, he beckoned me forward.

'What's that, young man?' he snarled accusingly.

'Nothing, sir?'

'*Nothing*? How can it be nothing? It's not nothing... it's something?!'

'It's an album, sir.'

'*Stamps*?'

'No, sir.'

'If not stamps, then what?!'

'People, sir.'

'*People*?!'

'Yes, sir.'

'How can it be people?! Show it to me!'

Gingerly, I passed over the people collection.

Slotting his monocle into place, the retired major regarded the pages fast, grunting with disdain – while I prayed.

My prayers were not answered.

Cheeks flushing beetroot in rage, his mouth snarled, his monocle popped out and dangled on its chain.

'How dare you?!' he roared.

'Very sorry, sir.'

Thrusting left and right, he smashed the side of my head with the book.

'Going to burn it! Going to burn this wretched filth!'

Turning on his heel, the retired major stormed away, my people collection under his arm. It was a great sadness, and one I've never quite recovered from – not least because the final entry was incomplete:

*Major Smith: Grey hair. Pocket watch. Red and black zigzag tie. Calls lunch 'luncheon', and forces us to eat it with sliced white bread. Teaches maths. Cruel. Loud. Rude. Enjoys beating boys for no reason at all. Hope he goes to Hell...*

## Forty-seven

A terrible drought had afflicted the kingdom in which Nasrudin was travelling. In every village the livestock had perished, and the inhabitants were in a worse state than in the village before. Nasrudin's water reserves were almost gone. His flask barely contained enough to get through another day.

At dusk he came upon a traveller, weary from thirst and close to death.

'I was a fool,' the stranger whispered, almost too parched to speak. 'A day's walk east from here is a spring of fresh water in the grounds of a deserted palace. I should have filled my water bottles there.'

Nasrudin thanked the traveller for the information. Then, before lying down on his sleeping mat, he opened his flask and washed his face. At the sight of so much precious water being wasted, the traveller let out a last gasp.

'What a silly man,' Nasrudin thought to himself, 'how did he imagine I could set out for a palace without washing myself first?!'

# TRAVELS WITH NASRUDIN

I'm certain I reflect on my childhood more than most people.

The reason is that, the way I see it, the childhood years are a magical realm of delight – or at least they should be. A testing zone for ideas, emotions, sentiments, and all kinds of other interrelated components, they allow us to knead a lump of dough before it's baked into bread.

I believe we are born into the world with a default psychological setting, one that prepares us in the most perfect way for life. The problem is that Occidental society has reprogrammed itself to phase out the genius of our original calibration.

Through a decade or more of so-called 'education', children sit in class and are taught how to understand the society they'll inherit. However well-meaning, I believe the educational system doesn't prepare kids – because it's going about it in the wrong way.

When Ariane and Timur were young I fretted a great deal, anxious for them to evade reprogramming, and maintain the default setting of imagination with which they were born.

One evening, as I got them ready for bed, they asked me for a story. In my restless state, I remembered one my father used to tell us – a tale called 'When the Waters Were Changed'.

When they were in their pyjamas and tucked into bed, I told them the story.

This is how it goes...

There was once a land where the water was very sweet, and where everyone was very happy. The trees were tall, the flowers scented, and the mountain landscapes pristine.

One day, a man who lived in a remote valley had a dream. Through it, he learned that in the coming weeks the waters of the region would change overnight. The sweet water everyone knew and loved would be swapped for new water. It would look the same and taste the same, but the new water would change the way people would think.

Through his dream the man came to understand that he had to channel the existing water into a reservoir, and drink only from that supply. Without any other instructions, he did as he was bid to do by his dream. Accordingly, he filled a reservoir and made sure he only drank its water. Then, running through the kingdom, he warned others of the impending catastrophe, begging them to do as he had done.

A little time passed. Then, just as the voice in the dream had described, the waters of the kingdom were magically changed.

The old water was replaced by new water.

Instantly, the new water caused the people to think

in a different way. To the man who was drinking the old water – and who kept thinking the 'old' way – it was a terrible thing. He found the new thinking was at odds with everything he believed to be right. Everyone thought in the new way because of course, they were all drinking the new water – all except for him.

As the months passed, the people began to regard the man from the remote valley as insane. They couldn't understand it, but they knew he was strange and they were right. This conclusion was reached because there were more of them than there were of him.

More time passed, and the man who was drinking from his reservoir of old water found himself becoming more and more isolated. The people up on the plateau began to shun him when he ventured there. They grew increasingly bitter, asserting he was sick or mad, or both.

One day, the man could stand it no more.

He went over to the reservoir of old water he'd kept in secrecy, and drained every last drop. Then, anxiously, he moved up to the plateau and lived among the people there – drinking the new water just like they all did.

At first, they continued to shun him.

But with time, they saw he was quite sane. After that, they'd say to each other that the man had gone mad for a time but had eventually reverted to normality again thanks to the power of prayer.

### Forty-eight

asrudin suffered from delusions of grandeur. However hard he tried, he couldn't help himself.

As a child, he imagined ruling over the village where he lived.

Then, as a young man, he imagined being a provincial governor.

A few years later, he saw himself as a king.

Lying on his deathbed, he witnessed a vision of himself outstretched and feeble as he was, wearing the regalia and crown of an emperor.

'Damn you!' he wheezed with the last strains of life. 'Why did you wait until now to promote me to such high office?!'

TAHIRLAND, 1992

The idea of having my own country first came to me during a geography class at prep school.

As an excruciatingly dull lesson was getting under way, I happened to notice a curious paragraph in the textbook. It read:

'Between Egypt and the Sudan there lies a land known as Bir Tawil. It is an example of a *Terra Nullius* – a land unclaimed by any nation. Approximately 800 square miles in area, it was created in 1902 by border discrepancies between Egypt and the Sudan.'

Inspired by the thought of a realm in need of a ruler, I allowed my imagination to take over. Before I knew it, I was standing in a glorious valley, with luxuriant undergrowth all around. Although there were no buildings, there was a chair – or rather a throne. A golden throne adorned with peacock feathers and gems, and inscribed with the words:

'HERE SITS KING TAHIR'

Years passed...

From time to time the notion of *Terra Nullius*, and the unwanted realm of Bir Tawil, slipped into my mind. Turning it over for a few moments, I'd examine it, delight in it, and allow it to escape back into the ether.

As so often happens in life, an opportunity presented itself.

I had travelled down to Abu Simbel by boat, arriving there at the end of the holy month of Ramadan. A wealthy local businessman I'd met on the voyage invited me to stay at his splendid home. Named Youssef, he was one of the most generous people I've ever had the privilege to know.

After much celebration and feasting with his family,

he took me on a tour of the monuments – dating back to the reign of Pharaoh Ramesses II. Awe-struck, I enthused at length on and on about how spectacular they were, and how the journey south had been worth it.

'How I wish I'd been born a pharaoh!' I exclaimed, as we made our way back to the village of Abu Simbel. 'I've always secretly yearned to be a king.'

Youssef scratched a nail to his cheek.

'Every dream can come true,' he replied.

'Most dreams,' I said. 'But not me becoming a king of my own country.'

'Some dreams are far easier to realize than you would imagine,' Youssef replied cryptically.

Next morning, I woke early, and wondered how best to return to Cairo. The flight was expensive, but it replaced the need for many days of travel by boat and train.

'I'm going to check the price of flights,' I said at breakfast.

Youssef held out a hand, urging me to stop.

'If you will allow me, I want to give you something.'

'You've given me far too much already,' I replied. 'I can't accept anything more.'

'Not even if I were to crown you "King of Tahirland"?'

I balked, then sighed.

'Well, that's one thing I suppose I could accept,' I said with a smile, remembering the previous day's conversation.

For two days, Youssef hustled and bustled making preparations. I wasn't quite sure what was going on. Whenever I asked a question, he would urge me to put my feet up and conserve my strength.

I noticed a pair of Land Cruisers being made ready at the side of the house, and masses of extra fuel, engine oil, and spare wheels. A substantial amount of food was prepared as well, in addition to reserves of drinking water.

At dusk on the second day, Youssef came to the room where I was taking an extra-long siesta.

'The team is ready. We leave at dawn!' he said.

'Where to?'

'To Tahirland!'

A ramshackle vessel bearing what looked like Russian markings ferried the Land Cruisers across the Nile.

The captain was rewarded with a wad of Egyptian pounds once both Land Cruisers were safely across, and promised the same amount again if he returned the next day.

Driving fast along rutted tracks for many hours, we found ourselves on a desert panorama as desiccated as any on Earth.

The vehicles were aimed at the horizon, their wheels churning up a storm of gravel and dust. As we tore ahead at full speed, I got a flash of the fantasy I'd first conjured back in my prep school's geography class. My imaginary kingdom of Bir Tawil had been tropical, awash with exotic plants and colourful birds.

The reality couldn't have been more different.

There wasn't a single creature, or even a single tree. It was as if the landscape was in lockdown, desperately waiting for a few precious drops of rain.

Youssef rode with me in the lead vehicle, Arab disco music blaring out through the speakers. Like the volume, the air conditioning was turned up high – chilling me to the bone. The thickness of a sheet of glass away, the temperature had reached forty-three degrees.

Late in the afternoon the driver jabbed a hand at the map.

'This is it,' Youssef announced. 'Your kingdom!'

'Dry, isn't it?' I replied uneasily.

'You'll need to irrigate.'

'It'll be a challenge.'

'A life without challenges is no life at all,' Youssef said.

The Land Cruisers were parked twenty feet from one another, and a canopy was unfurled between the two. While we took refuge in the ice-cool chill of the air conditioning, the team got the makeshift caravanserai ready with faultless efficiency – leading me to wonder whether this was the first time their boss had brought a would-be king to Bir Tawil.

Once the camp was ready, a signal was given, and we stepped out into the furnace-like heat.

Youssef invited me to sit in the Bedouin-style tent that had been erected at the side of the vehicles, the half-dozen staff busying themselves behind the tent.

In shock from transitioning between ice and fire, my body churned out a gallon and a half of sweat.

'This caravanserai will be your capital,' Youssef said grandly. 'Out there we will build pleasure gardens and a palace.'

'And a stadium,' I replied cheerily. 'I've always wanted a stadium.'

'So it will be.'

'And…' I said, wincing at my greed, 'I'd rather like a library – you know, a huge one, with every known book in the world.'

'It has been noted,' Youssef responded.

As the two of us reclined, I fantasized having a jinn at my disposal to materialize any whim.

Tea was served and, when we were refreshed, one of the support staff slunk forward and whispered in his master's ear.

'Excellent!' Youssef cried.

'What is?'

'We are ready.'

'Ready for...?'

Before I could complete the sentence, a pair of staff paced in subserviently with a plastic garden-chair-throne. It wasn't gold, encrusted with gems, festooned with peacock feathers, or as lavish as some thrones I've seen, but it was certainly the best throne in all Bir Tawil.

Another pair stepped forward bearing the regalia of supreme office.

The first held up a Bedouin robe for me to wear over my shoulders.

The second stood to attention, a cushion in his hands, a home-made crown on the cushion.

Youssef the kingmaker asked me to stand, and invited me to take my place on the ancestral throne. When I had done so, he stepped forward, took the crown from the attendant, and said:

'With this sacred coronet, I crown you, Tahir, king of Tahirland, to rule this great land as you see fit.'

Once the headdress was lowered into place, the staff whooped with joy, and Youssef kissed my hand.

'Your wish has come true!' he beamed. 'You're the king of your own country!'

For a few moments I sat there on my throne in silence, my mind whirring away as it came to terms with the responsibilities and tribulations of state.

There was so much to do.

Roads and schools had to be built, and public buildings – libraries, a stadium, and a palace. The legal system had to be laid out from scratch, as well as a constitution, a parliament, not to mention mass irrigation.

As I sat there, the crown weighing heavy on my head, I tasted bile on my tongue.

'Not sure I am ready to be king,' I mumbled in a faint voice. 'Don't get me wrong... I'm honoured to have my own country, and such a fine one as this. But it's quite a big undertaking.'

Kneeling, Youssef the kingmaker ducked his head in allegiance.

'Your Majesty,' he uttered tenderly, 'I would suggest you always remember something.'

'What?' I asked, peering down from my throne.

'To be wary of what you wish for,' he said.

### Forty-nine

One fine morning, Nasrudin was standing in the street wishing he had some new clothes, when a lovely white linen shirt blew down from a neighbour's washing line. Thinking it was a gift from the Almighty, the wise fool gave thanks, and quickly put it on.

In the afternoon of the same day, Nasrudin was loitering on a street corner reminiscing about the fun he'd had as a child with his cat. As he often did, he turned his hands upward in prayer, thanking Providence for the memory.

By chance, a fine tabby cat was at that moment prowling on a window ledge above. Losing its footing, the creature fell into Nasrudin's cupped hands. Catching it, he whooped with joy and rushed home to show the cat and the shirt to his wife.

Along the way, he needed to answer the call of nature. So, stepping behind a palm tree to relieve himself, he attended to his business.

As he stood there, the cat purring under his arm, a coconut fell from the tree and struck him hard on the head.

Stunned for a moment, he got to his feet, calmed the cat, and exclaimed:

'O Great Creator, your benefaction knows no bounds! You'd impressed me with the shirt and the cat, but now you're way ahead of me. I didn't even know I wanted a delicious fruit such as this!'

# TRAVELS WITH NASRUDIN

With my encounter with Marjorie of Alice Springs still very much in my mind, I climbed aboard the Ghan when it next rolled through town.

My one regret was not having been able to track down Outback Franc, the farmer-turned-English-teacher I'd known in Tokyo so many years before.

As the train rumbled heavily against the tracks, the awe-inspiring rust-red landscape of Australia passing me by, I found myself wondering what the purpose of it all could be. In my reflective state I felt blessed, confused, happy and sad, all at once.

Thoughts turning to my wise fool friend, I pondered how he had become me, just as I had become him.

Through thirty years of zigzag travels, our lives and characters had meshed together as though by some inexplicable alchemy.

By the time the Ghan deposited me at Adelaide I was melancholic, longing to know more about Marjorie and her family, just as I wished I could have found Franc.

I hadn't made a hotel reservation while on the train as the internet reception had been non-existent. So, on reaching Adelaide, I sat down on a bench at the station, and searched for a place to stay on my phone.

I was about to enter my credit card details, when I heard a voice.

A voice speaking my name.

Turning my head, I found myself looking at my bearded old friend, Outback Franc.

'G'day!' he blurted, grabbing me in a hug.

'How d'you know I'd be here?'

'Got yer message and thought you'd be on this one.'

'What if I wasn't?'

'I'd 'ave met the one next week.'

Franc hugged me again with the embrace of a man who craved nostalgia. I know, because I shared his yearning for the past.

'Dragging you to a posh dinner tonight,' Franc said. 'Don't even try and get out of it.'

'So long as it's not connected to my online entries,' I replied.

'They're nuts about Google in Alice, aren't they?!' Franc cackled as though speaking from first-hand experience.

'What's the dinner in honour of?'

'Tradition.'

'I love tradition,' I said.

'Yeah, well these are *new* traditions.'

'Huh?'

'I'm with the T.E.C.'

'T.E.C.?'

'Yeah.'

'What's that?'

'The Tradition Establishment Committee.'

'What does it do?'

'You'll see,' said Franc.


That evening, Outback Franc and I arrived at a fine colonial mansion on the edge of the city, both of us dressed up to the nines.

'It'll be Adelaide royalty,' Franc mumbled as we went up the stairs and into the building. 'Give 'em plenty of that Pom accent, they'll like that.'

'Think I could do with a bit more of a briefing,' I replied. 'Still not quite clear what T.E.C. does.'

'Told ya... we establish traditions.'

'But that doesn't make sense. The whole thing about traditions is that they just happen, you know with time... like the flavour in a chunk of tasty French cheese.'

'Yeah, well it doesn't work like that here in Adelaide,' said Franc.

Stepping into the packed salon, which was heaving with the cocktail set, we did our best to appear as though we were having a good time.

A recurring nightmare I've had since childhood hit me – arriving at a party in which I don't know anyone at all. The anxiety has somehow become attached to a secondary sense of trauma – the fear of not being picked for a team while at prep school.

Back then, I'd always be the last one to be chosen. They'd only take me if they could have Billings – the boy who excelled at everything.

'Let's mingle,' Franc blurted, handing me a flute of sparkling wine.

'I'm not much of a mingler,' I replied. 'Prefer to stand in one spot and let the party revolve around me, like planets orbiting stars.'

'They don't orbit in Adelaide,' growled Franc.

'Maybe we could start it... you know, like a new tradition,' I answered brightly.

'They don't do that kind of new tradition.'

'So what new traditions have they embraced?'

'Horseshoe hurling, thimble juggling... you know, that sort of thing.'

'Not sure I get you.'

'Just suck down the champers and smile as though you're having fun.'

So, I glugged the sparkling wine and forced a constipated grin.

Every so often, a member of Adelaide's gentry would bluster up to Franc, shake his hand, mutter congratulations, and swagger away.

'They all seem to like what you're doing,' I said.

'That's 'cos I've broken the records.'

'Huh?'

'Started more traditions in the last eighteen months than in the last fifty years!'

'That's great.'

'Yeah, well it's not the bed of roses it sounds like.'

'Why not?'

Draining his glass, Franc grabbed another from the waiter's tray.

'Jealousy,' he mumbled.

'Jealousy of what?'

'Jealousy of my imagination. I've got a knack at coming up with new traditions. Not sure how or why, but they just come to me – when I'm in the tub, or walking the dogs. I'm a natural.'

'Excellent,' I said.

'Yeah, well it would be if it wasn't for that bean-pole in blue over there.'

Looking towards the window, I spotted a suave man in a navy-blue suit. He looked as though he'd been stretched on a medieval torture rack.

'What's his problem?'

'Sabotage!'

'*Sabotage*...? In the ready-made tradition business?'

'Yup.'

'What kind of sabotage?'

'The kind aimed at making me a laughing stock.'

'Sounds like he wants to be the big chief.'

'Yeah, he does.'

'So why don't you trip him up... you know, sabotage him back?'

Franc swallowed hard.

'And lower myself to his level?'

'Don't see why not.'

'If I was found out, I'd be expelled from the Tradition Establishment Committee.'

Glancing around the room, I took in the throngs of phony faces, the fake laughter, and the way everyone seemed so ill at ease.

'I'm not sure that would be such a bad thing,' I said.

## Fifty

The harvest had failed again, and Nasudin's wife screamed at him as she'd done the previous year, and the year before that. Unfazed by the run of bad fortune, the wise fool strolled down to the teahouse in high spirits.

'Can't help noticing that you're remarkably happy,' said a friend.

'Oh, yes, that I am!'

'But I thought your crops had failed for the tenth year in a row.'

'Indeed they have!' exclaimed Nasrudin with glee.

'Then, how is it you could be so happy?
Anyone else would surely be suicidal by now.'

Turning to his friend, Nasrudin cracked his
knuckles.

'Well, having had my crops fail for ten years
in a row could mean only one thing.'

'That you're destitute?' the friend chipped in.

'No, no! Rather, that my fortune is about to
change!' roared Nasrudin.

ALGECIRAS, 2019

Three weeks ago I took Ariane and Timur to
Andalucía, and watched in sheer delight as they set
eyes on the Alhambra for the first time.

Both in their late teens now, they have inherited
my love of travel and stories, and my insatiable need
to unpick the details of the lands through which I
roam.

As they've grown up, and have been shaped
by experiences laid down layer upon layer, I've
marvelled at the freshness with which they regard
the world. Untainted by preconceptions and fears
that have shaped preceding generations, they begin a
new phase of their journey – a phase that I feel I have
myself completed.

Bidding farewell to Granada, we drove south to
the coast, and along the waterline until we reached

Algeciras. An hour early for the ferry across the Straits of Gibraltar to Morocco, I begged the kids to allow me a stroll down memory lane.

As I steered the car into the backstreets, the flat winter light seemed to yellow into a summer's day thirty-two years before. My mouth dried, and I sensed my pulse hasten, as I caught snatches of the familiar.

Having parked the car, we got out and made our way along a plush residential street, the buildings drenched in fresh white paint. Timur and Ariane must have wished we'd stopped for chocolate crêpes instead. They saw the very same details as me, but my eyes caught interwoven layers from another time.

Halfway along the street I made out the façade of a dear old friend – the glorious Hostal Magnífico. Unable to help myself, my mind's eye matched its current state to how I had known it in the days of the inimitable Doña Fernández.

My conclusion: not much change at all.

So we swanned up steps I'd first climbed in borrowed shoes and luggage-less, and found ourselves in the palace of kitsch once ruled over by the empress of low-budget hostels.

As soon as we were inside, I felt the ghosts of the French musicians robbed of their instruments, and the Dutch artist in painted-on boxer shorts.

And, for a fleeting moment, I saw María, her spectral form reclining on the threadbare couch.

An eager young receptionist blustered up, looked me up and down fast, and spat:

'*Sí*, señor?'

'We're not staying.'

'Oh.'

'You see, I'm on a journey down memory lane.'

'Oh.'

'D'you know what ever happened to Doña Fernández?'

'*Doña*?'

'*Fernández*... the proprietor. I imagine she's in hostel heaven by now. She was very old even then.'

'When?'

'Oh, gosh... let me think... it was early summer 1987.'

In a well-practised movement that no doubt impressed girls, the receptionist pulled a comb from his back pocket and slid it easily back through his quiff. He didn't reply, not in words. To a spring chicken like him, the 'eighties were ancient history taught in school.

So, with a prayer to past glory and the ghosts, we left.

Before going back to the car, I made a second pit-stop – at the building where Señor Chen had kept me alive with the house special.

A homeless man was sitting on a bench he'd jammed into the doorway.

Timur asked what I remembered of the place.

'I remember an especially fine conversation,' I said. 'And buying Señor Chen an equally fine set of German-made pots once my money finally came in.'

'Is that all?' Ariane asked.

'No,' I countered. 'There's something else.'

'What?'

'I remember being ready to take on the world,' I said.

'And did you?'

'Did I *what*?'

'Did you take on the world?'

Considering the question before answering, I replied:

'When I was young I used to feel no one would give me a chance. They kept people like me out at all costs. With time and experience, I learned how to work the system. None of that was especially important though.'

'What *was* important, Baba?' Timur asked.

Without even thinking, an answer offered itself:

'It's this: in your life there'll be times when you're up and times when you're down. The only certainty is that when you're riding high, you will be dragged down. And, likewise, when you're down, you'll get up again, so long as you remember the ultimate secret to life.'

'Which is?'

'To keep going at any cost.'

### Fifty-one

For fifty years, Nasrudin had hunted his nemesis, stalking him through teahouses and across deserts, along shorelines and even in and out of his own home.

Baffled at his arch-enemy's cunning, he'd made a careful study of his methods. And, tired of pursuing him, he had roamed the world in search of a quiet corner free from the wretched opponent.

Arriving in a new country, Nasrudin sat down in a modest *chaikana* and ordered mint tea. It wasn't long before one of the locals had engaged him in conversation, and asked the nature of his journey.

Glancing furtively from side to side, to check no one was listening, the wise fool answered:

'For half a century I've been followed by a terrible curse... a creature as cunning as any other, he always seems to know where I'll be.'

'How does he look?' the stranger asked, intrigued.

'He's always dressed in the same dark cape,' Nasrudin explained. 'Sometimes he's very short and at other times he's as tall as a house!'

'Have you ever tried to speak to him?' the man asked, sipping his tea.

'Yes, ten thousand times! I've tried to chase him, too. But when I do so he slips behind me until I run round in circles! All I can hope is that at last I've found a kingdom where I can escape him!'

The local sighed.

'Sounds as though you've suffered,' he said.

'Oh, yes, I have!'

'Well, it seems that fortune smiles on you.'

'*Really?*'

'Yes! You see, in this country we all have the very same dark nemesis.'

'Noooooo!' cried Nasrudin, hands clasped to his cheeks.

'Relax, my friend,' advised the local man calmly. 'There's nothing to worry about.'

'But why not?!'

'Because, we've learnt a secret way of coping.'

'Tell me! Tell me!' gasped the wise fool.

'Very well, but you have to do exactly as I say.'

'I promise!'

'It's quite simple really,' the local said. 'All you do is ignore him.'

Nasrudin's face was masked in terror.

'If I do that he'll devour me!'

The local stretched back on the sofa.

'Don't be so sure,' he said.


TANGIER, 2019

An hour and a half after leaving Hostal Magnífico, we were on the ferry traversing a short stretch of water and a vast chasm of cultural divide.

Standing on the deck, I got a flash of myself tossing my wooden clogs over the handrail, my name carved into them both.

'They may get washed up in China,' my father had noted.

'So should we go there?'

'Where?'

'To China?'

'What for?'

'To wait for them,' I'd said.

The muffled wail of the muezzin's call reached us before Tangier's medieval skyline was in focus, a pall of ink-black storm-clouds ominous and low.

Once we'd navigated through the ritual of

Moroccan customs, we drove out of town in search of the highway to Casablanca.

'Can't wait to see Zohra,' Timur said.

'Can't wait to swim in the ocean,' Ariane said.

'Can't leave Tangier yet,' I said.

Whipping the car round in a U-turn, I steered back to the port. Parking down at the boardwalk, I thanked the kids for their understanding.

'One day you'll have memory lanes of your own,' I whispered.

We turned left, walked up the steep hill that was the narrow rue de la Plage, and stopped at a metal door.

'This is it. Villa Calpe.'

'Where your grandfather lived?' asked Ariane.

'Yes, and where he died.' I pointed to the ground under our feet. 'Just here... struck by a reversing Coca-Cola truck fifty years ago.'

As the words left my mouth, something happened. A kind of alchemical reaction felt by no one except me. Noticing my forehead beading with sweat, Timur asked if I was feeling all right.

'It's ended,' I said. 'Just now. Ended as unexpectedly as it began.'

'What's ended, Baba?'

'The quest I began thirty years ago.'

'What quest?'

'The quest for Nasrudin.'

Unbuckling my canvas bag, I pulled out my journal.

Over the span of three decades I'd had dozens of similar notebooks – filled with scribbled comments taken down as I traipsed through jungles and over deserts, across mountain ranges, and from one city to the next.

Each time I bought a new journal, I transferred something from the old to the new without a passing thought. So familiar, I only ever noticed when it wasn't there.

Opening out my journal, I flicked through pages of random notes and observations until I reached it.

The tarot card… The Fool.

'What's that?' Timur probed.

'Something precious given to me by someone who'd been instructed to do so by my grandfather.'

'Is it Nasrudin, Baba?' Ariane asked.

'Yes it is… and it's so much more. You see, it's part of a chain of transmission that links me to you, and us to all those who came before us.'

'Who?' Timur asked.

'Admirers of wisdom and foolishness,' I said. 'The disciples of Nasrudin. But, as we stand here in this special spot where my grandfather drew his last breath, it's something else.'

'What, Baba?' Timur asked softly.

'It's the end of my journey and the beginning of yours,' I said.

Reaching out, I handed him the well-worn card...

The wise fool, Nasrudin.

### Fifty-two

Finding a crust of stale old bread on the ground, a beggar thanked his good fortune, dusted it off and put it to his lips. But even for a man as downcast and starving as he, the morsel was unappealing – for it was rock hard and covered in mould.

Glancing over his shoulder, the beggar noticed an expensive-looking restaurant, offering all kinds of culinary delights. The crust in hand, he slipped in through a side door and made his way to the kitchen.

The place was a hive of frantic activity as it was lunchtime – the head chef barking orders to his subservient team, all of whom were rushing about preparing the most sumptuous dishes the beggar had ever seen.

Amid the chaos no one seemed to notice the destitute soul pacing over to the stove, and waving his crust back and forth in the steam boiling off a pot filled with a rich sauce.

Within a minute or two, the dry crust had been transformed through a kind of alchemy into a tasty delight.

Just as the beggar was about to put it to his lips once again, a claw-like hand grabbed the bread, and another hand grabbed him.

'How dare you steal from my kitchen!' roared the head chef. 'You must pay for what you have stolen!'

The beggar explained he had merely been taking advantage of a little flavoured steam for his crust of third-rate bread.

Enraged, the chef dragged the beggar to the courthouse, along with the bread, which was the evidence.

As it was a quiet day, they were taken at once before the judge.

It just so happened the magistrate was none other than Nasrudin, who was standing in for a friend. He listened as the chef detailed how the beggar had been caught stealing vapour, and how he needed payment.

'As I understand it,' said Nasrudin, 'you're demanding to be paid for the smell of your sauce, rather than the taste.'

Even more irate than before, the chef nodded.

'Yes, that's right.'

'Very well,' declared the wise fool, 'I shall pay you myself, as the poor defendant has no funds of his own.'

Grinning with pleasure, the chef reached out to receive what was due to him. As he did so, Nasrudin took three coins from his pocket, jingled them on his palm, and put them away again.

'There you are,' he said. 'The sound of money in return for the smell of sauce.'


CASABLANCA, 2004, 2019

Fifteen years ago I scribbled a few questions relating to Nasrudin in a notepad.

Last week, while rooting through a file devoted to the wise fool, I happened upon it. Having read my questions through once, I read them again.

As my mind made sense of the words written long before in my own hand, I marvelled in absolute wonder.

In the very same file as my questions was the photocopy of a short, typed document. The text must have made its way into the file more than twenty years ago. Written by my father, it had formed part of his masterwork *The Sufis*, and provided answers to each of my questions:

*Question*: Who was Nasrudin?

*Answer*: Nobody really knows who Nasrudin was, where he lived, or when. This is truly in character, for the whole intention is to provide a figure who cannot really be characterised, and who is timeless. It is the message, not the man, which is important to the Sufis. This has not prevented people from providing him with a spurious history, and even a tomb. Scholars, against whose pedantry in his stories Nasrudin frequently emerges triumphant, have even tried to take the stories featuring him to pieces in the hope of finding appropriate biographical material. One of their 'discoveries' would have warmed the heart of Nasrudin himself. Nasrudin said that he considered himself upside down in this world, argues one scholar, and from this he infers that the supposed date of Nasrudin's death, on his 'tombstone', should be read not as 386, but 683. Another professor feels that the Arabic numerals used would, if truly reversed, look more like the figures 274. He gravely records that a dervish to whom he appealed for aid in this '...merely said, "Why not drop a spider in some ink and see what marks he makes in crawling out of it. This should give the correct date or show something."'

In fact, 386 means 300 + 80 + 6. Transposed into Arabic letters, this decodes as SH, W, F, which spells the word ShaWaF: 'to cause someone to see; to show a thing'. The dervish's spider would 'show' something, as he himself said.

*Question*: What's the function of Nasrudin and his stories?

*Answer*: Nasrudin is the classical figure devised by the dervishes partly for the purpose of halting for a moment situations in which certain states of mind are made clear. The Nasrudin stories, known throughout the Middle East, constitute one of the strangest achievements in the history of metaphysics. Superficially, most of the Nasrudin stories may be used as jokes. They are told and retold endlessly in the teahouses and the caravanserais, in the homes and on the radio waves, of Asia. But it is inherent in the Nasrudin story that it may be understood at any one of many depths. There is the joke, the moral – and the little extra which brings the consciousness of the potential mystic a little further on the way to realisation.

Since Sufism is something which is lived as well as something which is perceived, a Nasrudin tale cannot in itself produce complete enlightenment. On the other hand, it bridges the gap between mundane life and a transmutation of consciousness in a manner which no other literary form yet produced has been able to attain.

*The Subtleties of Nasrudin* manuscript has never been presented in full to a Western audience, probably because the stories cannot properly be translated by a non-Sufi, or even be studied out of context, and retain the essential impact. Even in the East the collection is used for study purposes only by initiate Sufis. Individual 'jokes' from the collection have found their way into almost every literature in the world, and a certain amount of scholastic attention has been given them on this account – as an example of culture drift, or to support arguments in favour of the basic identity of humour everywhere. But if because of their perennial humorous appeal the stories have proved their survival power, this is entirely secondary to the intention of the corpus, which is to provide a basis for making available the Sufi attitude toward life, and for making possible the attainment of Sufic realisation and mystical experience.

*Question*: How is Nasrudin perceived by Sufis?

*Answer*: In the development of the human mind, there is a constant change and limit to the usefulness of any particular technique. This characteristic of Sufi practice is ignored in repetitious systems, which condition the mind and create an atmosphere of attainment or nearness to attainment, without actually producing it. Nasrudin figures as the character in a story which seeks to make this clear:

The Mulla nearly fell into a pool of water. A passer-by saved him in the nick of time. Every time they met in future, the man reminded Nasrudin about how he had prevented him from getting wet.

Ultimately, unable to stand it any longer, the Mulla took his friend to the pool, jumped in as far as the neck, and shouted: '*Now* I am as wet as I would have been if I had never met you! Will you leave me alone?'

*Question*: What is the role of Fear and Humour in Nasrudin stories?

*Answer*: Another joke, found also in Cervantes (*Don Quixote*, Ch. 5), remains a joke although the technical term 'fear' is merely translated and not explained:

'I shall have you hanged,' said a cruel and ignorant king to Nasrudin, 'if you do not prove that you have deep perceptions such as have been attributed to you.' Nasrudin at once said that he could see a golden bird in the sky and demons within the earth. 'But how can you do this?' the King asked. 'Fear,' said the Mulla, 'is all you need.'

'Fear', in the Sufi vocabulary, is the activation

of conscience whose exercises can produce extrasensory perception. This is an area in which the formal intellect is not used, and other faculties of the mind are called into play.

Yet Nasrudin, in a manner wholly unique, manages to use the very fabric of intellectuality for his own purposes. An echo of this deliberate intent is found in the *Legend of Nasrudin*, where it is recounted that Hussein, the founder of the system, snatched his messenger-designate Nasrudin from the very clutches of the 'Old Villain' – the crude system of thought in which almost all of us live.

'Hussein' is associated in Arabic with the concept of virtue. 'Hussein' means 'strong, difficult of access'.

When Hussein had searched the whole world for the teacher who was to carry his message through the generations, he was almost at the point of despair when he heard a commotion. The Old Villain was upbraiding one of his students for telling jokes. 'Nasrudin!' thundered the Villain, 'for your irreverent attitude I condemn you to universal ridicule. Henceforth, when one of your absurd stories is told, six more will have to be heard in succession, until you are clearly seen to be a figure of fun.'

It is believed that the mystical effect of seven Nasrudin tales, studied in succession, is enough to prepare an individual for enlightenment.

*Question*: Were there traces of Nasrudin in Rumi's work?

*Answer*: Rumi tells a story which resembles Nasrudin's tale of the egg, but emphasises another significant factor. A king's son had been placed in the hands of mystical teachers who reported that they now could not teach him any more. In order to test him, the King asked him what he had in his hand. 'It is round, metallic and yellow – it must be a sieve,' the boy replied. Sufism insists upon a balanced development of inner perceptions and ordinary human conduct and usage.

The assumption that just because one is alive, one is perceptive, is denied by Sufism, as we have already seen. A man may be clinically alive, but perceptively dead. Logic and philosophy will not help him in attaining perception. One aspect of the following story illustrates this:

The Mulla was thinking aloud.

'How do I know whether I am dead or alive?'

'Don't be such a fool,' his wife said; 'if you were dead your limbs would be cold.'

Shortly afterward Nasrudin was in the forest cutting wood. It was midwinter. Suddenly he realised that his hands and feet were cold.

'I am undoubtedly dead,' he thought; 'so I must stop working, because corpses do not work.'

And, because corpses do not walk about, he lay down on the grass.

Soon a pack of wolves appeared and started to attack Nasrudin's donkey, which was tethered to a tree.

'Yes, carry on, take advantage of a dead man,' said Nasrudin from his prone position; 'but if I had been alive I would not have allowed you to take liberties with my donkey.'

*Question*: What's the relation between Nasrudin stories in the context of time and space?

*Answer*: Sufism, since it is the attunement with true reality, cannot be made closely to resemble what we take to be reality, but which is a really more primitive short-term rule of thumb. For example, we tend to look at events one-sidedly. We also assume, without any justification, that an event happens as it were in a vacuum. In actual fact, all events are associated with all other events. It is only when we are ready to experience our interrelation with the organism of life that we can appreciate mystical experience. If you look at any action which you do, or which anyone else does, you will find that it was prompted by one of many possible stimuli; and also that it is never an isolated action – it has consequences, many of them ones which you would

413

never expect, certainly which you could not have planned.

Nasrudin enables the Sufi Seeker to understand that the formal ideas current about time and space are not necessarily those which obtain in the wider field of true reality. People who believe, for instance, that they are being rewarded for past actions and may be rewarded in future for future doings, cannot be Sufis. The Sufi time conception is an interrelation – a continuum.

The classic story of the Turkish bath caricatures it in a manner which enables something of the idea to be grasped:

Nasrudin visited a Turkish bath. Because he was dressed in rags, he was cavalierly treated by the attendants, who gave him an old towel and a scrap of soap. When he left, he handed the amazed bath men a gold coin. The next day he appeared again, magnificently attired, and was naturally given the best possible attention and deference.

When the bath was over, he presented the bath keepers with the smallest copper coin available.

'This,' he said, 'was for the attendance *last* time. The gold coin was for your treatment of me *this* time.'

*Question*: How are Nasrudin stories related to understanding Sufi thought?

*Answer*: Money is looked upon by the Sufis as an

active factor in the relationship between people, and between people and their environment. Since the ordinary perception of reality is shortsighted, it is not surprising that the normal human use of money is equally limited in perspective. The joke about the frogs in the Nasrudin collection explains something of this flavour:

A passer-by saw Nasrudin throwing money into a pool, and asked him why he was doing it.

'I was on my donkey. He had slipped and was slithering down the side of this pool, about to overbalance and fall. There seemed no hope that either of us would survive a serious fall. Suddenly the frogs in the water began to croak. This frightened the donkey. He reared up and by this means he was able to save himself.

'Should the frogs not benefit from having saved our lives?'

Whereas on the ordinary plane this joke is taken to show Nasrudin as a fool, the deeper meanings are direct reflections of Sufi financial attitudes. The frogs represent people, who cannot use money. Nasrudin rewards them because of the general rule that a reward follows a good action. That the croaking of the frogs was accidental, seemingly, is another factor to ponder. In one respect, at least, the frogs were less blameworthy than ordinary people would be. They probably did not think that they were capable of using money, correctly or otherwise. This story is also used in the sense of 'casting pearls before swine', in answer to a questioner who asked a Sufi why he did not make his knowledge and wisdom available to all and sundry, and especially to people who (like the frogs) had showed him kindness and what they thought to be understanding.

In order to understand the wider aspects of Sufi thought, and before progress can be made along lines outside the web cast over humanity by the Old Villain, the dimensions provided by Nasrudin must be visited. If Nasrudin is like a Chinese box, with compartment within compartment, at least he offers numerous simple points of entry into a new way of thinking. To be familiar with the experience of Nasrudin is to be able to unlock many doors in the more baffling texts and practices of the Sufis.

As one's perceptions increase, so does the power of extracting nutrition from the Nasrudin tales. They provide for the beginner what the Sufis call a 'blow' – calculated impact which operates in a special way, preparing the mind for the Sufi undertaking.

Looked upon as nutrition, the Nasrudin blow is called a coconut. This term is derived from a Sufi statement: 'A monkey threw a coconut from a treetop at a hungry Sufi, and it hit him on the leg. He picked it up; drank the milk; ate the flesh; made a bowl from the shell.'

In one sense, they fulfil the function of the literal blow which occurs in one of the most terse of the Mulla tales:

Nasrudin handed a boy a pitcher, told him to fetch water from a well, and gave him a clout on the ear. 'And mind you don't drop it!' he shouted.

An onlooker said, 'How can you strike someone who has done nothing wrong?'

'I suppose,' said Nasrudin, 'that you would prefer me to strike him *after* he has broken the pitcher, when the pitcher and water are both lost? In my way the boy remembers, and the pot and contents are also saved.'

Since Sufism is a comprehensive work, it is not only the Seeker who must learn, like the boy. The work, like the pitcher and the water, has its own rules, outside the mundane methods of arts and sciences.

Nobody can set off on the Sufi path unless he has the potentiality for it. If he tries to do so, the possibilities of error are too great for him to have a chance of bringing back the water without breaking the pot.

Sometimes Nasrudin stories are arranged in the form of aphorisms, of which the following are examples:

It is not in fact so.

Truth is something which I never speak.

I do not answer *all* the questions; only those which the know-alls secretly ask themselves.

If your donkey allows someone to steal your coat – steal his saddle.

A sample is a sample. Yet nobody would buy my house when I showed them a brick from it.

People clamour to taste my vintage vinegar. But it would not be forty years old if I let them, would it?

To save money, I made my donkey go without food. Unfortunately the experiment was interrupted by its death. It died before it got used to having no food at all.

People sell talking parrots for huge sums. They never pause to compare the possible value of a *thinking* parrot.

Finding my questions again as I did last week, together with the answers in my father's typewritten manuscript, reminded me of something important.

Much of the time we bluster through life searching for answers to questions. In assuming the answers can only be hunted down on a journey through a distant realm, we forget that often the answers we require are ready and waiting within arm's reach beside us.

Information we have known our entire lives is invisible to us because we are not sufficiently prepared to recognize it as the key we're searching for.

Over the years since my father's death, I have lost count of the number of times I opened a book or a file and found a scrap of paper that answered a precise question I was preoccupied with right then.

At first, I used to think it was a kind of magic – my father sending me signals from beyond the grave.

But as time has passed I've come to understand that, although magical, the process takes place as it does not because of my father's ability to read my thoughts – but because I am sufficiently ready to receive the material he left behind.

*FINIS*

# GLOSSARY

**Achiote**
Tropical seed crushed by the tribes of the Upper Amazon, and used as a ceremonial face paint.

**Arau**
So-called 'Field of Reeds', the realm in Ancient Egyptian society to which the souls of mortals journey after death.

**Ayahuasca**
Powerful hallucinogen found in the Peruvian Amazon made from the lining of the caapi liana. Also known as 'The Vine of the Dead'.

**Bazaari**
Someone who works in a bazaar.

**Cantonment**
Military area, particularly in a former British colony, where military staff work and live.

**Chaikana**
Teahouse in Afghanistan, or elsewhere in Central Asia.

**Chitrali**
Being from the town of Chitral, in the northern mountains of Pakistan.

**Chonta**
Wood of an Amazonian palm, used for making nails with which to bind tree trunks together when making rafts.

**Chooha**
Hindi word for 'rat'.

**Durian**
Large fibrous fruit found especially in tropical regions of the Far East, known for its potent smell.

**Field of Reeds**
See *Arau*.

**Ghan**
Nickname for the camel caravans that once criss-crossed the Australian Outback. Now the name for the train running north–south from Darwin to Adelaide.

**Hodja**
Turkish appellation for Nasrudin.

**Jelaba**
Long, flowing robe worn in Morocco.

**Joha**
Moroccan appellation for Nasrudin.

**Kajar**
Dynasty that ruled Persia from 1794 until 1925. Relating to the artistic style prominent during that time.

**Kashikoi-bakka**
Wise fool found in the culture of the Ainu people of Japan.

**Kurta**
Loose cotton shirt worn in India.

**La Vache Qui Rit**
Popular brand of French processed cheese packaged in miniature triangles.

**Mapacho**
Black tobacco smoked in the Peruvian jungle.

**Masato**
Alcoholic beverage served in the Upper Amazon, made from masticated manioc.

## Mellah
Area of a medina in Morocco, traditionally reserved for the Jewish population.

## Melungeons
People of mixed-race ancestry from the south of the United States.

## Momo
Tibetan dumpling, often made with yak meat.

## Muezzin
Person who recites the call to prayer in Islam.

## Mulla
Person learned in the intricacies of Islamic teaching.

## Mutton do pyaza
Literally 'mutton two onions', refers to a concoction that fulfils a need at hand.

## Nauruz
Afghan New Year, celebrated on 21st March each year.

## Paan
Chewed stimulant popular in the Indian subcontinent, made from a folded betel leaf, containing a variety of chopped ingredients.

**Paratha**
Fried flat bread of the Indian subcontinent, often stuffed with cooked vegetables or meat.

**Parsi**
Community that fled Persia with the arrival of Islam, dedicated to following the Zoroastrian faith.

**Peccary**
Pig-like mammal found in the Upper Amazon, and regarded as a prized food.

**Puja**
Religious ceremony, particularly one occurring in the Hindu faith.

**Pundit**
Religious scholar overseeing a Hindu ceremony.

**Riad**
Literally 'garden', the word has come to represent a traditional courtyard home, especially those found in Morocco's old cities.

**Rouss**
Afghan appellation for the Russian invaders during the Soviet occupation of Afghanistan.

**Salwar**
Baggy cotton trousers held up with a drawstring, worn in Pakistan and India.

**Santería**
Faith found through parts of the Americas, revering deities linked to African gods, brought to the New World during centuries of slavery.

**Sasquatch**
Otherwise known as 'Bigfoot', a mysterious ape-like creature said by some to hide in the mountain forests of North America.

**Sehur**
Moroccan word for 'magician'.

**Shuar**
Name of a tribe native to the Upper Amazon, formerly regarded as notable for their tradition of shrinking the heads of their enemies so as to tame their avenging souls.

**Thuggee**
Cult of stranglers that killed hundreds of thousands of travellers until they were suppressed by the British Raj.

**Tripoint**
Border at which three countries meet.

**Vine of the Dead**
See *Ayahuasca*.

**Walla-walla**
Australian term for an unpleasant medical condition associated with subcutaneous bleeding.

**Weiss beer**
White beer popular in Germany and its former colonies.

**Yakuza**
Japanese mafia, known for their intricate tattoos.

**Yezidi**
So-called 'People of the Peacock Angel', a Kurdish sect once wrongly thought to be associated with Lucifer, native to northern Iraq, Syria, Armenia and the surrounding region.

**Zeligier**
Expert in the craft of making hand-cut Moroccan mosaics.

*Recommended Reading*

The following titles by my father are available in standard and limited editions, published by The Idries Shah Foundation.

By Idries Shah:

*The Exploits of the Incomparable Mulla Nasrudin*

*The Pleasantries of the Incredible Mulla Nasrudin*

*The Subtleties of the Inimitable Mulla Nasrudin*

*The World of Nasrudin*

*The Sufis*

Please visit: www.idriesshahfoundation.org

# A Request

If you enjoyed this book, please review it on Amazon and Goodreads.

## Reviews are an author's best friend.

To stay in touch with Tahir Shah, and to hear about his upcoming releases before anyone else, please sign up for his mailing list:

 http://tahirshah.com/newsletter

And to follow him on social media, please go to any of the following links:

 http://www.twitter.com/humanstew

 http://www.facebook.com/TahirShahAuthor

 http://www.youtube.com/user/tahirshah999

 http://www.pinterest.com/tahirshah

 http://tahirshah.com/goodreads

 https://www.instagram.com/Tahirshah999/

# http://www.tahirshah.com

Lightning Source UK Ltd.
Milton Keynes UK
UKHW011014270919
350576UK00001B/77/P